Praise for *Activate Your Money*

"I am delighted to see *Activate Your Money* breaking down barriers that keep women from being confident, inspired investors. This book can empower all of us."

— Rachel Robasciotti, Founder & CEO, Adasina Social Capital

"As women, we have the ability to use our financial power to shape an economy that truly works for all people and the planet. In this empowering book, you'll find the inspiration and information you need to flex that power!

— Alisa Gravitz, President and CEO, Green America

"I have sought to better align my investments with my values and have been looking for a roadmap to do so. *Active Your Money* is a detailed, hopeful, and inspiring compilation of information for others, like me, who see greater potential in the world and are determined to be part of the positive change."

— Lynn Frair, Nurse and Founder, fihealthcare.com

"*Activate You Money* is about more than putting your money where your values are — it offers a roadmap for ethical investing, regardless of how much money you make. This is a must-read book to make sure your financial portfolio is good for you and good for the world."

— Joe Sanberg, Entrepreneur and Co-Founder, Aspiration Partners

"*Activate Your Money* shares Janine's personal journey and will give you the knowledge, confidence, and inspiration to start in her footsteps and end by creating your own path."

— Eileen Freiburger, CFP®, Partner, Abacus Wealth Partners

"This book really spoke to me emotionally in a way that I was not expecting. I think it's going to help a lot of women and their families."

— Cheryl Contee, CEO, Do Big Stuff and Author, *Mechanical Bull: How you can Achieve Start-up Success*

"Financial fulfillment is about more than having enough money. It means feeling confident about your investments and knowing that your money is working as hard as you are to leave the world a better place than you found it."
— Kat Taylor, Co-Founder and Board Chair of Beneficial State Bank, a Community Development Financial Institution and Certified B Corporation

"So excited to have Janine Firpo's voice and the voice of so many smart, engaged contributors helping us all on our path to activate and build a better world with our financial resources. Tools like this are just what we need to inspire us to action, help us to know how it's done and learn from our peers."
— Suzanne Biegel, CEO Catalyst At Large & Co-Founder GenderSmart.

"Many women believe they are not good investors and shy away from discussions about money. This book busts that myth and shows that not only can you do this, you don't have to go it alone. There is a growing community of women you can tap into that will help you and cheer you on."
— Michelle Best, Director, Social Impact Partnerships, Facebook

"For generations, women have faced systemic barriers to building wealth; for women of color, it's been centuries. By exercising our own financial power with the guidance in *Activate Your Money*, each of us can build a better world for ourselves and our families and, collectively, we can create an equitable financial system that works for all."
— Heather McCulloch, Founder and Executive Director, Closing the Women's Wealth Gap

Activate Your Money

Activate Your Money

Invest to Grow Your Wealth and Build a Better World

BY JANINE FIRPO

WILEY

Published by John Wiley & Sons, Inc., Hoboken, New Jersey.
Published simultaneously in Canada.

For general information on our other products and services or for technical support,
please contact our Customer Care Department within the United States at (800) 762-
2974, outside the United States at (317) 572-3993, or fax (317) 572-4002.

Wiley publishes in a variety of print and electronic formats and by print-on-demand.
Some material included with standard print versions of this book may not be
included in e-books or in print-on-demand. If this book refers to media such as a
CD or DVD that is not included in the version you purchased, you may download
this material at http://booksupport.wiley.com. For more information about
Wiley products, visit www.wiley.com.

Library of Congress Cataloging-in-Publication Data is Available:

ISBN 9781119777083 (Hardback)
ISBN 9781119777090 (ePub)
ISBN 9781119777106 (ePDF)

Cover Images and Design: Noushin Pourmirza

SKY10028021_070821

Activate Your Money is dedicated to my strong, fierce mother, Kay Firpo, and all the women like her who came before us to pave the way and to make our roads less rocky.

My mom taught me about money from an early age and set me on the path to financial freedom. I am so appreciative of her openness and transparency around the subject of money. She took it from being a taboo subject to something we spoke about freely. She taught me to save, live below my means, and to invest wisely. She also taught me to step out of my comfort zone and take informed risks. I would not be where I am today without her.

"When money flows into the hands of women who have the authority to use it, everything changes."

—*Melinda Gates*

Contents

Welcome to a Brave New World

Women have been left out of the financial conversation for far too long, and it is time for our voices to be heard and our needs to be addressed. Collectively, our money has the power to change the economy and create a world that better addresses our needs and priorities.

You picked up this book because you want to know more about how to invest your money in a way that resonates with your values. Putting your money to work this way is called values-aligned investing. Just because this is not the way that investing has been traditionally practiced does not mean it cannot be the way you invest. It is time for women to own their assets and to become confident investors while using their money to create a world that reflects their values. This book will show you how to invest with confidence and invest your values—without giving up your financial returns.

You may be single, partnered, or married. You may be a parent, childless, or an empty nester. You may be well informed about money, or you may be just a beginner. You may have a financial advisor or be in the market for one. Regardless of your personal situation, this book is intended to help you feel empowered around your money and help you think—and act—in new ways around your investments and your ability to use them as a force for good.

Feel Good About Your Financial Decisions

We all want to feel good about our financial decisions, and increasingly we want to know that our money supports the things we care about. Yet, many of us are unsure. Perhaps you don't think you have enough money to invest. Maybe your usual reaction to conversations about money is throwing up your hands in despair because you simply don't know what to do or you don't have the time to figure it out. You might find the thought of taking responsibility for your investing overwhelming and fear inducing. Maybe you are ashamed, because you think you should know more than you do, or you incorrectly believe that other people are just smarter than you are about money. Or maybe you already take responsibility for your investing and just want to know more.

I'm here to tell you that you can learn to invest wisely, just like you have learned everything else in your life. If you lack confidence, don't worry. There are lots of other women who are in the same boat as you. Even women who are worth tens of millions of dollars, women with MBAs, and women who work in the financial industry can feel uncomfortable when it comes to making investment decisions about their own money.

These feelings are not surprising, given our history as women. We are often not trained in finance and investing, but that doesn't mean that we are incapable. When we do take control of our money, we outperform men by as much as 0.40% to 1.8%, according to recent studies conducted at the University of Warwick and Fidelity Investments.[1] [2] While this may appear to be a minor difference, it can have a significant impact over time. The old messages about our abilities with math, numbers, and investing are fallacies. Not only can we do well when we invest, we can do better!

Live Your Values

If you've picked up this book, chances are you're someone who lives her values. You care about your family, friends, and communities. You want to see the world be a better place for future generations. You care about the planet—the quality of the air, the water, and all living things. You are interested in sustainability and justice. You already do a lot to live your values, through the choices you make and the way you spend your money. You're beginning to realize that how you invest your money, and what you support with your assets, matters. And now you are ready to know more.

This book will help you build your confidence about investing *and* show you how to invest in ways that support the things you care about *without* giving up financial return. I am a testament to this practice. I have been working to align all of my money with my values for more than 10 years, but I am not a professional financial advisor. For that reason, I reached out to the incredible network of women that I have developed over my professional career. More than 150 amazing women (and a few men) contributed to this book. Some wrote a few pages, others a chapter, and still others served as reviewers, commenters, and thought partners. I could not have created this book without them, and I owe them all an enormous debt of gratitude.

How This Book Came to Be

This book grew out of my own investment journey. I wrote it to make investment know-how more transparent and easily understandable. I didn't want learning how to invest according to your values to be the steep uphill climb for you that it was for me.

In 1995, after a four-month solo backpacking trip through sub-Saharan Africa, I stepped out of a successful career in the computer industry to redirect my work toward addressing issues of global poverty. Not only did I take a significant pay cut when I embarked on this new venture, I also left the high-tech industry just as the Internet came on the scene. Some of my former colleagues thought I was crazy. But I was passionate about making the world a better place, and I was willing to bet my future on the potential that I saw. Over 20 years later, I couldn't be happier with the outcome of that choice.

Among other things, my new career gave me entree to many of the early discussions about transforming philanthropy and what became known as impact investing. One of the premiere conferences related to these conversations was the Global Philanthropy Forum. Around 2009, I stood up at their annual meeting and announced to the audience of foundation CEOs, ultra-high-net-worth individuals, and large institutional investors that I wanted to invest my own assets in alignment with my values. I was greeted with mute surprise. The impact investing community at that time was not a place for those without *very* deep pockets, which I did not have. But I was unfazed. After all, I had made a major career pivot to align my life's work with my values. Why should my money be supporting the social injustices I was striving to change?

Since then, I have been working to align all of my assets—from my checking and savings accounts to stocks to real estate—with my values. I want all of my financial resources to support the things I care about—the things I would like to see created, elevated, and empowered. Over the years, I have worked with three different financial advisors, all of whom assured me they would help me reach my goals. Unfortunately, *they didn't.* The reasons are as varied as the advisors themselves, but after a decade of depending on them, I found that less than a third of my assets were helping to create the world I wanted to see. The majority of my money was still in the service of banks, financial institutions, and companies I did not want to support. In some cases, my investments were upholding industries and companies I actually abhor. Now I'm changing that, and I'm finding it does not have to be that hard.

How did this happen? Why wasn't I more successful sooner? The answer to those questions is partly an issue of timing. When I started on this path 10 years ago, there were not many socially responsible investment options for individuals, particularly if you did not have extraordinarily high net worth. Fortunately, things are changing. As you will discover in this book, socially responsible investing is becoming mainstream, and there are investment options across all asset classes. With the passage of the 2012 JOBS Act, investment opportunities that were previously available only to people with $1 million or more in net worth are now available to anyone. There has been a sea change in terms of values-aligned investment opportunities over the past 10 to 15 years, and the level of innovation is accelerating.

In addition to the timing issue, I think I was less successful back then than I wanted to be because I was trapped between wanting to trust my financial advisors and wanting to wait and know more before I invested. I did not feel comfortable just doing as I was told. I wanted more knowledge, but my advisors were not providing me with the depth of information that I needed to feel secure and confident. It seemed the only way to learn was to figure the details out myself. Crazy, right? So I asked my advisors to hold off making investments until I had the time to learn more. Other things got in the way, time passed, and my money sat in cash or other low-yielding assets, waiting for me to make a decision.

This pattern was extremely frustrating, and I found it difficult to find the time to get educated. The financial knowledge I craved was hard to locate. It was dispersed among a wide variety of sources, presented in a complex manner, and challenging to distill in a meaningful way. My advisors weren't that helpful, either. I once asked my advisor about the risk related to an investment they were recommending and was told there was no risk. I knew that could not be true, but when I asked for more detail, I was told the risk was complicated to explain and I should just trust the advisor. I did not make that investment, because I didn't want to invest in something that I couldn't understand.

Although it was often slow going, over the years my knowledge grew. As a result of my self-directed education, I interacted with many leading thinkers in social investing, some of whom are contributors to this book. They helped me learn. And in late 2017, when I retired from my career in international development, I reclaimed control over most of my assets. Since then, I have been moving toward my values-aligned goals at an accelerated pace.

I've learned that investing for positive impact does not have to be difficult. You shouldn't have to tease out information about values-aligned investment options from the knowledge banks of financial advisors or disparate online sources. Through direct experience, I know it is possible to invest with conscience as a guide *and* to achieve market-rate financial returns across most asset classes.

How to Use This Book and Our Companion Website

There is no silver bullet to achieving financial freedom. If you want to achieve financial fulfillment, you're going to have to do some work. You're going to need to learn things and practice what you've learned. This is a process. But it does not have to be onerous or fear inducing. Nor does it have to be mind-numbingly boring. It can actually be fun, particularly if you join other women and learn together. As you see your money growing and positively influencing the world, it can give you great joy as well.

The book is divided into three parts. You can read the book cover to cover, or you can jump to a section or chapter that most appeals to you. Each chapter has a stand-alone quality, enabling you to approach the book in the manner that seems most appropriate to your needs. You can pick it up, take some action, put it down, and then pick it up again when you are ready.

- **In Part 1, Establishing Your Foundation**, you'll learn what values-aligned investing is and discover how you can engage in socially responsible investing. You'll identify beliefs around money that may be sabotaging you and can select the values you would like to integrate into your future investments.
- **Part 2, Crafting an Aligned Portfolio**, will walk you through each asset class in which you might want to invest—from cash to stocks to real estate and beyond—to help you understand their dynamics. Each chapter in this section will show you where to find values-aligned investment options, regardless of the amount you want to invest.
- **Part 3, Building a Community of Support**, will show you how you can work with financial advisors, friends, and employers to strengthen your investing muscles. We love the idea of shifting discussions of money from being taboo to something that empowers you and builds your confidence. And that can happen as you build trust with family, friends, and trusted advisors.

This book will introduce you to a new way of thinking about money. It will show you that you have a choice about how—and where—you invest your assets. Your investment choices can bring your money into alignment with your values. When you feel good about what your money is doing in the world, it makes the entire process of investing more fun and engaging.

Our companion website, *activateyourmoney.net*, has downloadable resources that build on the themes introduced in each chapter. Be sure to visit it when you find a topic of particular interest as you are reading. Here you will find worksheets, spreadsheets, and other tools to help you take actionable steps toward your investment goals.

While writing this book, the contributors and I took great care to include information that was current. Given the dynamic nature of finance and the investing world, some of the information in this book, such as interest rates, returns, and fees, was obtained at the time the book was written and is subject to change. Therefore, we encourage you to check the current rates and fees, in case anything has changed since this book was written.

We're excited to take this journey with you. By investing according to your values, you can literally change the world.

Let's get started.

A Final Note

This book is designed to provide information on the subjects of personal finance and values-aligned investing. The information is offered for general educational purposes only and is not intended to provide financial planning, legal, tax, accounting, or investment advisory services. Each person's financial needs, goals, and circumstances are unique. Therefore, if financial, tax, legal, and other advice is required, a licensed professional should be consulted.

The information in this book was gathered from sources deemed reliable at the time of writing. However, accuracy and completeness cannot be guaranteed. Tables reflect only a snapshot in time and do not indicate future performance, which may vary substantially. References to companies and investments are for illustrative or informational purposes and do not constitute a recommendation or endorsement of any kind. Neither the author nor the publisher will be liable or have responsibility of any kind for any loss, expense, or other damage you incur, either directly or indirectly, as a consequence of the use or application of any of the contents of this book. Any investment you make is at your sole discretion and risk.

In keeping with the collaborative nature of this work, the author is donating 100% of the net income from sales of *Activate Your Money* to organizations that are advancing women's economic empowerment and values-aligned investing.

Endnotes

1. https://www.wbs.ac.uk/news/are-women-better-investors-than-men/.
2. https://www.fidelity.com/about-fidelity/individual-investing/better-investor-men-or-women.

Establishing Your Foundation

In Part 1 you will be introduced to key concepts that will be referenced throughout *Activate Your Money*. You'll learn what values-aligned investing is, how it works, and why women should care. In addition, you'll discover how the pieces of a values-aligned portfolio fit together and become inspired to incorporate this type of investing into your own financial life. Along the way, we will debunk several myths related to values-aligned investing and show how you can achieve both financial and social returns.

You will also have an opportunity to identify the beliefs you have around money that may be sabotaging you, as well as to consider the values you would like to integrate into your future investments.

Even though this book is not intended to teach the basics of personal finance, there are a few critically important concepts that anyone diving more deeply into their investments needs to understand. The final chapter in Part 1 touches on those fundamentals. It also explores the theory behind portfolio diversification and asset allocation. And, finally, it steps you through the process of taking an inventory of your current investments and points you to tools you can use to set realistic savings and retirement goals.

CHAPTER 1

Values-Aligned Investing
Step into Your Financial Power

Whether you realize it or not, you're already an investor. Your money is having an impact somewhere, somehow. This is true even if all you have is a savings account. Every entity in which you save or invest your money is using your assets for some purpose. The question is whether this supports the things you value—or undermines them.

When you take greater responsibility for understanding your investments, you can use the power of your capital to make a difference in the world. Values-aligned investing, while novel, is not a new practice. In the US, it can be traced back to 1758 when religious societies like the Quakers didn't allow their members to invest in companies involved in the slave trade.[1] The momentum picked up in the 1960s when opponents of the Vietnam War blacklisted weapons manufacturers and continued into the 1980s as students demanded divestiture from South Africa as a response to apartheid. Today many people are interested in "voting with their dollars" and boycott companies that do not support their values and patronize the ones that do.

In the best-case scenario, 100% of your portfolio would be invested in the things that matter to you. Personally, I have made a pledge to invest all of my assets in alignment with my values. But you don't have to make the same commitment I did. You might prefer to make a smaller commitment initially and take this step-by-step. Perhaps you could start by shifting some of your assets into investments that create positive change. Or you might decide to keep the investments you already have and allocate all your new assets to values-aligned financial products.

As you learn, you'll gain more confidence and may decide to move even more money into alignment with your values. That is what happened to me. My increased desire and ability to reallocate my money to funds, companies, and financial institutions that deliver positive results is an outgrowth of gaining more confidence in my overall investing knowledge and skills. Follow whatever approach and timing feels right for you. We're not here to tell you what to do. Instead, we want to give you the tools you need to feel empowered and to make more informed investment decisions.

Before digging into what values-aligned investing is and how it works, let's take a look at the dynamics around how women currently invest, what they want, and the potential women have to change the world for the better based on the investment choices they make.

Women Think Differently About Money

Our current economic model has led to a world that does not work for all of us. It enables businesses to maximize financial gain without full consideration of the adverse impacts their operations have on people or the planet. Since these damaging effects do not have a direct financial cost to the business, they are often ignored or underreported. Even worse, businesses have been known to obfuscate, refuse blame, or actively cloud an issue to avoid having to pay the full cost of their negative impacts.

This has led to environmental degradation, social problems, and other adverse consequences that are known as externalities. In economics, a negative externality is a cost that affects a third party who did not choose to incur that cost. An example would be a manufacturing plant that contaminates a nearby lake but does not pay for its cleanup. The cost is ultimately paid, but it is borne by the people who live near the lake, taxpayers, or both—not the company that created the problem. This approach is not sustainable, and it does not bode well for our health, happiness, or prosperity—or for that of our children and grandchildren.

Today's financial system also undervalues the priorities of women. As wage earners, we garner only 81 cents on the dollar compared to men.[2] As entrepreneurs, we get a mere 2.2% of the venture capital funding.[3] And as money managers, women serve as the exclusive managers for only 2% of mutual funds.[4] Across the board, the situation is even worse for women of color. We are also living in a country where the top 1% of the population holds more wealth than the entire middle class.[5] However, it doesn't have to be this way.

The prevailing winner-takes-all mentality is not the way women show up in the world. It's not who we are. We are collaborators, coalition builders, and promoters of win-win scenarios. We definitely want to see our money grow and achieve great financial returns, but not at any cost. Of course, we want to make money through our investments, but it's not enough for us to simply receive a competitive return. We want more, and guess what, so do our children.

In 2017, a Morgan Stanley study found that 84% of women and 86% of millennials were interested in sustainable investing.[6] Two years later, their biennial report showed interest had grown even more: 95% of millennials said they wanted to invest in alignment with their values, and 50% of all respondents in the survey already had at least one sustainable investment.[7]

As women, we are clear. We want to direct our dollars toward a future of prosperity, inclusivity, and sustainability. We want to see our children, our communities, and our planet flourish. We want the ways that we show up to support our values. We want to walk our talk.

If enough of us align our money with our values, we can help change the face of the economy from a "profit at any cost" model to a more sustainable and equitable approach. We can accelerate a movement to a financial system based more on long-term sustainability than on short-term gain. We can pivot markets to a model that works better for people and the planet, not just shareholders. We can also dramatically increase the number of women-led businesses that receive funding, and we can underwrite the development of products and services that meet our needs as well as those of our children. And we can do all that without giving up financial return. Our combined potential is bigger than you think. In fact, it is incredible!

You Already Have a Lot of Financial Power

As women, we already control more than 50% of the personal wealth in this country, and that percentage is expected to rise to 65% by 2030.[8] As of this writing, 45% of millionaires in the United States are women, and the number of wealthy women in the country is growing at twice the rate of wealthy men.[9] We have become a financial force, and that financial power can create great change. But that change will only come when we decide to take more control of our assets and invest in ways that make us feel good.

With *#MeToo* and other female-focused movements, women are galvanizing change. While advances have been made in many areas, women are still lagging when it comes to their money, even though their overall wealth is growing.

When you think about your money, you probably consider what it will buy, what you and the people you love need and want, how much you have or don't have, whether you'll have enough to retire, and how to get more of it. Regardless of how much money you have, you probably stress about it—in one way or another. You probably worry about whether it is invested wisely, whether it is safe, whether it is growing, what will happen in the next economic downturn, and whether you are getting good financial advice.

Money is a constant theme in our lives. If you are like many women, you probably wish you didn't have to worry about it at all. To many of us, managing and investing our money seems overwhelming, hard, and often the least favored item on our to-do list. You might wish that someone else would just handle it for you. And that is what a lot of women do. They leave their money in the bank—and hope for the best. Or they hand their financial agency over to someone else. We all do this. But at what cost?

The first cost is to our ability to grow our wealth over the course of our lives. Many women know there is a gender pay gap but might not be aware there is also an investment gap. Not only do men earn more, they also retire with three times more money than we do, even though we save more.[10] According to a 2018 study by BlackRock, women keep 71 cents on the dollar in savings rather than take the risk of investing, and possibly losing, it.[11] Meanwhile, men invest and grow their wealth. They're more willing to take the risk, whether they feel fully confident or not.

Our lack of confidence in our ability to invest and build our wealth is hurting us. This gap has led women to hand financial authority over to the men in our lives—husbands, male relatives, and financial advisors. When we pass responsibility for our money to others, we're putting ourselves at risk. We're also giving up our agency, our financial security, and the potential to change where money flows—and what it affects. Even worse, we're setting up our daughters and granddaughters to be uninformed as well. It's time for us to take back our financial agency, and this book will help you do just that.

When we invest, we do it differently than men. When we hand our agency to men, we are letting them invest in the way that works for them, not for us. Women tend to be more cautious and more analytical as we assess potential investments. We want to understand risks before we take them. We are more willing to collaborate, whereas men are more likely to trust their gut and go it alone. Our approach serves us well, and we create broad networks of colleagues along the way. This makes investing more fun and more effective, because it exposes us to additional knowledge and new opportunities.

We also have a greater propensity to invest in the things that matter to us, and increasingly we want advisors that listen to, and educate, us. Ask yourself, What would it be like to feel skilled, competent, and self-assured about my money? And how would it feel to be confident enough to teach your children how to be investment-savvy?

Eventually, you will most likely be put in a position where you have to take on responsibility for your money, whether you want to or not. As a woman, you will probably be alone at some point in your life—because you stayed single longer, or divorced, or outlived your spouse or partner. Whom will you trust when the person (usually a man) overseeing your finances is no longer there to guide you? When the sands start to shift beneath your feet is not the right time to start learning. If you're going to have to learn to be a better investor at some point, why not start now? And why not do it in a way that actually makes you feel good?

What About Financial Returns?

Some of you may be wondering if you have to give up financial return to invest with your values. No, you do not! Yet, perceptions of a trade-off between sustainable investing and financial gain have proven stubborn. People who argue that you will give up financial return when you invest consciously are most often referring to investments made in the stock market. These naysayers are not even considering other asset classes, such as cash, fixed income, private investments, or alternatives, where the trade-off can be hard to find. They are primarily focused on stock funds that incorporate ESG (environmental, social, and governance) criteria, and even there, they are wrong.

The evidence supporting ESG investing is mounting. In 2019 *Cornerstone Capital Group,* a women-led financial advisory and research firm, undertook a comprehensive review of research papers that looked at the potential trade-off between ESG criteria and financial performance. They analyzed over 2,200 studies conducted since the 1970s and found the research consistently concluded that ESG standards do not compromise investment performance.[12]

A 2017 study by Nuveen TIAA Investments, 2016 research by Barclays Research, and three meta-studies in 2015—one by Deutsche Asset & Wealth Management, another by Oxford University and Arabesque partners, and a third by Morgan Stanley—provided similar results.[13] The Morgan Stanley study looked at more than 10,000 mutual funds over a seven-year period. Their analysis showed that investing in sustainability not only met, but often exceeded, the performance of comparable traditional investments. This was true on both an absolute and a risk-adjusted basis. And it was true across all asset classes over the period studied.[14] Follow-on research by Morgan Stanley in 2019 provided further support to these earlier studies.

Even with all this evidence, some people continue to argue that ESG results in lower returns. One of their arguments was that we didn't know what would happen in a serious economic downturn. As a result of the market collapse in early 2020, now we do know. We learned that ESG funds performed better during this period, according to research by Morningstar, MSCI, BlackRock, and other leaders in the finance industry.

You don't have to take our word for it. As we progress through the book, you will learn how to compare social impact scores and financial returns across the most commonly traded index, exchange-traded funds, and mutual funds in the US stock market. You will see for yourself that there doesn't have to be a trade-off between values-alignment and financial return in the stock market and that this is the case with other asset classes, too.

Some Terms You Need to Know

Impact investing, ESG, socially responsible investing (SRI), green investing, conscious investing, and mission-driven investing are all terms used to describe aspects of values-aligned investing. If you ask five people what a specific term means, you're likely to get five different answers. This book uses the definitions that follow.

Terminology

Conscious Investing

Investing in such a way that an investor is aware of the impact their money is having on the environment and society. In conscious investing, the investor makes a conscious, aware choice.

Socially Responsible Investing (SRI)

One of the earliest terms coined. Often associated with negative screening in the public equities market—negative screening focuses on what is not included in an investment.

ESG

Environmental, social, and governance criteria that are used to evaluate companies for investment purposes. Research shows that companies with higher ESG scores have improved returns because they represent lower risk.

ESG Investing

The act of investing in high-scoring ESG companies. Although some consider ESG investing to be an approach across all asset classes, it primarily refers to investments in fixed income and public equities (also referred to as the stock market).

Green Investing

Investments specifically related to conservation of natural resources, production of alternative energy sources, and other environmental sustainability goals.

Impact Investing

While some use this term to refer to social investing across all asset classes, it usually refers to debt and equity investments in private businesses that have a mission directly tied to intentional positive impact.

Mission-driven Investing

Investments that align with the mission and values of an organization, usually a foundation or endowment. Mission-driven investments are often concessionary and made out of a special pool of money that is set aside for this purpose. Also called program-related investing.

Social Investing

An investment strategy that seeks to consider financial return and social/ environmental good. Also referred to as sustainable investing, socially conscious investing, and ethical investing.

Sustainable Investing

Investments that lead to sustainability for people and the planet.

Values-aligned Investing

A comprehensive approach in which investors seek to align their money with their values across all asset classes.

Even Small Investments Make a Difference

The first person you need to be satisfying with your investments is yourself. If it matters to you that your money supports the things you care about, then it matters, regardless of how much you have to invest. It also matters on a larger scale because small things add up in a big way. Our greatest impact is a collective one. It is felt most acutely when large numbers of us choose to move our money where our hearts are. And when enough of us make that choice, things change.

Although investors have been voicing concerns about sustainability for several decades, it's only recently that they have been translating their words into actions. And those actions are making a difference. *The Harvard Business Review* states that in 2006, 63 investment companies with $6.5 trillion in assets under management (AUM) signed a commitment to incorporate ESG issues into their investment decisions. In 12 years, there were 1,715 signatories representing $81.7 trillion in AUM. And today, more than half of global asset owners are implementing or evaluating ESG considerations in their investment strategy.[15]

Don't underestimate the power of the purse. If women in the United States shifted an average of $20,000 in existing savings and investments into financial products aligned with their values, an additional $2.56 trillion of assets would move,[16] and that would definitely cause the investment companies that manage our assets—as well as the business entities themselves—to take notice. While some of us do not have $20,000 in assets, many of us have considerably more.

How you invest your money also matters because it is a reflection of who you are. It mirrors your deepest values. It brings you into integrity with other aspects of yourself. And it is the part of your road to financial freedom that will bring you joy and make the entire process of investing deeply satisfying. The ultimate metric for your investments is how they make you feel.

How can you know if you're having a positive impact with your investments? Sara Olsen, one of the leading thinkers in measuring socially responsible investments, says there are three fundamental impact issues to understand:[17]

1. The effect your investments have on you and how they make you feel;
2. The effects they have on the world, particularly in terms of avoiding harm and benefiting a wide range of stakeholders; and
3. The degree to which the investments are living up to their social contract by contributing to solutions to pressing social and environmental problems.

The degree to which you incorporate all three of these factors into your investments depends on the amount of money you are investing as well as the type of investment. If you make a $10,000 investment in a stock fund, for example, the research you did to determine whether the fund was aligned with your values (e.g., no fossil fuel companies, gender equity, social justice) may be enough for you to feel good about that investment. If you invest $500,000 into a private equity fund, then you probably want to push further and seek more assurances that the fund managers will invest in companies that are creating viable solutions for problems that matter to you.

We'd all like to think that managing our investments and growing our wealth is easy and risk-free. We want simple, quick solutions. We're excited to read blog posts that promise five easy steps to financial freedom. Those essays extol financial basics like living below your means, saving as much of your money as you can as early as you can, and taking advantage of matching funds in employer-sponsored retirement funds.

While this is valuable advice, those tenets do not help you invest. Nor are they sufficient for the long term. Investing wisely takes time. You need to learn, experiment, and take risks. You need to build your confidence and skills. Smart, successful investing and wealth creation is not a one-to- five-step sprint. It's more like a marathon. The training starts slowly and then builds over time until you are amazed that you are about to run 26 miles! And then, it becomes an enjoyable lifestyle. The same is true of strengthening your investment chops. But it doesn't have to be overwhelming, boring, or anxiety provoking. It can actually be fun.

Investing and investing with your values do not have to be two separate things. In today's world, they can be one thing. When you invest with your values, you are just making different choices in the banks where you save your money and in the financial products you buy. When you know where to look for values-aligned investment options, making values-aligned investment decisions becomes as easy as making non-values-aligned decisions.

Attaining Financial Fulfillment

You're probably familiar with the concept of financial freedom, which means having enough money to afford the lifestyle you want even into your retirement. This is a goal that we all aspire toward.

Suze Orman took this concept even further in one of her podcasts. In it she claimed that financial freedom is not the goal.[18] She believes the true goal is financial independence, which she describes as having knowledge about your money, being involved in financial decisions, and not being financially dependent on others. It's interesting to note that some women who are financially free are still financially insecure. They may have enough money for their current and future needs, but they still don't feel safe.

If you leave the management of your assets to others, you are depending on them to make the right decisions for you. Even with the best of intentions, no one else is going to care about your money, or how it's invested, as much as you do. I learned this the hard way more than once.

In one instance, my financial advisor suggested I put 25% of my total assets into what I considered high-risk investments. Since I'd been doing my homework, I knew that most advisors recommended only 10% of a portfolio be invested this way. I did not feel comfortable with my advisor's recommendation, and because I had that knowledge, I pushed back, refusing their advice. If I hadn't known better, I would probably have agreed to the 25%, even if my intuition caused me to have a sinking feeling in my stomach. I would have been fearful of challenging my advisor.

Another time, an advisor told me that my stock fund was aligned with my goals—one of which was related to climate change. I trusted him. My money sat in that fund for five years. At some point, I decided to look at the companies held in the fund. Imagine my shock when I discovered that about 20% of my holdings were in oil and gas companies! I felt betrayed. If I hadn't taken it upon myself to look, I would never have known what was really in that fund. I decided I would never be that uninformed again. It was time for me to get directly involved with my money and my investments. And I encourage you to do the same.

When you invest with your values, you can move beyond financial independence to what I call financial fulfillment. Financial fulfillment offers the joy that comes from knowing your investments are a true reflection of your values and the deep contentment that comes from recognizing that your money is working for you and for the world.

So is this hard? Yes and no. Creating financial fulfillment takes time and attention, but you don't have to do everything at once. In fact, I encourage you to take one step at a time. By working your way through each chapter in this book, you can learn and get comfortable with one part of your portfolio before moving on to the next. Your confidence around investing will grow, and you will gain agency and invest for a better world as an ongoing practice that moves at your own pace.

Just as you do not need to do everything at once, you do not need to do everything yourself. Engage your friends, learn together, support each other, share the work, and enjoy the process. Seek additional support from your family members, colleagues, peers, and financial advisors. If women learn together and remove the taboos that we carry around money, then we can learn how to be financially free, independent, and fulfilled. And we can change the world for the better at the same time.

Prepare to Learn, Experiment, and Have Fun

There's no silver bullet when it comes to investing, and the road is not without potholes. Expect that you'll make some mistakes. I guarantee at least once in your lifetime, the stock market will go down—possibly way down. The government will change the tax rules. And what you thought would happen won't and what you never imagined will. The best advice I can give you: Roll with it. You can't control what's coming down the pike. What you can control is how you approach uncertainty.

Be smart, be watchful, learn, experiment, make mistakes, pick yourself up, and try again. Being smart about your money, learning, investing, and growing your wealth is a practice. And like any other commitment you make, it is achievable.

If you are young and just starting to invest, you're in an enviable position, because you are starting with a clean slate. That means you can make values-aligned investment choices from the outset. For someone like you, there is really no reason not to invest this way. If you are older and have existing investments, you'll need to decide whether you want to sell some or all of those assets to reinvest them in a more values-aligned manner. You may not be prepared to sell assets that have embedded capital gains, which is completely understandable. In this case, you can focus on cash, tax-deferred retirement accounts, or investments with limited gains. You can also sell during a market downturn, which is what I did in March 2020 when the stock market had its biggest decline since the 2008 financial crisis.

Prior to that market drop, I had a plan to sell all the stock funds I owned that were not aligned with my values. Since some of those assets had significant embedded gains, I decided to sell them over a five-year period to minimize my tax burden in any one year. When the stock market collapsed as a result of COVID-19, many of my gains had turned into losses. So I sold them, harvested the losses, and immediately bought back into the market. But this time I invested in stock funds that aligned with my values. It felt great to have such a positive outcome during an otherwise extremely difficult time.

I realize not everyone will choose to sell all their current holdings, even during a market downturn, and that's fine. You don't have to move everything into alignment if that feels like too much. Do what feels right to you. I am confident that as you do, as you learn, you will be motivated to do more. That is what happened to me and to many of the women who contributed to this book.

Take Action

After reading this chapter, take some time to think about your impressions. What resonated with you the most? What steps can you take to move forward? Make a list of action items and move at a pace that feels right for you.

No investment is too small. Whether you decide to start with $100 or have $10 million to invest, values-aligned investing is smart investing, particularly when you think about the long term. It can also be fun, creative, and something that you do in community with other women.

For the sake of your financial fulfillment and a better world for all of us (and our children), the time to start is now!

Endnotes

1. https://russellinvestments.com/-/media/files/us/insights/institutions/non-profit/evolution-of-sustainable-responsible-investing.pdf.
2. https://www.payscale.com/data/gender-pay-gap.
3. https://news.crunchbase.com/news/q1-2019-diversity-report-female-founders-own-17-percent-of-venture-dollars/.

4. https://hbr.org/2019/03/when-will-we-see-more-gender-equality-in-investing.
5. https://www.brookings.edu/blog/up-front/2019/06/25/six-facts-about-wealth-in-the-united-states/.
6. Morgan Stanley Institute for Sustainable Investing. Sustainable Signals: New Data for the Individual Investor. August 7, 2017.
7. Morgan Stanley Institute for Sustainable Investing. Sustainable Signals: Individual Investor Interest Driven by Impact, Conviction and Choice. Sept 11, 2019.
8. https://www.theglobeandmail.com/business/careers/leadership/article-will-the-transfer-of-wealth-to-women-take-sustainable-investing/.
9. https://thequantum.com/financial-facts-for-womens-history-month/.
10. https://capitalandmain.com/10-shocking-facts-about-inequality-in-america.
11. https://money.com/investing-finance-gender-gap-pay-inequality/.
12. https://cornerstonecapinc.com/sacrifice-nothing-a-fresh-look-at-investment-performance-of-sustainable-and-impact-strategies-by-asset-class/.
13. https://www.ussif.org/performance.
14. https://www.morganstanley.com/press-releases/new-morgan-stanley-report-challenges-misperceptions-regarding-sustainable-investing-and-performance_32620b34-1e1c-47ef-a722-c8d1e43f5288.
15. https://hbr.org/2019/05/the-investor-revolution.
16. Calculation assumes 330 million adults in the United States, 77.6% of whom are adults (i.e., over the age of 18). Of that amount, i.e., 256 million, one can further assume 50% are women. That gives 128 million adult women, each saving an average of $20,000, which provides the $2.56 trillion figure.
17. Emerson, J. *The ImpactAssets Handbook for Investors*. Anthem Press. 2017. p. 188.
18. https://omny.fm/shows/women-and-money-with-suze-orman/s2-e3-financial-independence-part-1.

CHAPTER 2

Your Relationship with Money
Invest with Your Heart and Mind

Everyone has personal beliefs about money. Developed in our formative years and throughout our lives, these stories guide our financial decisions for better or worse. By understanding our money stories, we can discard self-destructive behaviors and adapt new positive practices. While there is little you can do about the past, you can rewrite your stories from this day forward.

For years, my financial habits were dictated by the trauma my Depression-era parents experienced around money. They both suffered through poverty in their youth, with my dad often saying he had grown up "dirt poor." My earliest money memory was the recognition that we did not have enough. We clipped coupons, saved pennies, and wore used clothing. So it's not surprising that as I became an adult, I believed I would always have to do without. I was a saver from the get-go, because I didn't want to end up as an impoverished 80-year-old woman living under a bridge eating cat food. Even as I became a better earner, owned my own home, and had excess money, I still clung to my fear that I would never have enough to avoid future poverty and hunger. That disempowering belief stayed with me through my fifties! It's only when I took control of my own money and began investing in the things I cared about that I was finally able to dispel my fears and embrace something more empowering.

The way you choose to reimagine your relationship with your money will determine the future of your financial life and the way you feel about it. You have an opportunity to create a story of empowerment that brings you joy and puts you into integrity with your values. This chapter will start you on a process of uncovering any of your self-limiting money behaviors and set you on a path to identify and integrate your values with your money.

We All Have Money Stories

Think back to when you were growing up; what was the most significant principle you learned about money? Perhaps you can even hear the voice in your head of the person who drilled it home. Or maybe you remember a time when a money belief was first imprinted on your psyche. Often, these rules take the form of something like "you should always" or "you should never."

Spending as a Guilty Pleasure

Barbara, a former colleague and friend, shared one of her early money memories with me. Whenever her mother bought her a new dress or some other longed-for item, she always said, "Don't tell your daddy." The secrecy surrounding these purchases created a conflict in Barbara's mind. On the one hand, she realized spending money was dangerous, because she and her mother could get in trouble if her father found out. But on the other hand, she experienced great pleasure from her new treasures. From an early age, Barbara associated shame with spending money on herself. These feelings of guilty pleasure followed her into adulthood. Even today when she buys something for herself, she always experiences a level of remorse. She only finds true joy when she spends money on others.

Sometimes our most influential and entrenched money stories are more mundane or can even emerge from pleasant memories. Rather than an explicit admonishment, our stories can evolve from what we pick up around us—from behaviors in our families to social cues to others' opinions. We may not even be aware that we're piecing together a story about our money along the way.

Not Allowing Rules to Bind Us

Suzanne Andrews, a contributor to this book, has a pleasant early memory of her father sitting at the dinner table balancing the family checkbook. It was just a matter-of-fact act, something he did on a regular basis. Knowing that her dad was taking care of things made Suzanne feel safe and secure. She listened to him when he gave her the financial advice to always spend less than you earn. If she did this, he told her, "you will always be fine."

Suzanne took that lesson to heart, and it served her well for many years. But the situation changed when she got a divorce. After 13 years as a full-time mom, she was put in the position of having to figure out how to support herself and her children. Much to her chagrin, she realized she needed to pull money from her savings accounts to pay the bills. Every time Suzanne did this, her dad's refrain played in her head. It made her anxious, and she even experienced shame, because she knew she was no longer abiding by her father's edict.

Around this time, Suzanne picked up a copy of Lynne Twist's book *The Soul of Money* and started reading it. This was a pivotal moment for Suzanne, because the book described a completely different way to think about money. It articulated an approach that Suzanne had never considered before. Lynne suggested the accumulation of money is non-linear. Sometimes it ebbs, and sometimes it flows. Lynne believes this is just the natural order of money. This concept was incredibly freeing for Suzanne, and it released her from strictly adhering to her father's rule. It also released her from the anxiety and shame she was feeling, because she began to trust that even if she pulled money from her savings now (an ebb), there would be future deposits (flows) to balance it out. And that is exactly what happened.

Suzanne now has a career in financial services that she loves. She is also a passionate angel investor, who supports female entrepreneurs. Suzanne believes that the shift in attitude she experienced after reading Lynne's book played an instrumental role in helping her develop a new set of stories around money. Suzanne still appreciates her dad's principle and thinks it has value, but she is no longer bound by it.

The Eight Financial Archetypes

Our money stories are revealed in our lives through our financial behaviors, which can carry both strengths and weaknesses. As Suzanne's story demonstrates, the way we show up around our money can also change over time as a result of circumstances and our conscious decisions. To be more intentional with our finances, it helps to understand these behaviors and to discover what drives them.

In his book *It's Not About the Money*, Brent Kessel, CFP and founder of Abacus Wealth Partners, introduces eight financial archetypes that describe the money behaviors that people most commonly display. The archetypes provide insight into the stories that might be driving our attitudes, beliefs, and behaviors around money. Each has a set of key attributes, positive gifts, and potential pitfalls. The gifts associated with each archetype highlight the strengths you carry, while the pitfalls point toward obstacles that might be blocking your way to a completely satisfying financial future.

No one archetype is superior or inferior to another. In fact, we are all more than one, sometimes a blend of three or four. As you read through this section, try to be compassionate with yourself if you notice negative patterns in your behaviors. Balance them against the gifts that are also present. You might find that through increased awareness you can modify your behaviors to minimize pitfalls and maximize the gifts that have emerged from your money stories to date.

The following narratives are composites of real women who exemplify each of the archetypes. You will meet some of them again in later chapters where they are used to illustrate key points or concepts.

THE GUARDIAN—ALERTNESS, PRUDENCE, THOROUGH ANALYSIS FOR SAFETY

Anika is 27 years old and single. She watched her parents struggle to make ends meet. Sudden, unexpected expenses—like a major car repair—could put the family in financial crisis for months. Anika grew up believing that money was scarce and could disappear at any moment. Now, she is vigilant with her money and saves aggressively. Most of her savings are in cash, because that is what she feels is safest. Anika believes her financial situation is precarious, even though she has enough money set aside to cover all her expenses for one year and is maxing out her employer's retirement fund.

THE PLEASURE SEEKER—ENJOYMENT, RELAXATION

Sydney is a 45-year-old life coach. She makes enough money for her needs and even has some left over. She derives great pleasure from clothes, her home, and weekend getaways. Sydney often treats when she and her friends go out to dinner. She knows she is not saving enough for her future and sometimes it worries her, but Sydney has a really difficult time turning down invitations to dinners, events, or minivacations.

THE IDEALIST—DESIRE TO CREATE SOCIAL OR ENVIRONMENTAL TRANSFORMATION

Jade is 32 years old, married, and part of Financially Independent Retire Early (FIRE), a lifestyle movement whose members have the goal of achieving financial independence and retiring early. Based in a coastal area, she and her husband, Denzel, are environmentalists and make their purchasing decisions accordingly. Because they plan to retire in their early 50s, they have chosen a simple lifestyle. They expect to have children but are concerned about the world they will be bringing them into.

THE SAVER—SELF-SUFFICIENT, SECURE FUTURE

Toni is a 73-year-old retired nurse with three adult children, one of whom has special needs. She and her husband saved consistently throughout their lives, and now have enough money to carry them through a pleasant retirement. Even though they don't touch their principal and live off dividends and Social Security, they worry constantly about their financial future. As a result, they scrimp and obsess about their daughter, Nina, who will need to be cared for when they die.

THE STAR—LEADERSHIP BY EXAMPLE, INFLUENTIAL, VOCAL   Natalie is 35 years old and recently married. She works in sales for a major corporation and was recently promoted to a leadership role. Natalie's leadership begins with herself, and she strives to set an empowering example of what is possible. She's proud to share her experiences with others, using her voice on different platforms to do so. She thrives on being seen as relevant and influential. She loves to share what she has learned. Natalie wants her money to nourish all parts of herself and wants to use it to help others.

THE INNOCENT—SIMPLICITY, TRUST, NETWORKS, COMMUNITY   Cynthia is an unmarried 58-year-old former schoolteacher turned educational consultant. Her work takes her around the country helping low-resource communities strengthen local education systems. Professionally, she is very well connected, creative, and accomplished. Yet when it comes to her money, she avoids looking at it. Instead, she relies on her friend and CPA to tell her what she needs to know. Because she prefers not to think about money, Cynthia doesn't have a handle on her actual income, expenses, or level of investments. She doesn't really know what amount she needs to retire or how to get there.

THE CARETAKER—COMPASSION, EMPATHY   Ava is a 46-year-old mother of two children in middle school. She dropped out of the workforce when her first son was born and relished the years she stayed home. She is now divorced and reentering the workforce. Ava needs to rebuild her career and gain control of her financial life. Although she was a tax attorney and good with numbers, she left all the investment decisions to her husband when they were married. A friend suggested Ava hire a financial advisor, which she is considering.

THE EMPIRE BUILDER—INNOVATION, ENDURANCE   Maria is 51 years old. She lives with her current partner and two teenage daughters. Her parents were immigrants who worked hard, but in low-wage jobs. Her upbringing was loving but financially stressful. Through hard work and grit, Maria became an engineer. She ended her career as a co-founder in a recently acquired company, leaving Maria a multimillionaire—an outcome she never expected. Always driven, Maria thrives on being relevant and influential.

Special Note

While our money stories and archetypes can influence us, most people are not incapacitated by them. However, that is not true for everyone. Some of us feel truly paralyzed or traumatized around money. If you are one of those people, you might want to know that there are certified psychologists, psychiatrists, and social workers that specialize in assisting individuals with their deep-rooted distress around money. These professionals can help uncover internalized fears, beliefs, and money stories that are resulting in destructive behaviors or irrational fears. They can help their clients work though these self-defeating attitudes to achieve greater success in their financial and personal lives.

You likely noticed a few familiar patterns as you read. Perhaps you are pleasantly surprised and ready to forge ahead, or maybe you're beating yourself up over your negative patterns. Regardless of your reaction, I invite you to continue exploring your money stories and the behaviors they engender. Table 2.1 lists each financial archetype, along with their

TABLE 2.1 The Eight Financial Archetypes

Archetype	Key attributes	Positive gifts	Potential pitfalls
The guardian	Always alert and careful, fear of financial loss	Alertness, prudence	Worry, anxiety
The pleasure seeker	Prioritizes immediate pleasure and enjoyment	Enjoyment, pleasure	Hedonism, impulsiveness
The idealist	Values creativity, social justice, and compassion	Vision, compassion	Distrust, aversion
The saver	Seeks security through accumulating money	Self-sufficiency, abundance	Hoarding, penny-pinching
The star	Spends, invests, or gives to increase self-esteem	Leadership, style	Pretentiousness, self-importance
The innocent	Avoids focus on money, hopes for the best	Hope, adaptability	Avoidance, helplessness
The caretaker	Gives and lends money to express compassion	Empathy, generosity	Enabling, self-abandoning
The empire builder	Thrives by creating enduring value	Innovation, decisiveness	Greed, domination

attributes, gifts, and challenges. If you want more information about your own financial archetypes and to gain insight into how you can change behaviors that are not working for you, visit abacuswealth.com/quiz and take their five-minute quiz to reveal your primary archetypes.

Our money stories and financial archetypes influence how we behave around our money. As you begin to recognize behaviors that may be holding you back, know you can change them. You can create new stories around your money. New stories about how to earn it, control it, save it, and invest it. You don't have to stick with what has been true in the past or with the status quo. The way you manage and invest your money is an expression of your "how." As you learn, you'll be able to bring more awareness to your "how" and make more informed investment and money management decisions.

Integrating Your Values

Just as the way we manage and invest our money is an expression of our "how," our values and what we choose to invest in are an expression of our "why." They guide how we show up in the world and drive our actions and choices. Each and every day, as a friend, partner, parent, consumer, and citizen, you are living your "why" through the choices you make about where you put your time, attention, and resources.

Yet, this "why" has been left out of most investment decisions and discussions. Just because it has been that way for a long time, does not mean it has to be that way going forward. Our "why" is connected to our hearts, to our deepest-held feelings and values. Do we really want to leave that out? Particularly if we do not have to give up financial return?

When you invest with both your heart and mind, you can step into your real power around money. If you are reading this book, you probably want to see a world that supports you, your family, your community, and the planet. Most of us strive in our daily lives—in big and small ways—to make the world a better place than we found it. We are committed to justice. We are committed to equity. We are committed to sustainability. We want the world to be a healthy place to live and to offer even more opportunity to our children and future generations than it has for us. Not surprisingly, people everywhere have the same ideals, dreams, and visions.

In recent years, a framework has emerged that is connecting organizations and people around the world to a global movement that has a shared vision for our collective future. You can use this framework to clarify your values and prioritize the ones you want to inform your investment decisions.

The SDGs: A Powerful New Way to Think About Your Investments

This framework is referred to as the Sustainable Development Goals, or SDGs. It originated at the United Nations Conference on Sustainable Development, which was held in Rio de Janeiro in 2012. Representatives from over 30 countries were involved in the design of the SDGs. The designers of the framework aspired to create a set of universal goals that addressed the most urgent environmental, political, and economic challenges facing all of us. On September 25, 2015, the SDGs were ratified by the 193 member countries in the United Nations.

The SDGs provide a new model for how you can put your money to work. They offer a simple way to prioritize the values you want to see reflected in your investments. Because they are straightforward and easy to use, the SDGs are becoming a de facto standard among many values-aligned investors. When you use the SDGs to guide your investments, you become part of a movement that is larger than yourself. You join governments, businesses, and citizens from around the world who are working toward a common set of goals. By participating, you can amplify the impact of your investments.

As shown in Figure 2.1, there are 17 SDGs that range from ending poverty to tackling climate change to providing peace and justice for all. Each goal is broken down into a set of measurable indicators that are being used to track progress.

FIGURE 2.1 Sustainable Development Goals

How I Applied the SDGs to My Own Investment Decisions

I was first introduced to the SDGs through my work in international development where they were frequently discussed. As the SDGs became better known in those circles, impact investors also discovered them. Over time, these investors began to realize the SDGs offered a great way to think about and organize their values-aligned investment decisions. Like many others, I decided to use them as a framework to inform my own investing.

Since it was challenging to wrap my head around 17 goals, I decided to focus my investments on just five SDGs. Now, whenever I consider a potential investment, I evaluate it against my goals. The investment either fits or it doesn't, which makes my decision about whether to invest or not much clearer. As a tool, the SDGs empower me to advance the causes that I care about. As a result, I am more engaged with my investments than I was when I was only considering returns or more generalized impact goals.

The SDGs have been such a powerful tool for me that I frequently recommend them to others. I also recommend choosing no more than five, a number that has turned out to be both manageable and broad enough to address many of my key interests. That is not to say that I don't care about the other goals under the SDGs. I do. But I believe my impact will be greater when my investments are more directed, and I have chosen to use this method to achieve my investment goals. You might decide to choose fewer than five, a completely reasonable option. Not everyone uses the SDGs the same way, nor should they. The framework is actually quite flexible and can be used in a variety of ways.

Using an Investment Lens Approach with the SDGs

Some people prefer to make their investment decisions with an overarching goal in mind. They look at every investment through that perspective, or "lens." Gender lens investing is a great example. In this case, the investor seeks financial return while also considering the social well-being and economic opportunities available to women and girls. Multiple SDGs support this lens. Figure 2.2 shows how SDGs can be applied to four common impact lenses. If you want, you can create your own lens and assign the SDGs to it that you believe support that goal.

Gender Lens Empower all women and girls	Climate Lens Action to combat climate change
■ No poverty (SDG 1) ■ Zero hunger (SDG 2) ■ Good health and well-being (SDG 3) ■ Quality education (SDG 4) ■ Gender equality (SDG 5) ■ Decent work and economic growth (SDG 9) ■ Reduced inequalities (SDG 10)	■ Clean water and sanitation (SDG 6) ■ Affordable and clean energy (SDG 7) ■ Industry and infrastructure (SDG 9) ■ Responsible production (SDG 12) ■ Climate action (SDG 13) ■ Life below water (SDG 14) ■ Life on land (SDG 15)
Social Justice Reduce inequality within countries	Locavesting Investments in a local area
■ Good health and well-being (SDG 3) ■ Quality education (SDG 4) ■ Gender equality (SDG 5) ■ Clean water and sanitation (SDG 6) ■ Decent work and economic growth (SDG 7) ■ Reduced inequality (SDG 8) ■ Sustainable cities and communities (SDG 9)	■ No poverty (SDG 1) ■ Zero hunger (SDG 2) ■ Good health and well-being (SDG 3) ■ Quality education (SDG 4) ■ Clean water and sanitation (SDG 6) ■ Decent work and economic growth (SDG 7) ■ Sustainable cities and communities (SDG 9)

FIGURE 2.2 Applying SDGs to Investment Lenses

Putting Your Heart and Mind into Your Investments

If you're like most people, you've probably been taught there are two things you can do with the money that you don't spend—you can either invest it to maximize your return or you can give it away as charity. This is known as "two-pocket thinking." Money that goes into one pocket is for wealth creation and what goes into the other is for creating positive change. Unfortunately, this reasoning does not accurately reflect what is really happening.

Far too often the dollars invested to grow wealth and maximize return actually contribute to the very problems the charitable dollars are intended to address. What's more, the amount in the "grow wealth" pocket usually dwarfs the amount in the "do good" pocket, raising questions about which is realizing the greatest impact—the invested or the charitable dollars.

Values-aligned investing moves beyond this limited, two-pocket perspective. As Figure 2.3 shows, it is a new landscape that has emerged between the pillars of traditional investing and traditional philanthropy. Values-aligned investing brings together the best of both—the informed mind of the investor and the heart of the philanthropist—to offer investment opportunities that are completely new. And it does so without giving up financial return. Because of this, we no longer have to choose between doing well financially and doing good for society.

TRADITIONAL INVESTING	VALUES-ALIGNED INVESTING			TRADITIONAL PHILANTHROPY
	Prioritize Maximizing Financial Returns & Achieving Social Impact			
Prioritize Maximizing Financial Returns	**LEVEL 1** Do No Harm	**LEVEL 2** Benefit Stakeholders	**LEVEL 3** Develop Solutions	Prioritize Achieving Social Impact
	Excludes companies that do harm	Includes companies benefiting a broad base of stakeholders	Includes companies creating new solutions	
	Negative screens	ESG Scoring Impact Lenses	Targeted Impact	
	DEPTH OF POSITIVE IMPACT			

FIGURE 2.3 Values-Aligned Investing Landscape

The values-aligned landscape stretches across all the asset classes, or categories of investments, that we will be discussing in this book. As you will discover, there are opportunities for you to move your money into alignment, regardless of whether you are using cash, stock, or any other investment vehicle. For example, let's consider gender lens investing again. This goal could be addressed by moving:

- Cash into community banks;
- Fixed income into municipal bonds;
- Stock investments in to companies that advance gender diversity and leadership;
- Private investments into women-led start-ups;
- Alternative investments to support affordable housing;
- Philanthropy to nonprofits that improve the lives of women and girls.

These are not the only options for gender lens investing but rather a sample of what's possible. Similar lists of potential investments can be created for other lenses or for your SDG priorities, with some caveats. Because the market of values-aligned financial products is still growing, it's not yet possible to find a full array of investment options for every SDG or investment lens. However, the rate of new product introductions is accelerating, and there are already a lot of options to be excited about.

Levels of Impact

Referring to Figure 2.3, you'll see there are three levels of impact within the values-aligned investing landscape: do no harm, benefit stakeholders, and develop solutions.

- **Level 1: Do no harm** is closest to traditional investing. Investments at this level eliminate involvement in selected industries, such as tobacco and weapons, from your portfolio. This approach, which is also known as negative screening, was the first way that socially responsible investments were designed.
- **Level 2: Benefit stakeholders** moves to the next level of impact by actively selecting only those companies that adhere to ESG best practices. As values-aligned investing has become more mainstream, fund managers are shifting from "considering" ESG in their investment decisions to integrating these criteria as a central element of their investment philosophy.
- **Level 3: Develop solutions** is the most impactful approach to investing. At this level, investments support companies that are creating solutions that result in positive social and/or environmental change.

You can't achieve all levels of depth with every investment—at least for the time being. But you should be able to find options in every asset class that can move you closer to your values and impact goals. I firmly believe our options will broaden and deepen going forward. As more of us actively shift our money into alignment with our values, the faster that change will come.

Take Action

This section provides some action steps you can take to deepen your understanding of your relationship to money. Choose one or two to do this week.

1. Explore your money stories

   If you haven't already, take the archetype quiz mentioned earlier in this chapter to learn more about your financial archetypes or download one of the toolkits on our companion website, *activateyourmoney.net*, to engage in another method of exploring what money means to you and how it fits in your life.

2. Bring clarity to your values

   Find a quiet place and grab a pen and paper. Then write your answers to the following question, taking care to be as thorough as you can. What changes would you like to see in our society over the next 20 years? Think about your community, the country, the economy, the environment.

   Once you complete your writing, look back at the SDGs in the previous section to see which of them are most related to your vision. Now, explore which resonate the most with you and pick your top three to five. Then put your list away and return to it in a few days.

   Do the SDGs you chose still feel like your top priorities, or has something changed? If they are the same, you're ready to move forward. If they changed, reflect on why.

   Perhaps you realized one or two really stand out and you want to use them as your lenses. Perhaps you dropped a few and added others. Assuming you feel good about your choices, move on. If you're still wavering, you might want to sit with them a bit longer.

3. Engage with others

   Start a conversation with a few of your female friends and ask them about the early childhood messages they received around money and how those messages are still influencing them today. Alternatively, have a conversation about the SDGs and aligning your investments with your values.

Special Note

The biggest taboo around money tends to be how much we have or don't have. So if that is really uncomfortable for you, as it is for many of us, don't include it in your conversations. You can talk about your money without divulging how much you have. I have been in two investment clubs in my life, one in the early 1990s that was inspired by the book *The Beardstown Ladies' Common-Sense Investment Guide* and another during the mid-2010s. The second club was focused on values-aligned investing. We talked at length about our investments, our financial advisors, our successes, and our failures. Nothing was left off the table. After five years of membership, I still had no idea how much money each of the other members had, and I didn't care. I gained tremendous value from just being in the conversations, and so can you.

CHAPTER 3

Your Financial Foundation
Master Some Core Principles

You need the same knowledge and tools to make sound investments, regardless of whether they are values-aligned or not. Since our society has not done a great job of educating women about basic investment concepts, investing can be intimidating or overwhelming for a lot of us. Lisa Leff Cooper, an investment expert and contributor to this chapter, has witnessed over and over again how knowledge about a few key investment concepts can go a very long way toward empowering individuals in making wise and informed investment decisions. She has found this to be true for all types of investors, such as recent graduates new to saving and investing, mid-term careerists, newly single women, recipients of new wealth, and women entering retirement.

Even though this book is not intended to teach the basics of personal finance, there are a few important concepts that anyone diving more deeply into their investments needs to understand. This chapter touches on those fundamentals. After reading it, you'll know if you're ready to invest, where you stand financially, and what your investment priorities are. You will also be introduced to the major asset classes as well as the concepts of portfolio diversification and asset allocation. When you complete this chapter, you'll have the foundational elements you need and the beginnings of your own investment strategy.

If you feel confident with your overall investing knowledge, feel free to skip ahead to the next chapter. If you want even more information about the basics after completing this chapter, you will find additional resources on our companion website.

Before You Invest

This book assumes you're ready to invest and already have some of the basics of your financial life in order. You're ready to invest once the following qualifiers are true:

- Your income comfortably covers your ongoing expenses;
- You have manageable debt, which means you can avoid high-interest debt and comfortably afford your monthly debt repayments; and
- You have at least three to six months of readily available (e.g., "liquid") funds to cover needed expenses in case of an emergency or other unexpected event.

If you're not quite there yet, don't worry or be ashamed. Whether you are young or old, you're not alone. A study by Charles Schwab[1] found that only 28% of Americans have a written financial plan. Those who do, however, feel more financially stable and demonstrate better saving and investing behavior.

Saving Is Important, But It's Not Enough

As women, we tend to save. That's what we've been told to do by family, society, and personal finance gurus. The good news is we've listened. The bad news is we're more likely than men to keep our savings in cash, because we're worried about losing our money.[2] Unfortunately, keeping the bulk of our money in cash or low-risk/low-return investments is usually not sufficient to achieve our financial goals, particularly over the long term. When we keep our money in cash, inflation outpaces the interest we are being paid. So we're actually losing money year by year. Even more significant is the asset growth that's being left on the table.

Five Requirements to Building Your Wealth

When you know how much money you need to meet your goals and meet the following five requirements, you're well on your way to building your wealth:

1. Spend less than you make;
2. Pay off debt;
3. Save;
4. Invest; and
5. Monitor your investments.

Assume you save $500 per month in a bank that's paying you 1% interest per year. Over a 30-year period you will have accumulated $210,000. If that money had been placed in a bond fund that returned 3% per year, you'd have $294,000. But if the money went into investments that returned 6% over the same term, you'd have more than $500,000.[3]

To build your wealth, you should be putting aside as much money as you can as soon as you can, and you should be investing your money rather than putting it in a savings account. While virtually any form of investing is going to be riskier than just putting your money in a bank, chances are you will not reach your financial goals without it.

How Much Money Do You Have?

It's going to be impossible for you to invest your money wisely if you don't know how much money you have and where it is. You'd be surprised by how few of us actually know where all our money is being held and what it's invested in. So the first thing to do, if you haven't done so already, is to take inventory. If you haven't done this, we'll help you get started in the "Take Action" section at the end of this chapter.

The hardest part of this exercise might be pulling together all the sources of information you have about your money. Once you are done, though, you'll have a way to keep all the information in one place, going forward. You'll also know what you own, what you believe is values-aligned, and how your money is spread, or allocated, across different asset classes.

Where Do You Stand Compared to Other People?

When you calculate how much you have, where it is, and your financial net worth, you might be interested to know how your level of wealth compares to other Americans. Many people do not have a realistic sense of what wealth—or a lack thereof—looks like in this country.

According to data from the Federal Reserve's 2016 Survey of Consumer Finances (SCF), the median net wealth of households in the United States was $97,300.[4] Thus, half of Americans had a net wealth below this number and the remainder had a net wealth above it. Table 3.1 highlights how much money the average household needed to be in the top 50 percentile, top 20 percentile, and top 10 percentile by age.

The same SCF study concludes that only 7.6 million, or 6% of, households have $2 million or more, 1.3 million, or 1% of, households have $10 million or more, and a mere 84,000 households in this country have a net wealth of $50 million or more.[5] A different study looking at individuals showed that by the end of 2019, 45% of millionaires in the United States were women.[6]

TABLE 3.1 Wealth Percentiles

Age	Top 50%	Top 20%	Top 10%
18–25	$4,000	$22,750	$65,510
26–30	$12,000	$82,500	$142,710
31–35	$30,400	$144,950	$259,780
36–40	$47,700	$218,400	$464,100
41–45	$85,600	$379,000	$721,800
46–50	$131,590	$546,200	$1,173,100
51–55	$134,920	$586,470	$1,224,500
56–60	$188,250	$998,100	$2,456,300
61–65	$209,700	$1,015,350	$1,957,700
66–70	$218,500	$852,300	$1,712,000
71–75	$255,900	$990,500	$2,118,600
76–99	$259,900	$1,003,800	$2,079,069

This data is important because part of our money beliefs relate to where we think we stand relative to others. Since so much about money is taboo, we don't actually know. So we make up stories about our personal situations. Perhaps you're young and already have a few hundred thousand dollars stashed away in retirement funds and other investments, and you think that everyone else is in the same situation. Or maybe you have a few million dollars, but you don't think you're rich, because you compare yourself to those who are much wealthier than you. Only a small fraction of the population are millionaires, and only the top 1% has $10 million or more.

How Much Will You Need to Retire?

While some Americans are set up to enjoy a comfortable retirement, far too many are woefully unprepared to support themselves in their later years because they aren't planning sufficiently and aren't on track to reach their goals. Social Security can play a role in filling the gap, especially for those at the lower end of the wealth spectrum. However, Social Security alone is often not enough to cover expenses through the retirement years, particularly with growing concerns about the continued availability and sustainability of this government funding.

So how much is enough? Well, that depends. Different people have wildly different points of view. One of the men who kicked off the Financially Independent, Retire Early (FIRE) movement, "retired" in his early 30s with only $800,000.[7] He and his family had a low-cost lifestyle and pulled their annual expenses from the dividends and other revenue that their portfolio generated each year. On the other hand, a well-known personal finance pundit initially hated the FIRE movement because, among other things, she thought it left too many unknowns unaccounted for. In her view, you need at least $10 million to retire early.[8] Whereas, Schwab 401(k) participants believe they need $1.7 million, on average, to retire.[9] So who's right?

There is probably no right answer. How much you need to retire is a very personal decision. It is based on your current age, earning potential, expected return on your assets, age of retirement, expected cost of living at retirement, and a number of other factors. At first glance, it seems difficult to know all of those variables, particularly if you are still young and in the earlier stages of your career. So much can happen between now and the time you retire. How can you possibly know? Fortunately, the power of technology makes it easy to get a reasonable estimate of your long-term financial situation. You simply enter some key data, which you should be able to easily gather, into any one of the retirement calculators that you can find online, and the tool does the rest.

The retirement calculators allow you to play what-if games. By entering different values in the calculator, you can determine the impact that lifestyle changes would have on your long-term goals. For example, if the calculator shows you aren't going to meet your retirement objectives, then you could consider getting a better-paying job, saving more of your assets, taking additional investment risks, reducing your expenses in retirement, or working longer than you had planned. For those close to, or in, retirement, another calculator can determine how long your existing assets will last at your current spending rates.[10] You'll find the links to these tools on our companion website.

A Few Words of Wisdom on Retirement Funds

Like many people, you probably have some of your assets in tax-deferred or tax-exempt retirement accounts. Since each type has varying tax consequences, you might want to consider using them for different types of investments.

For example, you might place investments that you expect to pay the highest returns in tax-exempt accounts, like Roth IRAs. You might also use tax-deferred accounts for investments that you intend to buy and sell more frequently, since you won't have to pay taxes until you retire and withdraw the funds. Similarly, investments that you plan to hold for long periods, or that have limited tax implications, could be held in your taxable accounts. These types of considerations can play a role in growing your wealth over time.

Your Investment Criteria

As you begin your investment journey, it's helpful to clarify your priorities and tendencies. There are three essential criteria to consider: your personal investment objectives, your time horizon, and your risk tolerance. As you consider these criteria, ask yourself: What do you want to do with your money? How much time do you have? How much risk can you handle?

The way you answer these questions will guide just about every investment decision you make going forward.

What Are Your Investment Objectives?

Investing is highly personal. Each of us has our own goals for deciding how we invest and spend our money. For example:

- Do you want to put a down payment on a house?
- Are you saving for your children's education?
- Are you planning for a long and secure retirement?
- Does your money need to generate regular cash flow to support you or someone else, now or in the future?

Defining your personal financial goals can be highly challenging! A lot of people simply think, "More is better" when it comes to money, without recognizing there can be significant trade-offs to seeking high levels of growth, particularly in terms of portfolio safety and stability. Others—especially those with newly acquired wealth—approach the goal-setting process by saying, "Well, what *can* my money do?" without first delving into the question of where they would like to make an impact. While money can provide the means for reaching your goals, it can't provide answers about what those goals are. That's something only you can decide.

How Much Time Do You Have?

Another important criterion to specify is the length of time you're able and willing to invest. This is known as your time horizon. In other words, how long can your money stay invested and grow without your needing to tap into it for funds? This is an important question, because there are big differences between appropriate investment strategies for money you may need in a near-to-intermediate time frame and for money that can stay invested long term.

Finance professionals refer to short-, medium-, and long-term time horizons. Short-term time horizons are up to 3 years, while mid-term horizons are 3 to 10 years, and long-term is considered to be 10 years or more. If you have a short time horizon, you will likely want to minimize the risk of loss and invest conservatively. If your investment horizon is longer, your portfolio will have time to weather shorter-term ups and downs, giving you the opportunity to withstand a higher level of risk, which allows you to earn higher returns over time.

Many investors and investment professionals overlook the importance of time, especially in periods when markets are making dramatic moves. We saw this during the 2008 financial crisis and again with COVID-19 when many people pulled their money in panic, only to watch the market recover. History has demonstrated that market downturns are followed by recovery—and if you have time to weather downturns, staying invested produces the best outcome, typically by a significant amount.

Time Is a Powerful Force

Consider the 10-year period between January 2007 and December 2017—a period that includes the great recession of 2008. If you had $100,000 invested entirely in US large-cap stocks at the beginning of the 10 years and simply held onto those stocks for the full 10-year period, your $100,000 would have grown to $238,447. However, if you'd gotten nervous and pulled all your money out of the market in early 2009, which turned out to be the market bottom, and put it in cash for the remainder of the 10 years, your $100,000 would be worth only $55,125. And if you'd pulled out of the market for just one year, until things "calmed down," then reinvested, your $100,000 at the end of 10 years would be $155,356, which is 35% less than the optimal situation.

Some investors believe they can choose exactly when to move money in and out of markets, investing when prices are at a bottom and exiting at high points before a crash. This strategy is known as market timing. In practice, it rarely works out well. Most investment professionals urge investors to focus on "time in the market" rather than "timing the market."

The amount of time we have in the market has particular significance for women, because, on average, we live longer than men and need our money to last longer. We also tend to have fewer years in the workforce (e.g., taking time away to have children), resulting in less time to accumulate wealth. Combined, these factors present an added challenge for women and contribute to the wealth gap that we face relative to men.

What Is Your Risk Tolerance?

All investing involves the risk of loss. Some types of investments are subject to more risk, whereas others are subject to less. There is generally a trade-off between the level of risk associated with an investment and the potential return of that investment. This is known as the "risk-return trade-off." As an example, speculative small-cap stocks involve a higher level of risk but also the possibility of higher returns. High-quality bonds, on the other hand, tend to offer increased certainty but only low-to-moderate returns.

Your tolerance for risk is determined by a number of personal factors, including your time horizon, your financial capacity to withstand losses, and your emotional response to seeing the value of your portfolio fluctuate or drop. For many investors, the emotional component plays a significant, sometimes oversized, role in investment decision-making. A fear of loss generates strong emotions. We tend to remember our financial losses more than we do our financial gains. Being aware of this emotional bias can help you mitigate your own fears, as will increasing your investment knowledge and experience.

In general, each type of investment tends to have a unique position along a risk-return continuum. Figure 3.1 identifies the relative positions of cash alternatives and some types of fixed income and public equity investments.

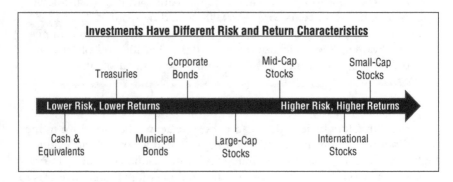

FIGURE 3.1 Risk-Return Spectrum

There are special considerations for women around risk. Generally speaking, we can be more conservative investors than men. The problem with this too-conservative approach is that it can lead to low portfolio growth over time, or even a portfolio that struggles to keep up with inflation and taxes. This presents a significant risk of not being able to meet long-term financial goals, such as buying a house, putting children through college, or being prepared for retirement.

Introduction to Asset Classes

Once you have a sense of what you want your money to do and you have insight into your time horizon and risk tolerance, it's time to consider where and how to invest. For better or worse, you have a very wide array of options from which to choose, and investing can get complex. The goal of this section is providing a basis for your choices by introducing you to the major asset classes, each of which will be explained in detail in the next part of the book.

In general, each asset class offers a distinct combination of risk-return characteristics. But this is not a hard-and-fast rule, because there can be variations within a single asset class. What's more, there can be wide fluctuations from one year to the next. Table 3.2 shows the average returns for several asset classes over the 15-year period from 2005 to 2019.[11] It also shows the best and worst returns in any one year during that same period. Notice the dramatic shifts that can occur, particularly with emerging markets and high-yield bonds. Also note the relative stability afforded by high-grade bonds.

TABLE 3.2 Asset Class Returns

Asset Class	Average	Best	Worst
US large cap	9.00%	32.4%	−37.0%
US small cap	7.92%	38.8%	−33.8%
International developed	5.33%	32.5%	−43.1%
Emerging markets	7.85%	79.0%	−53.2%
Investment-grade bonds	4.15%	7.8%	−2.0%
High-yield bonds	7.11%	57.5%	−26.4%
Cash	1.30%	4.7%	0.0%

Cash

Cash provides immediate liquidity. Your funds are extremely safe, as they are federally insured up to $250,000 in any certified financial institution. However, returns are usually well below the rate of inflation. Thus, over time, funds left in cash decline in value.

Cash Alternatives

Cash alternative investments include money market funds, certificates of deposit (CDs), and some specialized financial products. These investments tend to be relatively safe, and some are even federally insured. They provide less liquidity than cash, tying up your assets for 3–12 months. In turn, they tend to offer a somewhat higher return than you will get from your savings or checking accounts. Cash alternatives can play an important role in a portfolio by providing safety for capital that you will need in the short term, but they should not be expected to provide real growth over time.

Fixed Income

Fixed-income investments include longer-term CDs, promissory notes, bonds, and bond funds. When you invest in fixed income, you're essentially making a loan to a borrower. In return, the borrower vows to pay you back with interest. Most often, their payments are made on a regular schedule. Fixed-income investments usually carry low to modest risk—more than cash but less than public equities. But they also provide more modest returns than stocks. Some types of bonds, however, carry higher risk. This is an example of the diversity and differing risk-return trade-offs that can exist within a single asset class. The most common reason for adding lower-risk fixed income into a portfolio is to provide stability and safety while generating a predictable stream of reliable income.

Public Equities

When you buy stock in a company, you own a portion of the company. That portion is allocated to you in shares and represents your ownership, or equity, in the firm. As the value of the company goes up or down, so does the worth of your shares. Most public equities trade actively throughout the day and offer a high degree of liquidity. You can basically buy and sell these assets whenever you want. However, there can be exceptions, especially in the cases of smaller companies, which may have fewer interested buyers, making these stocks harder to sell and therefore less liquid.

The purpose of including stocks, or public equities, in a portfolio is to deliver growth over the long term. However, stocks can be volatile, with lots of ups and downs in the shorter term. This volatility makes them a riskier asset class than cash or fixed income.

Private Investments

Private debt and private equity are investments in companies that are not traded on the public stock market. The restaurants, shops, and businesses in your neighborhood are prime examples, as are the technology start-ups that we hear so much about in the news. Because these companies are not publicly traded, it's much harder to find buyers and sellers. The difficulty in selling your shares in a privately held company is what makes these assets illiquid.

Private investing can be a lot of fun. What makes investing in this asset class engaging is that you can target your investments directly to the entrepreneurs, start-ups, and other early-stage businesses that excite or inspire you. You can also choose to invest in companies that have high social impact, are located in your community, and/or are run by traditionally underfunded founders, such as women and minorities. You can actually engage with the entrepreneurs directly. Depending on the size of your investment, you could even take an observer or board seat to provide assistance and oversight to the business.

Private investments can offer high returns and compelling targeted opportunities for social impact, but they also often involve considerable risk, because most companies go out of business within their first five years of operation.[12] In addition, private companies are not bound by the same disclosure requirements as public companies, so it can be harder to access financials and other key information that an investor needs to assess risk.

Alternative Investments

A number of additional asset classes that investors can use to diversify their portfolios are grouped together under the term "alternatives." This broad category includes virtually anything that can be traded and that doesn't fall into one of the other asset classes. Currency markets, commodities, real estate, natural resources, and collectables are all examples. Many of these investments require specialized knowledge to achieve a successful outcome and tend to have limited liquidity. As you might expect given the range of options, risk levels and return potentials of alternative investments can vary widely.

A Note on Accredited versus Non-Accredited Investor Status

In the US, investors are separated into different categories based on their annual income and net worth. Individuals can be non-accredited, accredited, or qualified investors. These designations are set by the US Securities and Exchange Commission (SEC) to protect smaller investors from putting their money into high-risk ventures, such as private and alternative investments. The SEC traditionally believed that only financially sophisticated investors had the knowledge and financial resources to invest in these riskier financial products. This changed, to some degree, with the passage of the 2012 JOBS Act, which opened private and alternative investing to everyone. However, there are limits on how much a non-accredited person can invest in these opportunities.

Investor Designations

An accredited investor is anyone whose income exceeded $200,000 (or $300,000 with a spouse) in each of the prior two years and who reasonably expects the same for the current year. Or it is someone who has a net worth over $1 million, either alone or with a spouse, excluding the value of the person's primary residence. An even higher bar is the qualified purchaser, who is an individual or legal entity with at least $5 million in investments.

If you do not meet these criteria, then you're a non-accredited investor. Although many private and alternative investments are limited to accredited investors, there are a growing number of opportunities that are open to both accredited and non-accredited investors.

Designing Your Portfolio

Now that you have a basic understanding of your own financial situation and the different asset classes open to you, let's look at how you can put them together into a portfolio that is designed to fit *your* specific goals, time horizon, risk tolerance, and investor class.

Don't Put All Your Eggs in One Basket

One of the first things to understand is the importance of diversifying your portfolio, which means dividing your money across different investments and asset classes. Diversification is one of the most powerful concepts in investing. It can help you build a portfolio that's more resilient to market downturns. While diversification does not eliminate the risk of losing money, it does reduce the risk by spreading funds across different asset classes that behave differently under certain market conditions. Diversification, however, can also reduce the overall return of the portfolio. The goal is to introduce enough diversification to reduce risk without adding so much that you undermine your investment returns. There are opportunities for diversification *across* different asset classes as well as *within* a particular asset class.

Diversification is essentially adding an *uncorrelated* asset to a portfolio. This is basically an asset that behaves differently from the rest of your portfolio. When you add an asset with a lower correlation to your current portfolio, the asset has the potential to increase the portfolio's expected return and simultaneously decrease its overall risk.

For example, large-cap and small-cap stocks are closely correlated. Their values tend to move in the same direction under similar market conditions. When the US economy is healthy and employment levels are high, these assets do well. But when economic growth is lagging, they tend to suffer. Under these conditions, the government may lower interest rates to stimulate renewed growth. When interest rates go down, the value of bonds goes up. Thus, in an economic downturn, the value of stocks and bonds moves in opposite directions. By holding stocks and bonds, you alter the level of correlation in your portfolio, thereby reducing your overall risk. Including other asset classes, such as private investments and alternatives, can decrease the level of correlation even more and further diversify your portfolio.

Professional investment managers use diversification as they seek to deliver the highest level of return relative to risk. A typical professionally managed portfolio will contain a mix of some, if not all, of the asset classes outlined here. These managers can also bring additional diversification into a portfolio through a single asset class. For example, investments in public equities could be segmented by company size, geographic location, and business sector. Other asset classes have similar diversification potential.

Individually managed portfolios often lack an appropriate level of diversification. Most often portfolios are not diversified enough. Having too much of your money in a single investment or asset class can have a negative, potentially disastrous, impact on your entire portfolio if something goes wrong with the few investments you hold. You can also over-diversify a portfolio. Investing too broadly across a wide range of investments can reduce the return of your overall portfolio. The goal is to find a balance between risk and return.

Diversification is used to mitigate risk in most economic conditions, but it's not a silver bullet. Even a well-diversified portfolio cannot protect us in all circumstances. In certain economic situations, asset classes that normally react differently to market conditions can unexpectedly all move in sync.

This was the case in 2008, when many asset classes were affected by the mortgage crisis.

Include Asset Allocation

Asset allocation is a strategy for portfolio management that splits assets among broad categories of investments, such as cash, fixed income, public equities, and alternatives.

You decide which asset classes you want to hold and how much money you will invest in each. When you allocate your money, you are literally determining the percentage of your total assets you want in cash, fixed income, public equities, and so on.

Establishing asset allocations lies at the heart of designing your portfolio. Your goal is to choose a mix of asset types, which, over the long term, will deliver a high probability of meeting your financial goals while exposing you to a manageable level of risk. Ideally, your asset allocation should seek to tap the power of diversification so your assets are distributed across relatively uncorrelated asset categories.

Asset allocation typically involves setting a target allocation for each asset class, along with tolerance bands that specify the minimum and maximum amounts you want in each asset class. This allows for fluctuations that are likely to take place in your portfolio over time.

Asset Allocation Examples

To help illustrate, let's revisit some of the sample investors you met in Chapter 2 and see how asset allocations play out for them. These allocations are based on each woman's investment priorities, time horizon, and risk tolerance.

JADE: A FIRED-UP IDEALIST   Jade and her husband are saving for a downpayment on a two- to three-unit building that will include their housing and provide an additional income stream. They are more than halfway to their goal and expect to have the full downpayment in three to four years. Jade and Denzel are non-accredited investors; however, they enjoy making investment decisions together and want to allocate some of their assets to public and private companies that align with their environmental values.

As you can see in Table 3.3, their current asset allocation is *extremely conservative* because of their immediate savings goal. However, it also takes into account their interest in investing a bit of their money in the public and private equities markets. After Jade and her husband buy their property, their financial priority will shift to investing for an early retirement, and their asset allocations will become more aggressive, reflecting their young age, upward career potential, long time horizon, and comfort with risk.

TABLE 3.3 Extremely Conservative Asset Allocation

Asset Class	Target	Minimum	Maximum
Cash / cash alternatives	75%	50%	100%
Fixed income	10%	5%	50%
Public equities	13%	0%	85%
Private investments	2%	0%	10%
Alternatives	0%	0%	10%

TONI: A RETIRED SAVER   Toni is retired and lives with her husband and disabled daughter, Nina. Although neither she nor her husband had high-paying jobs, they lived simply and saved their money from an early age. They rarely touched their assets and let them grow over time. As a result, they are now accredited investors and have enough money to meet their monthly needs without having to touch their principal. Their primary goal is to safeguard the funds they have for the remainder of their retirement and to have enough left over to ensure Nina's safety and happiness after they die.

Toni and her husband's risk tolerance is low, and their asset allocations are *conservative*. They are worried, however, that this strategy may not provide sufficient capital for Nina's life expectancy. As a result, they are reconsidering the allocations shown in Table 3.4.

TABLE 3.4 Conservative Asset Allocation

Asset Class	Target	Minimum	Maximum
Cash / cash alternatives	5%	2%	20%
Fixed income	60%	40%	70%
Public equities	35%	25%	45%
Private investments	0%	0%	0%
Alternatives	0%	0%	0%

AVA: A CARETAKER AND "RETURNER"   Ava is a recently divorced mother of two, who is reentering the workforce. While married, her husband managed their assets and was invested primarily in the stock market. She decided to hire a financial advisor, who is now working with Ava to diversify her portfolio. Ava needs some of her money to supplement her income until she finds a job. She also wants some portfolio growth to ensure she can have a comfortable retirement, even if it has to be delayed slightly.

Ava's advisor is moving her toward a *moderate* asset allocation, highlighted in Table 3.5. Given her lack of familiarity with investing, Ava's risk tolerance and time horizon are medium.

TABLE 3.5 Moderate Asset Allocation

Asset Class	Target	Minimum	Maximum
Cash / cash alternatives	5%	2%	20%
Fixed income	30%	5%	40%
Public equities	55%	50%	70%
Private investments	0%	0%	5%
Alternatives	5%	0%	10%

ANIKA: A YOUNG GUARDIAN   Anika is under 30 and hypervigilant with her money. Her primary goal is a comfortable retirement, for which she has a long time horizon (30+ years). When she started saving, Anika was reluctant to invest. However, a mentor has been helping her understand investing, which is building her confidence. As a result, her risk tolerance is higher than it used to be, because she now understands the benefits of a long time horizon and compounding. With her mentor, Anika developed an investment strategy and plan. This has helped her relax a bit around money.

Anika's asset allocation, depicted in Table 3.6, is *moderately aggressive,* given her young age, long time horizon, and remaining level of discomfort with risk.

TABLE 3.6 Moderately Aggressive Asset Allocation

Asset Class	Target	Minimum	Maximum
Cash / cash alternatives	5%	2%	20%
Fixed income	20%	5%	25%
Public equities	75%	60%	85%
Private investments	0%	0%	5%
Alternatives	0%	0%	5%

MARIA: AN EMPIRE BUILDER   The start-up business Maria co-founded was recently acquired, making her a multimillionaire. As a result, Maria's investment goals of financing her daughters' college educations and having a comfortable retirement are already covered. She realizes that she has enough wealth now to do more. Maria is grateful for her good fortune and wants to use her wealth to create deep impact. She is an accredited investor and a qualified purchaser.

Maria's asset allocation is ***aggressive***, thanks to her overall level of wealth, high-risk tolerance, and minimal needs for income and liquidity. As you can see in Table 3.7, Maria is in a good position to invest in private and alternative investments.

TABLE 3.7 Aggressive Asset Allocation

Asset Class	Target	Minimum	Maximum
Cash / cash alternatives	3%	2%	10%
Fixed income	17%	5%	25%
Public equities	30%	25%	60%
Private investments	20%	10%	25%
Alternatives	35%	10%	40%

While these examples are designed to be instructive, your specific situation is likely to be different. There's no exact formula for determining an appropriate asset allocation, as each case depends on your investment objectives, time horizon, and risk tolerance. It's also important to realize your asset allocation is likely to change over time, as your life situation, goals, and time horizon shift. It may also change as you become more confident with your investing. A financial advisor may add a great deal of perspective and value to this process.

Make Time to Rebalance Your Portfolio

Once you've established your asset allocation targets and built a portfolio to meet them, you'll need to monitor and make adjustments to keep your allocations in line. This is an important part of managing your investments. Even in relatively calm times, market movements are likely to create shifts in your portfolio's asset allocations over time. For example, if you—like Anika—set your allocation to public equities at a targeted 75% and the stock market then enjoys a particularly strong period of relative returns, the percentage of your portfolio allocated to public equities will rise to some level higher than 75%. This can expose your portfolio to unintended risk. When this happens, a prudent strategy is to *rebalance* your investments back to the targeted allocations.

While there are no hard-and-fast rules around when to rebalance, many investors and financial advisors do so either quarterly or annually. Some investors have a policy of rebalancing when there's a big swing in the markets, so a move in any single asset class—say, up or down 10%—serves as a trigger to rebalance. Many advisors suggest investors rebalance at least once a year to keep their portfolios appropriately allocated. If you have a financial advisor, you may want to confirm they are performing this service for you on a routine basis.

Tracking How Your Investments Perform

It's important for investors to be able to monitor their returns over time. Seeing whether your portfolio value has gone up or down is simple, but evaluating how your individual investments and overall portfolio have performed—compared with how they could, or should, have performed—is a more complicated exercise. In addition, not all investments are equal when it comes to assessing performance.

Measuring investment returns for cash, cash alternatives, and private debt is relatively easy, because you receive regular dividends or interest payments. It's also relatively easy to calculate the total return on individual fixed income and public equities investments. This information is freely available online at any number of financial sites. When you get into private equity and some of the other alternatives, however, measuring return can be considerably more difficult because information is harder to find, track, and assess.

Challenges also exist at the overall portfolio level, where accurately measuring a portfolio's growth rate typically involves sophisticated calculations that take trades, cash flows, and other transactions that occurred in the portfolio into consideration. Providing meaningful reporting on investment performance is a valuable service investment advisors can provide.

To assess performance on a specific investment, it's critical to make sure you're looking at how your investment behaved relative to investments with similar characteristics over the same period of time. To do this, you'll use *benchmarks,* which are designed to reflect specific segments of the market. The S&P 500 is one of the best-known benchmarks for US public equities. You'll find more information about benchmarks and how to use them in Chapter 7.

Online Tools Make Investment Analysis Easy

If you want to better understand your public holdings, their performance, or how they compare to other investments, there are some wonderful online financial reporting tools, such as Google Finance and Morningstar. These free sites can provide a wealth of information about your investments, as the snapshot in Figure 3.2 shows.

Voya Russell Large Cap Growth Idx Port S IRLSX ★★★★ ⊞ Morningstar Analyst Rating
Quantitative rating as of Aug 31, 2020

Quote	Fund Analysis	Performance	Risk	Price	Portfolio	People	Parent

NAV / 1-Day Return	Total Assets	Adj. Expense Ratio ①	Expense Ratio
51.36 / ↑ 2.05%	1.4 Bil	0.680%	0.680%
Fee Level	**Longest Manager Tenure**	**Category**	**Investment Style**
Below Average	8.44 years	US Fund Large Growth	⊞ Large Growth
Min. Initial Investment	**Status**	**TTM Yield**	**Turnover**
0	Open	0.42%	19%

USD | NAV as of Oct 05, 2020 | 1-Day Return as of Oct 05, 2020, 2:30 PM GMT-07:00

FIGURE 3.2 Morningstar Snapshot

The Voya Russell Large Cap Growth fund is a values-aligned index fund. Its stock symbol, also known as the ticker, is IRLSX. The ticker is an easy way to identify a fund. When you search for IRLSX on Morningstar, you are rewarded with this summary screen. This snapshot from October 5, 2020, shows you that a total of $1.4 billion was invested in the fund. You can see that investors pay 0.68% per year to own the fund (*expense ratio*) and that this fee is considered below average (*fee level*). You can also tell that this is a US large-cap growth fund, which means it holds primarily large companies with growth potential. There is no *minimum initial investment* to buy into this fund, and it's available, or open, for purchase (*status*). By looking at the *turnover*, you can see 19% of the total holdings in the fund are sold, or turned over, on an annual basis. And you can tell that this fund received a 4-star rating from Morningstar.

And you learned all that just by looking at a single screen. If you go through the tabs immediately above this data to "Fund Analysis," "Performance," "Risk," and so on, you can find even more information about this fund. The "Performance" tab allows you to track the return on this investment over 1-, 3-, 5-, 10-, and even 15-year time horizons and provides information about the benchmark used with the fund. The "Portfolio" tab lists the companies held by the fund and shows Morningstar's sustainability ratings. If you try researching a few of your public equities holdings this way, you might be surprised by what you learn.

Your Investment Policy Statement

An investment policy statement (IPS) is a document that helps you put all the information you learned in this chapter together in one place. Your IPS will help guide your investment decision-making over time. This document, which can be as simple or as complex as you want, defines your investment goals, asset allocation targets, rebalancing objectives, and other key information.

Institutional investors, such as large foundations or university endowments, often have elaborate and detailed IPSs. Your IPS doesn't need to be fancy or lengthy. It just needs to address the critical elements that are most important to you and your financial advisor, if you have one. Some advisors use an IPS, or something like it, when they're establishing their relationship with new clients. An IPS is a living document, designed to be updated and revised as your lifestyle and goals change over time.

Take Action

The following actions are the foundational elements that you should consider developing if you want to take control of your financial future.

1. Determine what you have

Download the "What You Have Workbook" from our companion website. This Excel tool will provide you with full instructions and help you place your current holdings in appropriate asset classes. Once completed, the "What You Have Workbook" will show how much money you have invested in each asset class, along with the total monetary value of all your holdings. It will also automatically calculate your asset allocations, or the percentage of your total assets that are held in each asset class.

You can use the same workbook to enter your liabilities. The "Your Net Worth" tab will automatically calculate your net wealth.

2. Determine how much you need to retire

Use the retirement tools referenced on our companion website to get a better understanding of your current retirement situation and your retirement options. Play around with the calculators to see what happens under differing scenarios, such as retiring later, increasing your current income, and saving more now.

3. Determine your asset allocations

You have already reviewed the asset allocations for Toni, Jade, Ava, Anika, and Maria. If you want to know more or you don't feel those personas represented your situation, check our companion website. There you'll find references to more portfolios that you can study.

4. Track your investments' performance

If you have not done so already, delve into the details and performance history of some of your public equity and fixed income holdings using the Morningstar website or any other online platform.

5. Create your IPS

Building your own IPS is a helpful and important part of your investment journey. If you're currently working with a financial advisor or investment manager, you may already have a personalized IPS. Take it out and review it. Do you understand it? Does it still reflect your current situation and goals? If things have changed, it might be time to consider this document anew.

If you don't have an IPS yet, download the "IPS Template" and example from our website and work to develop your own document. Don't worry if you cannot fill everything out right now. As you get more comfortable with investing, it will become easier. This is also a great document to share with family, friends, and others with whom you discuss your financial situation. Once developed, you may want to revisit it on an annual basis to ensure it still reflects your goals.

Endnotes

1. https://content.schwab.com/web/retail/public/about-schwab/Charles-Schwab-2019-Modern-Wealth-Survey-findings-0519-9JBP.pdf.
2. https://www.ellevest.com/magazine/newsletter/2019-01-23.
3 These sums were obtained using a MoneyChimp calculator and assumed interest was compounded monthly. http://www.moneychimp.com/calculator/compound_interest_calculator.htm.
4. https://www.federalreserve.gov/econres/scfindex.htm.
5. https://dqydj.com/how-many-millionaires-decamillionaires-america/.
6. https://thequantum.com/financial-facts-for-womens-history-month/.
7. https://www.mrmoneymustache.com/2011/09/15/a-brief-history-of-the-stash-how-we-saved-from-zero-to-retirement-in-ten-years/.
8. https://affordanything.com/153-hate-fire-movement-suze-orman/.
9. https://www.aboutschwab.com/schwab-401k-participant-study-2019.
10. https://www.nerdwallet.com/blog/investing/how-long-will-your-retirement-savings-last/.
11. https://novelinvestor.com/asset-class-returns.
12. https://www.fundera.com/blog/what-percentage-of-small-businesses-fail.

Crafting an Aligned Portfolio

The second part of *Activate Your Money* contains the core of the book. In it, we will walk you through each asset class in which you might want to invest—from cash to stocks to real estate and beyond. Each chapter focuses on a single asset class, explaining how it works and providing you with key knowledge that you can use to make more informed investment decisions. You'll be introduced to tools and values-aligned investments that you can access today, regardless of the amount you want to invest.

Feel free to read through and apply the information in this section in any sequence that works best for you. Some readers may only be interested in diving into two or three asset classes—such as cash, fixed income, and public equities. Others may want to jump into private investing or alternatives. The chapters were written to maintain a stand-alone quality, allowing you to access them in the sequence that works best for you.

There is a lot of information in Part 2. If you start to feel overwhelmed at any time, simply put the book aside for a bit and come back to it. Nothing says that you have to absorb everything at once. Smart, successful investing and wealth creation is more like a marathon than a sprint. We are here to support your journey, but please be kind with yourself and proceed at your own pace. *Activate Your Money* and the companion website are a set of resources that are available for you whenever you choose to access them.

CHAPTER 4

Cash

Activate Your Savings and Checking Accounts

Over the next several chapters, we'll be discussing your investment options—asset class by asset class. We will look at what each class is, how it works, and the values-aligned investment choices you have. We'll start, in this chapter, with the first asset class: cash. Your cash should not be overlooked when you're thinking about a value-aligned portfolio. Like any other investment you make, it is being used for some purpose, and you have the right to choose a bank that uses your money to support the things you care about.

This chapter will help you think differently about your cash and the impact it is having on the world. It describes a range of banking options through which you can express your values, and it provides you with the step-by-step actions required to shift your assets from your current bank to a financial institution that is driven by more than the bottom line. By changing banks, you might also find that you receive higher interest, pay lower fees, and/or receive more personalized customer service.

In 2011, I transferred my savings and checking accounts from Wells Fargo and Citibank to New Resource Bank, which aspired to invest 100% of its loan portfolio in businesses that advanced sustainability. I loved New Resource Bank! They were small, local, and loaned my money to green businesses. When I started writing this chapter, my bank was in the process of being acquired by Amalgamated Bank, another values-aligned financial institution.

While I appreciated my new relationship with Amalgamated, I prefer smaller banks. So I moved my cash accounts to two different financial institutions, both of which support women-led businesses and underserved groups in my community. I also opened a third account with Aspiration Bank, because it is a digital-only values-aligned bank, and I wanted to test that, too.

Although I opened accounts at three banks, I'm not advocating that you do the same. I did it as an experiment. Bottom line? It wasn't that hard. I made the shift bit by bit and didn't close out my Amalgamated accounts until I knew all my deposits, bill payments, and transfers were being handled by my new banks. Since I wasn't in a rush, I gave myself about six months to complete the process, even though I could have done it much faster.

So far, I am very happy with my choices. I feel good about where my money "lives" and what it supports. I get updates about the impact these institutions are making, and my new banks even invite me to local events from time to time. In my view, that's a pretty compelling relationship to have with your bank!

Cash Is Ready Money

Cash includes any funds that are immediately available—in full—for any purpose. Cash is normally invested in savings, checking, and money market accounts. These investments are available from a range of financial institutions.

When you put your cash in the bank, it is safe, but chances are you aren't making money on it. In fact, since the rate of inflation is probably *higher* than the interest rate you receive on your cash, you're actually losing money. For example, if you're receiving 1.00% interest and the inflation rate is 3.00%, then in real terms* you're losing 2.00% of the value of your cash each year. Crazy, right?

Your bank, however, is using your money to make money for itself. How they are using it, what they are investing in, and who is benefiting from your money should matter to you. After all, it's your money. The question is: Are they supporting your goals and using your money in ways that align with your values? The good news is you have other choices if they aren't.

How Much Cash Should You Have?

A good rule of thumb is to have three to six months of your monthly expenses set aside as cash. Before retiring, I always kept six to 12 months in available cash, because I assumed it would take me at least six months to find another job, and I didn't want to be caught empty-handed. This is a personal choice. While I took a more cautious approach, some of you may be willing to take higher risks and have less cash on hand.

---

*Real rate of return is the rate you are actually earning, in this case from interest minus the rate of inflation, which is a measure of the rate at which the average price of a "basket" of selected goods and services increases over a period of time. If your earnings keep up with or exceed the rate of inflation, then your purchasing power increases. If your earnings do not keep up, then you have less money to purchase the same goods each year.

This is particularly important for women because we are savers. In other words, we often have more cash than we need to hedge against risks. According to an article by Ellevest, women keep 71 cents of every dollar in cash instead of investing it.[1] We tend to do this because we're saving for a future goal, we want to protect against lean times, or we just don't know where else to invest. So these funds are left in cash accounts—sometimes for years, even decades, without growing. I want you to know that it doesn't have to be this way. You can make the switch and start having your money work for you while supporting your values.

What Is Your Cash Supporting?

Banks make their money by using your cash deposits to make loans and investments. You'd better believe they earn far more on your money than the meager interest they pay you. Let's say your bank is paying you 1.00% interest on your deposits. They could be lending that money out at the rate of 4.75% for mortgages, 5.0% to 7.6% for student loans, or 14% to 20% for credit card balances. In other words, they're generating revenue on your money. They're also making money through the fees they charge you for your accounts, such as monthly service charges, fees for using out-of-network ATMs, and wire transfer fees. How different financial institutions invest (and profit from) the money they take in through your savings, checking, and money market accounts varies widely and depends on their size (that is, the amount of money they control), their business model, and their ownership structure.

Traditional Options: The Mega-Bank

Let's start by looking at the mega-banks, where many Americans have chosen to invest their savings, checking, and money market accounts. Four of the biggest banks in the US are Bank of America, Wells Fargo, Citigroup, and JP Morgan Chase. These four mega-banks have combined assets in the trillions of dollars, and they control half of all the banking assets in the country.[2] During the 2008 financial crisis, the economic power these banks wielded became apparent and the now-famous epitaph "too big to fail" became a household saying.

Too Big to Fail

As a result of the 2008 financial crisis, Congress passed a $700 billion bailout using our tax dollars for the big banks, because they were deemed "too big to fail," meaning the country would be too adversely affected should they go bankrupt. Several important mergers took place at this time, making the big banks even bigger. In 2010, the Dodd-Frank Act was passed to mitigate against future financial crises. At that time, any bank with assets over $50 billion was considered too big to fail. Forty-four banks met the criteria. In May 2018, Congress changed key parts of the Dodd-Frank Act. As a result, a bank needs an asset base of $250 billion or more to be considered too big to fail and thus eligible for government bailout funds.

How did we get to the point where a relatively small number of banks play such an outsized role in the US economy? In a word—consolidation. Through a series of mergers and acquisitions from 1990 to 2009, 37 banks combined into what are now known as the "Big Four."

These mega-banks tend to invest in what is known as the "financial economy," money that gets put to work in stock trading, global markets, investment banking, and similar financial services. Because mega-banks and other large banks are publicly owned and traded on the stock market, their investments must maximize return for the benefit of their shareholders. This requirement is a key driver of their business models, investment decisions, and customer focus—and it often doesn't leave a lot of room for people, the planet, or the other things that matter to many of us.

If you want your money aligned with your values, you need to know how your bank is investing your cash. Due to their size and complexity, there is little transparency as to how money deposited in mega-banks is actually used, which makes it hard to determine the values that drive the bank's business decisions. Putting your money in a mega-bank is like putting it in a black box. Chances are you're inadvertently supporting businesses, industries, and economic players that aren't aligned with your values. It's even possible that you're invested in the businesses and activities that you would boycott, petition against, and otherwise work to change.

While the mega-banks do offer a range of banking services, it's unlikely they're making us money—unless we're shareholders. And even then, it's unlikely they're a place where women, minorities, and the local community successfully obtain loans as they try to start—or run—small businesses.

These banks are so big, so much a part of our economy, and so ubiquitous in our lives that we just assume they're our only option for savings and checking accounts, credit cards, and other personal financial products. But that couldn't be further from the truth. And it wasn't always like this. Even today's mega-banks started out much smaller and focused on the needs of the average person. At one time, they were also centers for innovation. But as they grew, the banks' business models became more focused on large customers, economic growth, and shareholder profitability.

A Mega-Bank Origin Story That Changed the World of Finance

At the turn of the 20th century, most banks catered to big businesses and the upper classes—just like the big banks do today. Working people had little financial flexibility, and there were virtually no financial services available to them. The banking services we all take for granted now faced a major turning point in 1906 when the son of an Italian immigrant in San Francisco did the unthinkable.

Two years earlier, in 1904, A.P. Giannini, whose father had been killed in a disagreement over a $1 debt, launched the Bank of Italy. It was the equivalent of today's startup—scrappy, bootstrapped, and visionary. Giannini believed—against all odds—that the common man was a good bet. His bank was founded on the belief that "the small depositor of today often becomes the rich man of tomorrow." He intentionally chose to serve, not exploit, the hard-working people that he hoped would become his clients. But even his prospective customers were wary, and the bank grew slowly.

On the morning of April 18, 1906, one of the most devastating earthquakes ever to hit the Western states struck. San Francisco lay in ruins. Giannini rushed to his fledgling bank before the fires and looting that were engulfing huge sections of the city consumed his assets. He concealed all the cash and gold in the vaults of his nascent bank in a horse-drawn cart under a load of oranges and carted it away to keep it secure.

The next day, the bankers of San Francisco met to discuss the disaster and what they should do in response. Their solution: Close the banks for six months until things settled down and the financial situation stabilized. But Giannini was having none of it. He declared he was opening a branch of his bank on Fisherman's Wharf and would be giving loans to anyone who was ready to rebuild San Francisco. And that is exactly what he did! Operating from a plank placed across two barrels, Giannini approved loans on the spot with a mere handshake. His vision and trust in average men and women so endeared him to the hearts of his fellow citizens that the Bank of Italy prospered and grew into what we now know as the Bank of America.

Source: Chutow, Paul. VISA: The Power of an Idea.

Other Banking Options

Sadly, many financial institutions like Bank of America have long outgrown their founders' original visions. Still, there are plenty of others that use their capital to support local communities, the members of their institution, or specific values such as climate change and social justice. These alternatives to mega-banks include values-based banks, credit unions, and community development financial institutions (CDFIs). Some of these options are banks, some are member based, and some are nonprofits. These values-based financial institutions provide a wide range of banking services that often come with higher returns or lower fees than larger banks. Most of them ensure your deposits are federally insured up to $250,000, similar to mega-banks. And many have been in business for decades and are extremely viable options for socially minded individuals.

Is Your Money Safe?

Some of you may be concerned that values-aligned banks and financial institutions are not as safe as mega-banks, particularly during times of financial downturns or crisis. However, this is not necessarily the case. For one thing, not all the alternatives to mega-banks are small. Amalgamated Bank, the values-based bank referenced earlier, has over $40 billion in assets. Credit unions, another values-based option, have a combined asset base of over $1 trillion.[3] The Navy Federal Credit Union, currently the largest credit union in the country, has $95 billion in assets and over 8 million members.[4] It's hard to consider that small.

Even more important, there are two federal agencies that regulate financial institutions—the Federal Deposit Insurance Corporation (FDIC) and the National Credit Union Administration (NCUA). Both provide deposit insurance for financial institutions of all sizes up to a maximum of $250,000, but the types of institutions they cover differs. For example:

- The FDIC provides deposit insurance to regulated banks.
- The NCUA provides deposit insurance to regulated credit unions.
- Deposit-taking CDFIs can be banks, in which case the FDIC insures them, or they can be credit unions and be insured by the NCUA.

Should a financial institution of any size or type fail, if it is registered with the FDIC or NCUA, the funds deposited there are federally insured, and they should be safe.

How Does FDIC and NCUA Insurance Work?

FDIC insurance covers all deposit accounts at insured banks and financial institutions, including checking, savings, money market deposit accounts, and certificates of deposit (CDs) up to the insurance limit of $250,000 per depositor, per FDIC-insured bank.

When you deposit your money in a federally insured credit union, the National Credit Union Share Insurance Fund (NCUSIF) secures your funds up to $250,000. The NCUSIF is managed by the National Credit Union Administration (NCUA) and is a federal insurance fund that is backed by the US government. About 98% of credit unions in the US are insured by the NCUSIF. Credit unions without NCUA insurance must be privately insured.

Smaller Banks Support Local Businesses and Communities

With smaller banks and credit unions, your cash can be leveraged to support you, your communities, small businesses, women, minorities, and other social goals. Smaller financial institutions are often leading providers of home, auto, and consumer loans, particularly for underserved populations. And as we learned during the early stages of the COVID-19 pandemic, smaller financial institutions were often the ones that came to the rescue of local businesses that were struggling.

Smaller Banks Can Provide Greater Value

Values-based banks, credit unions, and CDFIs can offer you reduced fees, higher interest rates, and more personalized customer service. Let's start by looking at fees, which most of us don't like to pay, particularly when the fees are not transparent. Research shows that banks holding less than $5 billion in assets were more likely to offer free personal checking accounts than larger banks.[5] When you add in statement fees, overdraft fees, fees for currency exchanges, and money-wiring costs, it can get expensive to let your bank hold your cash. In fact, the average American pays hundreds of dollars each year in bank fees.[6] On top of that, you are probably earning interest rates on your cash accounts that are minimal to nonexistent. While your experience may be different, the customer service I received when I used mega-banks often equated to long hold times on customer support lines. Smaller banks can often do better across the board.

Digital-Only Banks

We have entered an era where much of our banking takes places online. As a result, we have seen the arrival of digital-only banks. A key benefit of these businesses is they often pay higher interest rates than brick-and-mortar banks and financial institutions. By lowering their overhead costs, online banks can pass their savings on to their customers in the form of lower fees and higher interest rates on their deposit accounts. However, most digital-only banks lack transparency in terms of how their funds are invested and are not the best options for values-aligned investors.

There are a few exceptions, however. Aspiration Bank, a green digital-only bank, is one example. From the beginning, Aspiration set out to provide its customers with ethical and sustainable banking services. Everything the company does is geared toward that objective. With Aspiration you can earn a higher rate of return than you would from most banks, and you can know that your deposits are fossil fuel free. The bank also offers cash back when you shop for impact and donates some of its profits to charity.

Before choosing a digital-only bank, you might want to verify it will meet all your needs. These financial institutions may offer a more limited range of banking services, which can be challenging if you transfer large amounts of cash, require a loan, or are considering this type of bank for your business. It may also be difficult to establish a personal relationship with your banker, as your interactions are likely to take place through email or online chat, which could lead to greater difficulty solving problems should they occur. That said, an online bank could be one tool in your cash toolbox.

Values-Aligned Banking Options

Choosing a values-based bank, credit union, or CDFI means you'll know how your bank is investing your money. In addition, you aren't giving up safety as long as you choose a financial institution where your money is insured. You may also pay less in fees and make more in interest. And in many cases, you'll receive a more intimate customer experience. That's a lot to like.

As a consumer of banking services, you have some control over the type of impact you make through your choice of a bank. You can choose a financial institution that supports a group you're affiliated with, provides loans to women and other underserved communities, or addresses environmental issues. All of those options are possible. Table 4.1 lays out some impact goals and shows the types of financial institutions that typically provide that level of impact. Please visit our companion website to locate values-aligned financial institutions near you.

TABLE 4.1 Impact Goals by Financial Institution

Impact Goal	Financial Institution
General values alignment	■ Global Alliance for Banking on Values (GABV) members ■ B-Corporations
Specific affiliations	■ Credit unions
Small business	■ Credit unions with small business and gender mandates ■ CDFIs
Local communities	■ Credit unions with local community mandates ■ CDFIs
Women/gender	■ Credit unions with gender mandates ■ CDFIs
Other	■ Specialized credit unions, such as Clean Energy Federal Credit Union or Maine Harvest Credit Union

GABV Banks

The Global Alliance for Banking on Values, known simply as GABV, was launched in 2009 as a direct response to the global financial crisis of 2008. The founding members were three financial institutions with social missions at the core of their business models. When the crisis struck, these banks realized there needed to be a global platform for likeminded financial institutions to come together and create a paradigm shift in banking and financial services. And GABV was born. As of this writing, the organization included 63 financial institutions from countries across the Americas, Europe, Africa, Asia, and the Middle East. Members had a combined asset base of over $210 billion and served more than 70 million customers.

For GABV members, business decisions start by identifying a human need. The banks then determine how to meet that need in a way that is sustainable from environmental, social, and economic perspectives. This includes sustainable profitability for the bank. Becoming a GABV member requires an in-depth due-diligence process to confirm the prospective bank has a business model that is driven by GABV principles. An assessment committee needs to see real commitment from the bank's senior leadership and governing board that it will advance GABV objectives within their business and through active participation in the GABV community. The financial institution must also pass high bars in terms of their regulations, governance structure, and financial sustainability.

When you bank with a GABV bank, you can trust that your financial institution is striving to be a deeply principled and socially responsible business. There are several GABV financial institutions in the US. Some are banks while others are credit unions.

GABV PRINCIPLES OF VALUES-BASED BANKING

Principle 1

A triple bottom-line approach is core to a values-based bank's business model.

Principle 2

Values-based banks are grounded in the communities in which they operate, and they serve the real economy.

Principle 3

Values-based banks establish long-term relationships and are directly involved in helping their customers analyze sustainability risks associated with their businesses.

Principle 4

Values-based banks have a long-term view to ensure they can be resilient and maintain their operations when exposed to external disruptions.

Principle 5

Values-based banks ensure their governance and reporting are transparent and inclusive. They consider all stakeholders, including customers, community, and other entities impacted by their business.

Values-based banks work to embed the five principles into the fabric of their companies, ensuring they're part of the culture and applied to all levels of decision-making.

Source: http://www.gabv.org/wp-content/uploads/Prinicples-of-Values-based-Banking.pdf.

B-Corp Financial Institutions

B-Corps, some of which are banks, are businesses that adhere to the highest standards of social and environmental performance, transparency, and legal accountability. To be designated as a B-Corp, a company must go through an extensive certification process that examines the entire business to ensure it meets the highest standards of social and environmental performance, transparency, and accountability. Some values-based financial institutions, including some GABV banks, have gone through the process of becoming B-Corps.

B-Corp Origin Story

The B-Corp concept and certification process grew out of B-Lab, a nonprofit formed in 2006 by three visionaries: Jay Coen Gilbert, Bart Houlahan, and Andrew Kassoy. The idea emerged after Gilbert and Houlahan sold their basketball shoe company, AND1, in 2005. The company had grown dramatically in less than 10 years into the second-largest basketball shoe brand in the US, second only to Nike. What really differentiated AND1 was the social mission that Gilbert and Houlahan integrated into their business from the very beginning. When they decided to sell their company, the two men watched as its new owner discarded the emphasis on employees, partners, and the local community in favor of higher profits. Although it pained them to watch this, there was little they could do.

After leaving AND1, the two partnered with Kassoy, a longtime friend, and started building a concept that would ensure a founder's social vision would remain an inherent part of their business even when the company accessed external capital or upon acquisition. There are now more than 3,500 B-Corps in over 70 countries around the world. Kickstarter, New Belgium Brewing Company, Eileen Fisher, and Patagonia are some examples you might recognize.

Credit Unions

A credit union is a member-governed, member-owned, nonprofit financial institution that has been established for the benefit of its members, that is, those who deposit their savings and checking accounts with the institution. Corporations and other entities can form credit unions, which can range in size from relatively small enterprises to very large financial institutions with millions of members and billions of dollars in assets.

In addition to providing bank accounts, credit unions offer loans and other financial services to their members and the broader community. Because these businesses are structured as nonprofits, any extra money earned is returned to the members in the form of reduced fees, increased interest rates on deposits, reduced loan rates, or other benefits. Regulated by the NCUA, deposits in credit unions are insured up to $250,000 per depositor.

Participation in credit unions is growing in the US. According to the Credit Union National Association (CUNA), a third of Americans are served by credit unions.[7] There are wonderful resources on the Web to help you find a credit union that meets your needs. Many of the listings provide information about the credit union, including eligibility requirements.

ELIGIBILITY   Since these are membership organizations, you must qualify to participate. Membership is often determined through an affiliation like your job, the town you live in, or association with a group you belong to. Some credit unions are very restrictive, while others are more flexible. You're eligible to join a nonrestrictive credit union if you belong to an "associated"

Nonrestrictive Credit Unions

- Clean Energy Federal Credit Union
- Digital Credit Union
- Kinecta Federal Credit Union
- Maine Harvest Federal Credit Union
- Self-Help Federal Credit Union
- United Nations FCU

membership organization. This option is often available for a relatively small, one-time fee. For example, if you join the Center for Community Self-Help—a nonprofit committed to economic and social justice—for a modest lifetime membership fee of $10, then you're eligible to become a member of the Self-Help Credit Union, which has branches in North Carolina, South Carolina, Florida, Illinois, Wisconsin, and California. Comprehensive lists of nonrestrictive credit unions are available on the Web.[8]

SOCIAL MISSION   The vast majority of credit unions strive to provide high-quality, personalized service to their members, and that may be where their impact stops. However, others have additional social objectives related to the types of clients they serve. Social justice is a common theme among credit unions, as many support underserved groups in their local communities with small business loans, mortgages, student loans, and other financial services.

It's exciting to see other specialized credit unions forming. The Clean Energy Federal Credit Union has a very unique investment objective. This financial institution provides loans to help people afford clean-energy products and services such as solar electric systems, electric vehicles, home-energy efficiency retrofits, electric-assist bicycles, and net-zero energy homes. You can join the Clean Energy FCU by first becoming a member of the American Solar Energy Society, a nonprofit that is working to advance solar energy. Another example is the Maine Harvest Federal Credit Union, which focuses on small farms and the new food economy in Maine. Given the advances of technology, you no longer need to be in the same physical location as your bank. This makes it possible for you to join credit unions such as the Clean Energy and Maine Harvest from any place in the US.

REACH Even though your credit union might be small or not close to you physically, if it participates in the CO-OP Network, it can use "shared branching," which allows members from one credit union to transact at more than 5,000 credit union branches across the country and around the world. They may also leverage the CO-OP ATM network, which offers access to over 30,000 ATMs.[9] In addition, there are other sharing programs your credit union may be affiliated with that expand their reach and service offerings. When researching credit union options:

- Confirm they are regulated by the NCUA to be sure your money will be federally insured up to $250,000;
- Check whether you're eligible to become a member;
- Determine if they're part of the CO-OP or other shared-branching and ATM network programs; and
- Look into the social mission of the credit union by finding out how they invest their deposits.

A Credit Union Forged in the Fight to Save Jobs

The 1970s were not a good time for many in Durham, North Carolina. Jobs in the cigarette factories and textile mills were disappearing, and many previously employed women and men were without jobs, opportunity, or hope. Newly minted from law school, 26-year-old Martin Eakes, his soon-to-be wife, Bonnie Wright, and a collection of their friends set out to do something about the social inequity they saw unfolding before them. With an initial goal of helping workers buy back ailing mills to transform them into worker-owned cooperatives, Eakes and Wright cofounded the Center for Community Self-Help in February 1980. Within months of opening, 32 companies in North Carolina announced closings, displacing almost 3,000 additional workers.

In the early days, Eakes was living with his parents and driving a white Audi that had been salvaged from a junkyard. He traveled around North Carolina to garner commitment to his cause. But restrictive government regulations, complicated business structures, and the need for consensus building slowed his progress. At the same time, some individuals desperate for income started small businesses or other entrepreneurial enterprises. Early on, Eakes and his team worked with

Percy White, an African American who had been a baker in the Navy, to help him buy an oven and start a bakery. Percy used his new oven to bake a fundraising cake that sold for $77 and provided the capital to start Self-Help Federal Credit Union.

From its modest beginnings in 1980, Self-Help Federal Credit Union has expanded beyond its roots in North Carolina to oversee two credit unions, totaling almost 60 branches in seven states. It also manages several revolving loan funds and other financial products that have about $3 billion in assets. These credit unions have invested or loaned almost $8 billion to families, businesses, nonprofits, and communities often overlooked by mainstream financial institutions. Despite their growth, these credit unions remain committed to their core ideals of social equity and the belief that ownership—of businesses and homes—is the best way for families to build wealth and financial security. Self-Help holds 15% of its assets in reserves, and their loan loss rate is only 35 basis points, which is less than 1% (1 basis point is 0.01%).

When you place your deposits with a financial institution in the Self-Help family, you help people like the couple who lived in their Chicago home for 40 years. When they needed an extension on their home-equity loan, their bank refused to offer an affordable option, despite the couple's stellar payment record. Faced with foreclosure, the couple confided in their pastor. He in turn spoke to a Self-Help Federal Credit Union branch, which refinanced their loan and helped them keep their home.

Sources: Covington, Howard E. *Lending Power: How Self-Help Credit Union Turned Small-Time Loans into Big Time Change.*

Interview with Steve Zuckerman, President, Self-Help Federal Credit Union.

Community Development Financial Institutions

Community Development Financial Institutions, or CDFIs, are financial institutions that offer affordable loans and small business advice to individuals and communities that are underserved by traditional banks. While some credit unions make an impact that extends outside their membership, *all* CDFIs have community-impact mandates. These financial institutions support small businesses, nonprofits, and other community-based organizations, stimulating the economy in underserved markets. CDFIs support businesses like your local dry cleaner, beauty parlor, and bagel shop, which are often run by women, who have a harder time getting business loans from banks than men.

CDFIs can be set up as for-profits or nonprofits. In all instances, they are profit making, just not profit maximizing, because they put community before shareholders. With a long history that accelerated in the 1990s, CDFIs have a proven track record in terms of strong financials and local impact.[10] Although CDFIs historically have higher loan delinquency rates, they also have lower total losses from their loans compared to other banks.[11] Since delinquency rates are generally calculated on a 90-day period, this data suggests that CDFI banks are more willing to work with their loan customers to ensure ultimate repayment, while traditional banks are more inclined to let those customers default on their loans (and the bank will then write off the losses). The CDFI approach translates into more dignity for the loan recipient and a better bottom line for the CDFI.

CDFI banks and CDFI credit unions can be found all over the country. The FDIC monitors CDFI banks while the NCUA regulates CDFI credit unions. In both cases, deposits at insured CDFIs are guaranteed up to $250,000.

Aligning Your Cash

At this point, you have learned that you have options about where you hold your savings and checking accounts. You also know that you can invest your cash in ways that support women, your local community, or other causes you care about. However, actually taking the time and energy to make these changes may seem daunting. Some of the women involved in writing this book went through the process just like I did. And, like me, they learned that it's not that hard to break with your current bank.

The biggest obstacle you are going to run into when moving your cash to a new bank will be inertia. We felt it, too, but as we started learning more about how our money could advance our goals, we got more and more excited to shift our cash into alignment with our values. Then, when we realized that we could make more money in interest and get more personalized customer support, many of us moved into action. And so can you.

If you're considering changing your bank, I'm sure you have a lot of questions. Here are some of the ones I considered when I first started to move my cash:

Isn't this Going to Take a Lot of Work?

It will take some work, but it doesn't have to be that much. It's going to take you a bit of effort to shift from one bank to another, but there are a number of resources that can help you make the transition easily. The most time-consuming aspects of this process will be:

- Deciding where you want to move your cash; and
- Establishing your automatic direct deposit and bill payment links with your new bank.

To simplify these steps and to hold yourself accountable for following through, you may want to go through the process with a few friends. Several of us did this together over a period of months, and we learned a lot in the process.

As a bit more incentive, you may find that changing banks saves you hundreds of dollars every year. Switching banks allows you to do some "financial housekeeping," because you will go through all of your recurring and automatic payments. You may find (as some of us did) that there are things you have been paying for on a regular basis that you completely forgot about and don't even need anymore.

How Long is this Going to Take?

Plan on a transition period of three to six months. Not because it must take that long—you could do this in a matter of days or weeks if you prefer. A longer time frame allows you to move through the process at a pace that fits your lifestyle. After you open your new account, you don't have to move all your assets at once. It can be easier initially to shift only a portion of your funds. By managing two accounts for a while, you can enter your automatic deposit and bill payment links into your new account over time. Furthermore, you can watch your old account after most of the funds have been shifted to be sure there are no unexpected deposits or withdrawals. Once you are comfortable that your new account is fully functional and funds are no longer needed in the old account, you can close it.

What if I Can't Find a Values-Aligned Bank that Provides all the Services I Need?

This can be a challenge if you do a lot of international travel, have business overseas, feel like you are tied to your bank due to a mortgage, or have unusual financial needs. Many credit unions offer additional services to their members through partnerships with Credit Union Service Organizations, so be sure to ask before assuming your needs can't be met.

If a values-aligned bank can't provide the services you need, you may want to have two banks. Most of your cash can be kept in a values-aligned institution, with a minimal amount kept in your current bank to ensure you have access to the key services you want to maintain or that your new bank cannot offer. This way, you will have most of your cash in alignment with your values, even though some of it will be in a nonaligned bank. If you set up a link between your banks, it will be easy to move funds back and forth. This can actually be a win-win scenario because you have access to the benefits of a community-based financial institution, the key services you need from your current bank, and the satisfaction that most of your cash is being put to work in support of the things you value.

What if I Hate My Current Bank, but I Love their Technology?

In the past, limitations related to online bill pay services or mobile phone apps were a hindrance in making the commitment to move cash to more values-aligned financial institutions. But this is changing.

Online banking capabilities are rapidly becoming the standard that all banks and credit unions need to meet. So more and more of them are upgrading their systems. If this is critical to you, be sure to address this issue when you are interviewing prospective banks.

What about ATMs? Won't I give up Access?

Not necessarily. Many credit unions and CDFIs are part of a broad network of ATMs. The ATM fees that values-aligned institutions charge for out-of-network ATMs can be competitive with major banks—even beating them in some cases. So don't assume that you will have less access or will pay more.

Won't Changing Banks Negatively Affect My Credit Rating?

Unless you're also applying for a new credit card or loan at the same time, the answer is no, because neither savings nor checking accounts are associated with lines of credit. Financial institutions don't report changes in these types of accounts to credit rating agencies unless you open up a new line of credit at the same time.

What's in Your Purse?

The use of debit and credit cards has become pervasive in our culture, and we currently use them more frequently than we use cash when we're making purchases—large and small. As a result, it's important to consider the source of these cards as you seek to move away from a dependence on mega-banks and align your cash with your values.

Debit Cards

Your debit cards are tied directly to the ATM cards that you were issued for your savings and checking accounts, and they operate as if you're writing a check. When your debit card is used for a purchase, the transaction amount is immediately debited from the account tied to the card. The retailer where you used the card is charged a nominal fee to process the transaction. When you change your bank, you will receive an ATM/debit card that is linked to your new values-aligned account.

Credit Cards

Credit cards function like a pre authorized loan, essentially giving you a financial advance or the ability to "float" your money. If you watch your spending and pay your entire credit card bill on time each month, you won't pay interest. However, if you do not pay off your credit card fully each month, then you can find yourself in an increasing level of debt as you pay a hefty interest fee on remaining funds. According to ValuePenguin,* women carry 22% less credit debt than men because we prefer debit cards.

In addition to their ease of use, credit cards often offer a range of benefits that are hard to give up. These benefits include protections against fraud, simplified dispute resolution, and rental car insurance. Loyalty programs that offer rewards for using our credit cards are among the most favored benefits. We usually don't even consider the financial institution behind the credit card that is issued to us from our bank, favorite airline, or retailer.

Big banks and bank-holding corporations, which are among the largest credit card issuers, compete aggressively for new credit accounts with enticing "activation" offers. Most provide a range of rewards cards that can include cash-back, rewards points, airline miles, or other perks for each dollar spent. How can we let all that go?

Values-Aligned Credit Card Options

You may not realize that many values-aligned financial institutions also offer credit cards featuring rewards points. While they aren't marketed as aggressively, the rewards earned through these alternative cards can still be substantial over time and may even support direct causes that

---

*https://www.valuepenguin.com/average-credit-card-debt#average-credit-card-debt-over-the-years.

matter to you. Start by talking to your new bank to determine what they have available, or ask them to suggest some values-aligned options. You can also reference the responsible credit card section of Green America's website. This nonprofit, which focuses on green business, not only offers their own credit card, they also provide links to cards that support endangered animals, clean water, protection of the Amazon, and green building.

Take Action

The following steps can be taken alone or in partnership with others if you prefer a more collaborative approach with shared responsibility and support.

1. Determine how much money you want to hold in your new savings, checking, and cash alternative accounts. If you have multiple accounts, consider whether you want to move forward in stages, moving one account first before tackling the next account.

2. Visit our companion website and create a short list of values-aligned financial institutions that interest you.

3. Interview your candidates to ensure they meet your needs and pick a new bank.
   - Download the questionnaire for this part of the process from our companion website and add any additional questions of your own.
   - Download the template spreadsheet to fill out as you conduct interviews.

4. Open your new account.
   - In some instances, you can open an account online, which makes this part of the process extremely easy. Most likely you'll need your SSN and some form of identification for this process.
   - Fund your new account with a deposit that's large enough to eliminate monthly fees.
   - Order your checks and ATM cards. They usually take one to two weeks to arrive.

5. If you're paid through direct deposits, have those—and any other automatic deposits—redirected to your new account. Do this as soon as you can after opening your new account.

- To make this process easier, get a direct deposit authorization form from your new bank. Make sure it includes your new account information. Give this to your employer or any company/individuals that make direct deposits to your account, along with a voided check (if requested) from your new account.
- Ask when the payment to your new account will take place. It could take one or more payment cycles, so be sure to watch your new account for the switch.

6. Once your direct deposits are being sent to your new account, update your automatic bill payment systems.
   - Make a list of any businesses that automatically debit your account for their bill payments. You can do this by going back through your bank statements. If you think you may have automatic deductions that occur less frequently, that is, quarterly or annually, you might want to look back through a year of statements.
   - Use this opportunity to do financial "housecleaning," eliminating any recurring services you no longer need or want.
   - To make this process easier, get an automatic payment authorization form from your bank. Make sure it includes your new account information before you send it to the businesses on your list.
   - If necessary, transfer more funds to your new account to be sure that as automatic withdrawals start taking place, there are sufficient funds in the account to cover the payments. Leave enough money in your old account to cover checks that haven't cleared or automatic payments that may still be made.

7. Capture any information about recurring payments that you have set up through your old online bill payment service. Enter this information in your new online service.

8. Once you have switched all your recurring transactions and bill payments and you are comfortable that everything is working, wait one to three months to ensure there are no unexpected transactions in your old account. Also confirm that all outstanding checks have cleared.

9. After your waiting period has ended, shift any remaining funds to your new account.
   - Before closing your old account, confirm that all outstanding checks have cleared and save PDFs of any statements you might need. If you think you'll need these records for tax purposes, check the IRS website to verify how long you should be saving these records, as circumstances can vary.

- Close your old account, following your old bank's procedures.
- **Caution**: Do not assume your account has been closed just because there is no money left in it. Your old bank will likely continue to charge fees on an empty account, unless you officially close it using their procedures.

10. Write a cordial letter to the CEO of your old bank explaining why you left. You can find a template for this on our companion website.

11. Pat yourself on the back for a job well done and think about all the people that you will be helping through your cash deposits, moving forward.

Endnotes

1. https://www.ellevest.com/magazine/newsletter/2019-01-23.
2. https://www.businessinsider.com/largest-banks-us-list.
3. https://www.ncua.gov/newsroom/Pages/news-2018-june-ncua-releases-q1-credit-union-system-performance-data.aspx.
4. https://www.navyfederal.org/about/about.php.
5. https://www.money-rates.com/research-center/bank-fees/.
6. https://www.chimebank.com/2018/01/19/should-you-switch-banks-when-you-move/.
7. Credit Union National Association. *The Credit Union Difference: 2019 Advocacy Briefing*.
8. https://www.depositaccounts.com/credit-unions/anyone-can-join/.
9. https://co-opcreditunions.org/locator/.
10. https://ofn.org/what-cdfi.
11. Opportunity Finance Network. "20 Years of CDFI Banks and Credit Unions: 1996–2015: An Analysis of Trends and Growth." Jan 31, 2017.

CHAPTER 5

Cash Alternatives
Yield Higher Returns for Idle Cash

In the previous chapter, we suggested you keep three to six months of expenses in cash for emergencies. Like many women, you might have even more in cash than you need for this purpose. Perhaps you're saving for a major capital expense, like buying a house or starting a business. Or maybe you just feel better with a larger cushion. Whatever your reason, you might want to consider putting your excess money into cash alternatives, which are relatively low-risk, short-term investments that provide a higher return than savings and checking accounts.

Let's say you wanted a one-year emergency fund. You could set aside the amount you need to cover several months of expenses in a savings account and put the remainder in cash alternatives that have a term of three to 12 months. The beauty of this approach is if you need that extra cash, it will be ready for you before your emergency cushion runs out, and it could be earning higher interest than if you had left it in your savings account.

I'm a perfect example of the situation in which many women find themselves. I, too, had more money than I needed in cash. In my case, it was because I was trying to figure out where to invest my assets. Since I didn't have the time to think about it, significant sums sat in cash accounts. When I asked my financial advisor about values-aligned alternatives to my current savings accounts, I was told not to worry, because it was just cash and it didn't need to be values-aligned. But there were meaningful balances in those accounts, and that answer wasn't good enough for me. I knew there had to be something better. So I did my homework and found several values-aligned, more lucrative cash alternative investments—and I moved my money. And you can, too.

What Are Cash Alternatives?

In this book, cash alternatives are defined as investments that are relatively low-risk and provide short-term liquidity, which means you have access to the capital within months from the time it was invested. Interest paid is usually a bit higher than you would receive for a cash account. Some of the investments described in this chapter are FDIC insured, while others are not. There are three primary differences between cash and cash alternatives:

- **Liquidity**: All the money in your savings and checking accounts should be available to you on request at any time. Funds in cash alternatives are "held" for 30 days to 1 year, depending on the investment. You cannot access your money during the holding period. Some cash alternatives automatically roll over at the end of the term, initiating a new holding period. If you need your money in the short term, be sure to check on this feature before investing.
- **Risk**: Money in savings and checking accounts in federally regulated financial institutions is insured up to $250,000. Some cash alternatives are federally insured, but some are not. Uninsured investments will carry a higher level of risk but can also provide higher returns.
- **Return**: Although interest rates can change from bank to bank, if you take inflation into account, you're most likely losing money on your savings and checking accounts. Cash alternatives pay somewhat higher returns. Not surprisingly, there is usually a direct correlation between the return you will receive and the level of risk in any investment.

You can purchase cash alternatives at values-aligned banks and financial institutions as well as through some financial product innovators.

Fully Insured Cash Alternatives

Federally regulated banks and financial institutions offer money market deposit accounts and certificates of deposit (CDs). These investments can provide values-alignment as well as high levels of liquidity and security. As long as they're held at federally regulated financial institutions, these assets are insurable up to $250,000.

To be fully insured, the total value of all the accounts that you hold with a single financial institution cannot add up to more than $250,000. Anything over that amount is not covered. If you have more than $250,000 in cash and cash alternatives, there are several ways to safeguard your money. First, you could simply move some of your assets to another bank, as long as it isn't a subsidiary of your current financial institution. Second, you could open accounts at your bank in different categories, each of which has its own $250,000 limit. These categories include single accounts, joint accounts, retirement accounts, and trusts.

To avoid the hassle of these options, you could also try a third option. Insured Cash Sweep (ICS) and Certificate of Deposit Account Registry Service (CDARS) are structures that allow large depositors to conveniently protect all their assets. Depositors maintain a relationship with only one bank, but their assets are split across a number of financial institutions, which enables you to receive the benefit of full insurance without the hassle. CNote, which will be described shortly, partners with CDFIs to offer an alternative to ICS and CDARS.

ICS and CDARS

When you invest through ICS or CDARS programs, you establish a relationship with only one bank. Your financial institution works on your behalf to divide your funds into $250,000 allotments that are deposited in multiple banks. This ensures that every $250,000 of value is federally insured. As the customer you receive one consolidated statement from your primary bank, which manages the assets on your behalf.

Funds in the ICS program are placed in demand deposit or money market deposit accounts, providing daily liquidity. Assets invested through CDARS are invested in CDs, which offer a higher return.

Not all financial institutions can manage ICS or CDARS. If this service is important to you, be sure to confirm this capability with your bank before opening an account. Fortunately, some values-aligned banks, like Beneficial State Bank, offer this service.

Money Market Deposit Accounts

Money market deposit accounts are a cross between a savings and a checking account. They are highly liquid, so you can withdraw your cash immediately or within a few days, depending on the terms set by your lending institution. As is the case with savings and checking accounts, the interest rates offered by your bank will depend on the rate set by the Federal Reserve System (Fed)* and vary over time. Depending on conditions, these accounts could return anything from slightly more to significantly more than savings accounts.

---

*The Federal Reserve System, often referred to as the Federal Reserve or the Fed, is the US central bank.

In 2019 I was receiving 1.91% interest on the money market deposit account I had at one of my financial institutions. That was almost 1.8% higher than what I was getting for my savings account at a different bank. A little over a year later, after the Fed cut interest rates multiple times in response to global economic conditions and the COVID pandemic, the return on my money market deposit account fell to 0.27%. This rate was much closer to the interest I was receiving on my savings account.

When you invest in a money market deposit account, your financial institution uses those assets for the same purposes that apply to your other cash deposits. So you can employ the same criteria you use in finding a values-aligned bank to determine where to open a money market deposit account.

Certificates of Deposit

CDs are time-bound cash deposits. These investments are made for a fixed term, and they pay a fixed interest rate during that time. CDs are available from banks, credit unions, and CDFIs. Funds in CDs are invested by the financial institution in the same way the money in any of their deposit accounts is used. Many values-driven financial institutions offer CDs. Some even offer green, sustainable, or other thematic options.

CDs are available in multi-month and multi-year durations. Terms from three months to five years are most common, although there are CDs with shorter and longer durations. It pays to shop around, as interest rates vary depending on the term of the CD and the financial institution selling the investment.

Non-Insured Cash Alternatives

Investments described in this section are not federally insured, there are limitations that can restrict liquidity, and they carry more risk. One way to assess risk is to understand the track record of the company and product in which you are investing. Unless you are comfortable with these factors, be thoughtful about how much of your cash you place in any of these investments.

Money Market Mutual Funds

Money market funds are often confused with money market deposit accounts. But these are two distinctly different financial products, as shown in Table 5.1.

TABLE 5.1 Money Market Deposit Accounts vs. Money Market Mutual Funds

	Money Market Deposit Account	Money Market Mutual Fund
Federally insured	Yes, up to $250,000	No
Liquidity	Immediate to a few days	Immediate to a few days
Principal at risk	No	Yes, although rare
How funds are used	By your financial institution to support its business mission	Invested in liquid cash securities with high credit ratings
Values-aligned	Based on bank's mission and values	Can be more difficult to determine
Return	Higher than savings account, linked to federal rate	Higher than money market deposit accounts

Money market mutual funds are usually acquired through an investment firm,* although they can sometimes be purchased through banks and even some values-aligned financial institutions such as credit unions. Assets in a money market mutual fund are invested in cash and cash alternatives that have high credit ratings. This makes them relatively liquid and relatively safe. However, you have limited visibility to the holdings within these funds, which can make it more difficult to tell whether the investments they hold are values-aligned.

Unlike money market deposit accounts, these investments are not insured, and you could lose money that is invested in them, although this rarely happens.[1] Because of this increased risk, returns on money market mutual funds tend to be higher than those on money market deposit accounts.

Community Investment Note®

The Community Investment Note is a product of Calvert Impact Capital, one of the oldest and most recognized names in the social investing space. Calvert Impact Capital was established as a nonprofit in 1995 to provide investors with more ways to support communities in the US and around the

---

*Investment firms are companies such as Schwab, Fidelity, TD Ameritrade, and Vanguard that sell financial products and serve as custodians by safeguarding your invested assets.

world. The Note's funds are used to finance affordable housing, community development, small business, and other sustainability goals.

You can invest in the Community Investment Note online for as little as $20, or through an investment firm with a $1,000 minimum. The Note has a perfect track record of repayment and a one-year rate of 0.50%. Since rates, terms, and other conditions change over time, please reference Calvert Impact Capital's website for up-to-date offerings and impact metrics.

Social Investment Fund

The Social Investment Fund is an offering of RSF Social Finance, a nonprofit that was founded in 1936. RSF was minimally active until its revitalization in 1984, when the organization began to dedicate itself to making loans to advance social enterprises working in food, agriculture, education, and the environment. Close to 45% of the loans in RSF's portfolio went to enterprises that were founded, or led, by women.

To date, RSF has had a perfect repayment rate, having returned 100% of all principal and interest to investors. RSF's Social Investment Fund has a $1,000 minimum, 90-day term, and has historically paid interest rates of 0.5% to 1.25%. Unlike most financial institutions that base their interest payments on the Fed's rate, RSF uses the combined wisdom of its borrowers and investors to set rates that are a win-win for all members of the community.

CDFI Loan Funds

In the previous chapter, we covered two types of CDFIs—banks and credit unions. A third type is the CDFI Loan Fund. These regulated financial institutions do not take deposits. Instead, they focus on providing low-interest loans and technical assistance for small businesses, housing, and community development in economically distressed locations.

Many of these organizations, which can be found all over the country, have maintained 100% repayment rates throughout their history. Minimum investment amounts can range from $1,000 to $250,000, while terms are usually 1 to 10 years in duration. Investors receive a modest, fixed rate of return that's determined by prevailing interest rates and the term of the investment. There can be a requirement that investors are accredited, and returns can be below market rate. If you consider investing significant amounts of capital this way, you might want to diversify across several loan funds.

CNote

CNote offers investors a way to diversify across multiple CDFIs with one investment. This innovative finance company was founded by Cat Berman and Yuliya Tarasava, two women who wanted to do something powerful and influential in the world of finance. They chose to start with cash because it's an overlooked asset class and they realized they could use it to help close the wealth gap in the United States. Both women come from immigrant families and believe that talent is universal, but opportunity is not. CNote allows any investor to achieve a greater financial and social return on their excess cash. Many of the loan recipients are women and minorities.

FLAGSHIP FUND   CNote's first product, the Flagship Fund, was launched in 2016. The investment is available to anyone for as little as $5. There are no fees. As of this writing, the Flagship Fund offers a 2.75% return with 90-day liquidity. There are a few conditions. First, the rate is not fixed and can vary. Second, liquidity is at management's discretion and dependent on the amount invested.

Here's how it works. CNote provides wholesale, or inexpensive capital, to highly vetted CDFIs, which then lend money to support their local communities. The CDFIs pay CNote an interest rate on the money they borrow. CNote then pays its investors their return based on the rate paid by the CDFIs.

To ensure investors are repaid, CNote has implemented several strategies to mitigate potential loss. First, CNote carefully vets its partners to ensure they have a strong repayment track record. CNote claims that not one of their partners has ever lost a single investor dollar—ever. Second, investments in CNote have exposure to more than 50 CDFIs across 37 states. And third, CNote has set aside a portion of its deposits as cash reserves to serve as a guarantee against loss.

Understanding CNote Liquidity

CNote has management discretion around liquidity. The company currently offers clients quarterly liquidity with 30-day advance notice up to $20,000 or 10% of invested assets, whichever is greater.

In other words, if you invest $20,000 or less, then you can retrieve all your capital 90 days after your initial investment. If you invest $40,000 or less, you can retrieve all your money in 180 days—the equivalent of two 90-day periods. And if you needed all your money back within one year, you would not want to invest more than $80,000.

CNote's Flagship Fund provides attractive returns for amounts up to $20,000 that you want to safeguard for three months and up to $80,000 for funds you want to invest for up to one year. Of course, you can invest larger sums. If you do that and think you'll need the money, please be sure you fully understand the liquidity implications.

CNote Helps Make Dreams Come True

Shavon Marley and her husband had long dreamed of leaving their jobs and starting a business that would allow them to set their own schedules, travel, and work from anywhere. That dream seemed impossible when Shavon was diagnosed with breast cancer in 2016. While undergoing long hours of therapy related to her treatment, Shavon plotted how to move her vision forward. Some of the people she met in treatment centers were businesspeople who gave her inspiration, hope, and confidence.

What Shavon didn't have as she recovered were the assets she needed to start her business. That's where the Carolina Small Business Development Fund, a CNote partner CDFI, came in. When Shavon first connected with the Fund, she had no idea how to develop a business plan. But by working together with the team at Carolina SBDF, Shavon and her husband were able to realize their vision. With the loan Shavon received from Carolina SBDF, Marley Transport & Trucking got off the ground and pulled its first load in April 2018.

PROMISE ACCOUNT   The Promise Account is a fully insured cash alternative that allows investors with more than $250,000 to distribute their capital across prequalified FDIC and NCUA insured CDFIs across the country. This account functions similarly to ICS and CDARS. Investors can deposit and insure up to $10 million through the Promise Account, while knowing that 100% of their cash is going to address housing, transportation, and other critical needs in low-income communities. There is a single dashboard that helps investors monitor their cash and its impact. Liquidity and returns are flexible.

Worthy Bonds

Worthy Bonds are a product of Worthy Peer Capital, a financial services company that launched in 2016 to provide a new type of investment vehicle. Sally Outlaw, the woman behind this business, wants the average non-accredited investor to have an opportunity to invest in private companies that are growing and providing high-yield returns. Until recently, these types of investments were only available to accredited investors and required minimums that started at $25,000.

Worthy Bonds are sold in $10 increments and pay 5% interest annually. An investor can purchase up to $100,000 of Worthy Bonds. These bonds are highly liquid, which means bondholders can withdraw all their capital with just a few days' notice and pay no fees or penalties. The bonds can be purchased online or through the Worthy app. By linking your debit or credit card to the app, you can choose to round up spare change from your daily purchases. Your extra cents are tracked, and once $10 has been accumulated, another bond is automatically purchased for your portfolio. Worthy is integrated into Mint and Dwolla, two popular FinTech companies that provide additional points of entry to this financial product.

Worthy lends the capital it raises through its bonds to small businesses. Each loan is secured by inventory, which means the companies that get loans from Worthy have tangible assets that can be sold in the case of delinquency. When you invest in Worthy bonds, your money is spread across multiple loans to diversify your holdings and minimize risk. Worthy also keeps assets in reserve to repay investors that seek redemptions or asset returns.

There are a number of values-aligned cash alternatives you can consider for your extra cash. They span from fully insured to higher risk solutions. Worthy Bonds' offering is the newest and least tested option, which makes it the highest risk solution described in this chapter. Some suggest that the increased risk makes this investment inappropriate as a cash alternative. However, the very low entry level, high liquidity, and 5% return potential could appeal to investors with a higher risk tolerance. Be sure to do your research on this, or any, financial product before you invest.

Table 5.2 compares minimums, terms, and expected returns for the products described in this chapter.

TABLE 5.2 Cash Alternative Product Comparison

	Federally insured	Investor type	Minimum	Term	Expected return
Money market account	Yes, up to $250,000	All	$0 to $100 common	Usually 1 day	Variable, tied to Fed rate
Certificate of deposit	Yes, up to $250,000	All	Variable, some $0	Variable, 30 days to 10 years	Variable, tied to Fed rate
Calvert Note	No	All	$20.00	Variable, 1 to 15 years	0.5%–3.5%
RSF Fund	No	All	$1,000	90 days	0.5%–1.25%
CDFI Loan Fund	No	Accredited investors	Variable, $1,000 and up	Variable, 1 to 10 years	0.5%–3.0%
CNote Flagship Fund	No	All	$1.00	90 days per $20,000	2.75%
CNote Promise Acct	Yes, up to $10 million	Accredited investors	$250,000	Flexible	Variable
Worthy Bonds	No	All	$10.00	2–3 days	5.00%

Take Action

Assuming you have more cash than you need for emergencies, consider try-ing one of the options listed in Table 5.2. You can start small and increase your investment over time if that feels better to you. That's what I did with CNote. I initially invested $5,000 with the company; then after six months I felt confident enough to increase my investment severalfold.

Regardless of the investment, be sure to do your homework first. As you consider your options, please remember to verify the status of term restric-tions, automatic rollovers, and limits on withdrawal sizes before you buy. This will help prevent any surprises when you're ready to withdraw your capital.

Endnote

1. https://www.investopedia.com/articles/mutualfund/08/money-market-break-buck.asp.

CHAPTER 6

Fixed Income
Grasp the Potential of Bonds

Fixed income is one of the two most important asset classes in many portfolios. It often pales in comparison to the stock market, which receives much more attention. Investing in stocks can be a bit like riding a roller-coaster, while fixed income is more like riding a merry-go-round. It's often the place where you put some money aside to safeguard it against potential market crashes. Many investors underestimate the wide variety available within fixed income and the potential this asset class has to generate significant positive impact.

Investments in fixed income are in the form of debts or loans. In most circumstances, investors are paid back over a fixed period of time (or term) at a fixed interest rate. In this book, we talk about loans with a term of one year or more as fixed income, while those of a shorter duration fall into the category of cash alternatives.

Fixed income is viewed as a counterbalance to public equities because it can offer relatively safe investments that are less correlated to the stock market than most other asset classes. These investments are often used to preserve wealth, generate income, and diversify portfolios. Due to the relative stability and predictable income stream of some fixed-income investments, we tend to see individuals who are approaching retirement age shift larger percentages of their total assets into fixed income, while younger people skew their portfolios toward investments that have more potential for capital growth.

It would be a mistake, however, to think that all fixed income is composed of relatively safe investments. This asset class is actually extremely diverse, offering everything from low-risk to highly speculative investments. So it's important to understand what you're buying and where it lands on the risk spectrum. Don't let fixed income's reputation for low risk fool you. You can lose money in this asset class as easily as you can in any other.

In this chapter, you'll learn about the different types of fixed income investments you can make, how bonds work, and values-aligned opportunities you have for this portion of your portfolio. Federal agencies, local governments, and even corporations are using debt to underwrite projects that green our environment, improve water quality, and better the lives of women and girls. Any one of us has the opportunity to support these goals with our fixed-income assets.

Non-Bond Options: CDs, CDFIs, and Notes

The terms "fixed income" and "bonds" are often conflated, which makes many people think they're the same thing. While bonds are the most common type of fixed-income investment, there are other options available. As you think about your fixed-income portfolio, you may want to include some of these products.

Certificates of Deposit

Certificates of deposit (CDs) were introduced in the previous chapter because they're available with terms of less than one year and can serve as a cash alternative. There are also CDs with longer terms, which you can purchase from most values-aligned banks and financial institutions. The return you receive will vary based on the prevailing interest rates, which are set by the Fed and the term of the CD. The longer the term, the more you would typically expect to receive in interest.

CDFI Loan Funds

Loans to CDFIs and CDFI Loan Funds tend to extend beyond one year, which makes them fixed-income investments. They're relatively low risk due to high repayment rates and tend to pay interest in the low single digits.

Racial and Gender Equity Fund

CNote offers a fixed-income product called the Wisdom Fund. This 5-year note focuses on racial and gender equality. The investment provides capital to female small business owners across the US and targets women of color. In addition to increasing access to capital, Wisdom

> Fund partners provide free business coaching to loan recipients. The fund is also gathering data to help reduce the underwriting bias that negatively affects female loan applicants.
>
> Like all CNote products, the Wisdom Fund invests in CDFIs that are helping to close the wealth gap in America. As of this writing, the fund is paying an adjustable interest rate of 3.5%. It's only available to accredited investors and requires a $100,000 minimum.

Impact Notes

Similar to CDs, impact notes are debt instruments that you can buy for varying terms, as shown in Table 6.1. They can be purchased through your brokerage firm or, sometimes, online. High-quality notes tend to be relatively low risk. The three organizations described here have invested more than $2 billion apiece, and they all claim they've maintained 100% repayment rates to their investors over their multi-decade histories.

TABLE 6.1 Impact Note Rates

Term	Calvert	Enterprise
1 year	0.50%	0.50%
3 years	1.50%	1.75%
5 years	2.50%	2.25%
10 years	3.00%	3.00%
15 years	3.50%	

As of Sept 21, 2020.

- **Calvert Investment Note**[1] invests in the US and internationally with an emphasis on community development, small business support, affordable housing, and microfinance. You can visit their website to see the organizations, countries, and programs they support.
- **Enterprise Community Impact Note**[2] invests in affordable housing, community health centers, and schools.
- **Reinvestment Fund**[3] is involved in neighborhood revitalization and community development. They invest in health, equitable food systems, and childhood education. Their website presents impact data and identifies the SDGs they're aligned with.

You can invest in the Calvert note for as little as $20. The Reinvestment Fund has a $1,000 minimum, while the Enterprise Fund requires an initial investment of $25,000. In each case, interest rates depend on the term of notes, which can run from 1 to 15 years. All these organizations track their impact and provide reports at least once per year.

Bond Basics

Bonds are the most common form of fixed income. They are debt instruments that have been standardized so they can be bought and sold on public markets. Governments, corporations, financial institutions, and other entities can all issue bonds. Money raised through a bond can be used to underwrite anything from corporate growth to mortgage lending to public goods.

You can choose to buy individual bonds and create your own bond portfolio, or you can invest in bonds by purchasing bond funds, which are single investments that hold multiple individual bonds. Many people do the latter, which simplifies decision-making and provides significant diversification through a few investments.

Bonds represent an emerging, but often overlooked, asset for impact investors. Since many bonds have specific, well-articulated objectives, they can deliver targeted impact and provide investors with transparency into the use of funds.

Bond Characteristics and Terminology

When an organization decides to raise millions, hundreds of millions, or even billions of dollars with a loan, they may issue a bond and establish its characteristics at that time. The bond is then sold through what is known as a primary market, and the issuer receives the money they intended to raise. At this point, the bond can move to a secondary market, where shares can continue to be traded throughout the life of the bond.

Characteristics of a Bond

Issuer: Jackson College, Michigan
Coupon: 2.50%
Maturity: 05/01/2044
Face Value: $100
Call: 05/01/2030 at par
Rating: Aa2 – Moody's / Standard & Poor's

The most important characteristics of a bond are the interest rate (coupon), maturity, face value, and rating. To help you understand these terms, let's consider a $11.3 million bond that was issued by Jackson College in Michigan. This bond was issued to help the college acquire more student housing and improve other buildings on campus.

The *issuer* of the bond is Jackson College, Michigan, which wanted to raise $11.3 million for campus improvements. This is the organization that's borrowing the money. So it's their obligation to repay.

The *coupon* is a fancy name for interest rate and is the amount that will be paid to investors each year. In this case, the coupon is 2.50%. Interestingly, the term "coupon" is a convention that goes back several decades. At that time, bonds were physical pieces of paper with coupons attached to them. Investors would cut off a coupon and take it to the bank to receive their interest payments. Fortunately, things are a bit easier today, but the term remains. In most cases, the coupon is established at issuance and does not change over time.

Maturity is the day when the bond term ends. It's the time when the initial investment, or principal, is due to be paid back to investors. Bonds can have short (1–5 years), intermediate (5–10 years), or long (10 years or more) terms. The Jackson College bond in this example matures on May 1, 2044, 24 years after it was issued, which makes it a long-term bond.

Face value is the amount that will be paid to a bondholder at the maturity date, assuming the bond doesn't go into default. It is usually $100 or $1,000. When you buy a bond, you may not pay the face value, because, over time, the price fluctuates based on the prevailing interest rate and other factors. You can always determine how much the price has changed by comparing the current value to the face value. *Par* is often used interchangeably with "face value."

Call is another important characteristic of bonds. In many cases, issuers have the right to pay off investors before the maturity date. The call is the date they can exercise that right by "calling" the loan and paying it off in full. In the case of a bond, the call date is specified and associated with a price that will be paid per share at that time. For example, the Jackson College bond could be paid as early as May 1, 2030, at the original par or face value.

A *rating* establishes the quality of the bond and is set by rating agencies. In this case, we're showing the rating that Moody's, one of three well-known agencies, has provided. The Aa2 rating in Table 6.2 is considered high investment grade, suggesting this bond would be a relatively low-risk investment.

Deciphering Bond Ratings

Bond ratings are a key metric you can use to determine where a bond or bond fund sits along the risk spectrum. The rating communicates the quality of the bond and the likelihood that the borrower will be able to pay back all the principal and interest by the maturity date. Risker bonds have lower ratings. Standard & Poor's (S&P), Moody's, and Fitch are the best-known rating agencies. They establish bond ratings based on an issuer's earnings expectations, credit history, leverage, and other criteria. S&P and Fitch use the same rating descriptors, such as AAA and BBB+, while Moody's uses different symbols to designate the same grade.

There are two basic rating categories: investment grade and non-investment grade, as shown in Table 6.2. Anything rated AAA through BBB– is considered investment grade and a relatively safe investment. Bonds with BB+ or lower ratings are considered non-investment grade. They can provide a higher return but also carry greater risk.

Non-investment-grade bonds are often referred to as high-yield, speculative grade, or less politely, junk bonds. They can be a productive sub-asset class if you invest with care, full knowledge of the associated risks, and frequent oversight. It's important to note that non-investment-grade bonds do not lend themselves to a "buy and forget" investment approach.

TABLE 6.2 Bond Ratings from S&P, Moody's, and Fitch

Investment Grade			
S&P	Moody's	Fitch	
AAA	Aaa	AAA	Prime High Grade
AA+	Aa1	AA+	
AA	Aa2	AA	High Grade
AA-	Aa3	AA-	
A+	A1	A+	Upper Medium Grade
A	A2	A	
A-	A3	A-	
BBB+	Baa1	BBB+	Lower Medium Grade
BBB	Baa2	BBB	
BBB-	Baa3	BBB-	
Non-Investment Grade			
S&P	Moody's	Fitch	
BB+	Ba1	BB+	Non Investment Grade Speculative.
BB	Ba2	BB	
BB–	Ba3	BB–	
B+	B1	B+	Highly Speculative.
B	B2	B	
B–	B3	B–	
CCC+	Caa1	CCC+	Substantial Risk, Extremely Speculative.
CCC	Caa2	CCC	
CCC–	Caa2	CCC–	In default with little prospect of recovery.
CC	Caa3	CC	
C	Ca	C	
D	C	DDD/DD/D	

Ratings are not foolproof, as we saw in the 2008 financial crisis when low-grade loans received high ratings based on the structure of the bond pool. This methodological inaccuracy was one of the many issues that led to the crisis. For this reason, in addition to using ratings to assess an investment, a good fixed-income advisor will perform their own credit research. If you're managing your own assets, it's wise to follow a similar course of action.

Finding Values Alignment in Bonds

Each bond issuer has a unique purpose for raising money. Sometimes the purpose addresses environmental and social issues, which make those bonds attractive to values-aligned investors. Bonds and bond funds can be found across all levels of impact. They do no harm (level 1) by excluding controversial sectors or companies, benefit stakeholders (level 2) by seeking favorable sectors or companies, or develop solutions (level 3) by supporting specific social or environmental outcomes. Some bond fund managers also engage directly with issuers to influence impact and outcomes. In this section, we're going to focus on the four bond types that are most likely to appeal to values-aligned investors: Treasuries, government agency bonds, municipal bonds, and corporate bonds.

Treasuries

Debt issued by the US government is called Treasuries. As shown in Table 6.3, it comes in the form of bills, notes, and bonds, each of which has a different term, or maturity. The US Treasury issues debt to fund the

TABLE 6.3 Treasury Bills, Notes, and Bonds

	Term/Maturity
Bills	a few months to 1 year
Notes	2 to 10 years
Bonds	more than 10 years

federal government's mandatory and discretionary spending each year. The Bank of England issued the first government bond in 1693 and used it to fund a conflict with France.[4] Similarly, the first bond in the US was used to finance the American Revolutionary War.[5]

Treasuries are considered one of the safest fixed-income investments, because they're backed by the full faith and credit of the US government. Investors are virtually guaranteed payment as long as the security is held to maturity. As a result, the interest rate paid on the US T-Bill is often referred to as the "risk-free rate." Interest rates on other bonds are often established by comparing the issuer's credit quality relative to an equivalent US Treasury. The closer a bond's interest rate is to the rate of a Treasury bond of a similar type, the lower the risk, whereas the further the interest rate is from the Treasury rate, the higher the risk. This difference is known as the "spread."

Government Agency Bonds

There are two types of agencies associated with the US government. Both issue bonds to finance public goods, such as home, small business, and education loans. The US Small Business Administration (SBA) and US

Department of Housing and Urban Development (HUD) are federal agencies established by the US government. They represent the first type of agency, and the bonds they issue are backed by the full faith and credit of the US government.

Government-Sponsored Enterprises (GSEs), such as mortgage lenders Freddie Mac and Fannie Mae, were created by the US Congress. However, they tend to be private companies. Although GSE bonds are frequently viewed as low risk, they do not carry the same full faith backing as federal agency bonds or Treasuries. These bonds are often securitized, which means they're backed by homes, automobiles, or other recoverable assets.

Municipal Bonds

State and local government and public entities, such as utility companies, school districts, and hospitals, all issue municipal (muni) bonds. These funds can be used to improve water quality, upgrade roads, build schools, and advance other important projects intended for the public good.

There are two types of muni bonds: general obligation bonds and revenue bonds. General obligation bonds are used to raise money for projects that are backed by the general taxing authority of the issuer, such as roads, bridges, and parks. In general, the interest and principal on these bonds are repaid through taxes and fees. The creditworthiness of the issuer and projected tax revenues are important in determining credit quality and risk.

Revenue bonds are used to fund projects that are tied to a revenue stream. Initiatives related to water quality, utility delivery, and higher education could all be funded this way. Investors are repaid through the revenue generated by the project, such as water/sewer bills, electricity bills, and tuition. Risk relates to financial assumptions, projections, and usage patterns.

Weighing the Tax Advantages of Muni Bonds

The interest on government-sponsored muni bonds is typically tax-free at the federal level. If you live in the same state where a bond is issued, the interest can also be tax-free at the state level. This feature of muni bonds can be an advantage for investors in higher tax brackets. However, the coupons (interest paid) on munis can be lower than those offered on other types of bonds. If you're in a low tax bracket, munis may not offer enough of a tax advantage to compensate for that difference.

You can use a simple formula to compare the interest you would receive on a federally tax-free muni bond with a fully taxable bond.

Muni bond interest rate / (1 – Your marginal tax rate) = Tax-Equivalent rate

Assuming a muni bond pays 3.0% interest and your federal tax bracket is 25%, then the tax equivalent rate would be 4.0%. Here's the math: 0.03/(1 – 0.25) = 0.04, or 4.0%. If another bond that interested you were paying more than 4.0% in interest, then you might want to consider it over the muni. If it were paying less, the muni could be a better option.

Now, assume the bond was also tax-free at the state level and your state tax was 7.0%; then you'd add the federal and state tax together before running the calculation. In this case, your total tax would be 32% (25% + 7%), and your tax-equivalent rate would be 4.4%. Here's the math: 0.03/(1 – 0.32) = 0.044, or 4.4%.

The tax-exemption potential should be just one element of your consideration in building a municipal bond portfolio. From a risk perspective, it's wise to hold muni bonds both in your state and outside of your state. For example, since I live in California, I hold several muni bonds that originate there, but I also have bonds from Texas, New Jersey, and North Carolina.

Corporate Bonds

Public and private corporations issue bonds to fund their operations, capital expenditures, and other business needs. A growing number have offered sustainable, social, green, and other impact bonds. Risk depends on both a company's prospects for future revenue and growth as well as the amount of debt it carries. If a company has no other types of debt, then corporate bondholders would be the first lenders to be repaid in a default scenario. However, if the company has other forms of debt that are prioritized, the corporate bondholders may never be repaid. All of these risks are considered in the rating of a corporate bond.

Starbucks Sustainability Bond

In May 2016, Starbucks Corporation issued the first US Corporate Sustainability bond. In 2019, they issued another $1 billion sustainability bond to support ethical coffee sourcing and the company's greener retail initiative. Starbucks is using bond funds to purchase verified coffee, support development centers in coffee-growing regions, and provide debt financing to coffee producers in Latin America, Asia, and Africa. Funds will also be used to advance Starbuck's Greener Stores commitments, which include advances in energy efficiency, water stewardship, and waste reduction. The company is also expanding its use of greener cups and packaging as a way to reduce waste and increase sustainability.

Investing in Individual Bonds

Many people invest in fixed income through bond funds. However, some prefer to own individual bonds as a way of gaining control over their portfolio. This approach can translate into increased values alignment and potentially higher returns. However, it requires more effort and/or more resources than a bond fund strategy.

You can invest in individual bonds on your own or with the help of a financial advisor. Although it's possible to proceed with less, you could need as much as $50,000 to build a diversified bond portfolio. If that's more than you have allocated to fixed income, you might prefer to invest through bond funds.

Taking a DIY Approach

While it's possible to build your own bond portfolio, the do-it-yourself (DIY) approach requires not only time but specialized knowledge. Bonds can be complicated. They aren't publicly traded like stocks, so you'll need to work with a broker. Unless you're experienced or have an advisor who can get good pricing, you could end up paying too much. You might also incur fees as high as 2.5%. What's more, you'll need to conduct your own research to identify the bonds you want to buy.

With the exception of Treasuries, which you can purchase directly from the US government for as little as $100, bond minimums tend to be in the range of $1,000 to $5,000. In some cases, you have to buy bonds in lots of 5, 10, 25, or 100. Thus, a $1,000 bond could end up costing $5,000, $10,000, or more. For example, a diversified portfolio that held 10 bonds could require an investment of $50,000.

Working with a Financial Advisor on an Individual Bond Portfolio

Some financial advisors can build an individual bond portfolio for you. They can identify investments, perform credit analysis, buy and sell bonds, and manage your account. They can also ensure that you are building enough diversification into this part of your portfolio. When I decided that I wanted to own a portfolio of individual values-aligned bonds, this is the approach I took.

During the course of writing this book, I met a financial advisor who specializes in impact bonds. She taught me about the benefits of owning an individual bond portfolio. None of my previous advisors had ever let me know this was even an option. As I realized the potential for cash flow, as well as the increased impact I could have, I hired her to manage some of my fixed-income assets. She selected investments that met my return and values goals and now oversees a portfolio of about 15 bonds for me. I am currently invested in a water treatment facility in my city, an upgrade to an elementary school in southern California, and the Lucille Packard Children's Hospital.

Not all financial advisors will have the interest or skills to help you build a values-aligned bond portfolio. Abacus Wealth Partners, Figure 8 Investment Strategies, Uplift Investing, and Zevin Asset Management were all contributors to this book. These firms are either women-led or have women in leadership positions. All of them offer this service, but investment minimums start at $50,000.

If you have more to invest: For those who have at least $250,000 to invest in an individual bond portfolio, you may want to work with an impact investment firm that specializes in bonds. Breckinridge Capital Advisors and Invesco both build and manage values-aligned bond portfolios, some of which focus on climate change and gender equity. In most cases, you'll work with these firms through your financial advisor. Should you choose this approach, you'll pay a fee to your advisor and another fee to the investment firm.

Values-Aligned Bonds

A World Bank article titled "From Evolution to Revolution: 10 Years of Green Bonds" sums up the current status of sustainable bonds beautifully when they say, "Issued in November 2008, the World Bank's first green bond created the blueprint for sustainable investing in the capital markets. Today, the green bond model is being applied to bonds that are raising financing for all 17 Sustainable Development Goals."[6] Green, social, sustainable, and thematic bonds are being issued by government and corporate entities. The best of breed are guided by a set of green and/or social principles and are validated by third-parties.

Green Bonds

Green bonds are used to fund environmental or climate-related projects. They were the first to the party, and they continue to dominate the market. In 2019, a record $258 billion worth of green bonds were issued globally.[7] This was a milestone that demonstrates the growing interest in this high-impact class of financial products.

Green bonds can range from very light green to dark green, according to the bond-rating categories established by BlackRock. On the light green end of the spectrum, bonds finance projects that yield only marginal improvements. On the other end, dark green initiatives are expected to result in a long-term, positive impact on sustainable energy consumption. That's quite a span, which is why it's important to pay attention to how bond funds are being used. Just because a bond is referenced as green doesn't make it so.

Beware of Greenwashing

Some financial providers are greenwashing, which means they're making unsubstantiated or misleading claims about the social benefits of their investment products. This practice, which can apply to any asset class, makes an investment appear more values compliant than it really is. The problem is compounded by the fact that there are currently limited standards defining the attributes of a sustainable, environmental, or social investment.

Before investing in a green bond, make sure you understand how the bond's proceeds are being used. For example, if a company is issuing debt under the auspices that it's a green bond, an appropriate use of proceeds could include green retrofitting its offices or investing in electronic vehicles for staff that get company cars. A green bond that allocates funds for general use should raise a red flag, because the proceeds could be used for anything. The use of proceeds in the bond's prospectus should explicitly specify an environmentally or socially aligned purpose.

Fortunately, standards related to green bonds have gotten stricter, and most issuers now follow the Green Bond Principles, a voluntary tool that is put out by the International Capital Market Association (ICMA). Third parties have also begun auditing green bonds to validate their claims.

You can find a wealth of information, including a database of green bonds on the Climate Bonds Initiative website.[8] Recently, green bonds have been aggregated into funds, making them easier to access and available to a broader range of investors. As an investor, don't hesitate to ask how proceeds will be used. It's also appropriate to consider the criteria that are being used to select the bonds included in a fund. Green bonds can target several SDGs, including affordable and clean energy (7) and climate change (13).

Sustainable Bonds

Since the United Nations estimates that between $2 and $3 trillion per year is required to achieve the SDGs in developing countries alone, there's an urgent need for private capital to address these problems.[9] Sustainable bonds are helping to fill this gap. Relatively new entrants to the market, sustainable bonds are pushing beyond pure environmental objectives to also integrate social and economic goals. Governments, corporations, and other organizations are stepping up to the challenge. Verizon is one example.[10]

Verizon Communications Has Bold Ambitions

In September 2020, Verizon Communications announced its second green bond. The $1 billion bond will be used to source power for cellular towers, data centers, and other parts of Verizon's mobile infrastructure from alternative energy sources, such as wind and solar. The company intends to obtain 50% of its energy consumption through alternatives by 2025 and to be carbon neutral in their operations by 2035. They also plan to provide 10 million youth with digital skills training by 2030. The company references four SDGs their efforts will advance: affordable and clean energy (7), decent work and economic growth (8), climate action (13), and peace, justice, and strong institutions (16).

Thematic Bonds

Gender-lens investing supports women-led companies, promotes gender equity in the workplace, and finances products and services that improve the lives of women and girls. Although rare, you can purchase bonds that are issued to finance women-led businesses or to foster women's leadership.[11] These bonds foster gender equity (5).

Another way to support gender values is by purchasing municipal or social bonds that underwrite affordable housing, healthcare, education, and community services—all of which have an outsized positive impact on women and girls. These types of bonds intersect with a number of SDGs, such as good health and well-being (3), quality education (4), and reduced inequities (10).

Social Bonds

Social bonds support projects designed to achieve positive socioeconomic outcomes for target populations. Often these bonds carry a strong gender component and hit many of the SDGs mentioned above. They can also align with sustainable cities and communities (11).

The exponential growth we've seen in values-aligned bonds over the past few years is expected to continue. That suggests we'll see even more opportunities in the years to come—not only in individual bonds but in bond funds as well.

Investing in Bond Funds

Many investors will enter the bond market via bond funds and ETFs, which can be purchased through public markets. ETF stands for exchange-traded fund, which is a type of financial product that holds a collection of securities such as other funds but is traded more like a stock. A number of these funds have no minimums, which makes them accessible to any investor. There are values-aligned bond funds and ETFs that allow you to have the best of both worlds: simplicity and impact. You can purchase these investments through an investment firm such as Fidelity, Vanguard, and Schwab, a robo-advisor, or a financial advisor.

How Bond Funds Work

There is tremendous variety within funds, each of which can hold hundreds or even thousands of individual bonds. You can find bond funds and ETFs that range across sectors (types of bonds), maturity dates, and ratings. To better understand how bond funds work, let's consider two very different values-aligned investments, as shown in Table 6.4.

TABLE 6.4   Bond Comparison

		ABIMX	EAGG
Sector	Government	–	35%
	Municipal	92%	–
	Corporate	5%	24%
	Securitized	–	24%
	Cash	3%	17%
Coupon range	0% to 2%	1%	22%
	2% to 4%	19%	46%
	4% to 6%	76%	13%
Maturity schedule	Short-term	4%	28%
	Mid-term	14%	14%
	long-term	79%	41%
Ratings	AAA	7%	48%
	AA	19%	9%
	A	36%	19%
	BBB	24%	19%
	NIG	14%	5%

Compiled using Morningstar data from August 31, 2020.

AB Impact Municipal Income (ABIMX) is an actively managed social bond fund. The fund supports solutions in education, water, and mass transit. Given this emphasis, this fund could be approaching level 3 impact. At the time the data in the table was captured, ABIMX held primarily municipal bonds (92%), although there was a slight allocation to corporate bonds (5%) and cash (3%). This is considered a long-term fund, as 79% of the assets fall into that category. ABIMX holds about 150 primarily investment-grade bonds—most of which range between AA and BBB. A portion (14%) are invested in non-investment-grade (NIG) bonds. Interest rates (coupon) paid on the bonds in this fund are in the higher end of the scale, which makes sense given the longer-term maturity schedule and rating choices.

iShares ESG US Aggregate Bond ETF (EAGG) is a passively managed fund that applies ESG screens to invest in government, corporate, and securitized bonds that receive favorable ratings on their environmental, social, and governance practices. This approach places EAGG at level 2 in terms of impact. The fund holds government, corporate, and securitized bonds in fairly equal portions. It's also relatively balanced across coupon range and maturity schedules. The fund has over 2,500 bonds, 95% of which are investment grade.

You might consider investing in ABIMX if you preferred an actively managed fund that is maximizing impact. You could, however, be accepting more risk, because the fund is skewed toward one bond type and includes more lower-grade bonds than EAGG. EAGG might be your choice if you're comfortable investing in bond ETFs and are seeking a high-rated investment with broad exposure across sectors and maturity dates.

The type of data contained in Table 6.4 is easy to find using online tools. You can look up any bond fund or ETF you own to better understand what it holds, the fees you are being charged, and other information. You can also use the tools to analyze investments you may be considering. A video on our companion website will show you how to locate this data for virtually any bond fund or ETF.

Comparing Bond Funds to Bond ETFs

Although bond funds and bond ETFs offer diversity across the bond market, have low minimums, and provide high levels of liquidity, there are some important differences between them. First, bond funds tend to be actively managed, which means investment decisions are made by portfolio managers. Bond ETFs, on the other hand, are passively managed and use technology to make investment decisions. Whether it's better to buy an active or passive fund is a choice that is frequently debated. The controversy is most apparent in the stock market.

The second difference is the way the funds are valued. The price of a bond fund is based on the value of the underlying bonds in the fund. In contrast, a bond ETF is influenced by additional factors, such as market momentum and speculative trading. An ETF can be traded more frequently than the underlying bonds it represents, which can create a disconnect between the ETF price and the value of the underlying assets. This dynamic, which is somewhat unique to bond ETFs, makes this investment more volatile and unpredictable than bond funds, particularly in times of market upheaval. As a result, some financial advisors recommend bond funds over bond ETFs and even shy away from investing in bond ETFs at all.

Values-Aligned Bond Funds and Bond ETFs

Sustainable, green, and other values-aligned bond funds and ETFs that anyone can invest in are relatively new. As a result, the number of investment opportunities is currently limited. What's more, some of these funds have track records of less than three years, which make them less attractive to investors who prefer to see more history. Although the shortened time frame would not stop me from investing, it certainly gives me pause and would cause me to do more diligence on a potential investment. In addition, some of these funds carry loads of 3.0% or more. A load is a fee or commission that is paid when the fund is purchased. I choose not to invest in funds that carry loads because the fees can have a negative impact on my return.

When you remove funds that have short track records or loads from the universe of values-aligned bond funds, it shrinks noticeably. That said, there are still a handful of opportunities for any investor. Unless otherwise noted, the funds in this section have minimums of $2,500 or less and no loads.

Trailing Returns: A Tool to Compare Funds

Rather than just listing the values-aligned funds that you can invest in, I wanted to present them in a financial context as well. To do that, I chose to display trailing returns in the tables that follow. These are backward-looking figures that cover a specific period of time. For example, a one-year trailing return dated September 18, 2020, shows how much an investment returned over the prior one-year period. A three-year trailing return captures a three-year window, a five-year return a five-year window, and so on.

The challenge with trailing returns is they're only valid at the point of measurement. If I captured the numbers a day later, they would be different because the next day's trading activity would change the window of time and the return value.

By the time you read this book, the trailing return data in it will be outdated. It's outdated even as I write this chapter. But I chose to include it anyway because I believe it's important to be able to at least get a sense of how different investments perform over time and how they compare to each other—even if all you're seeing is a snapshot of one point in time.

Sustainable Bond Funds

Sustainable funds currently offer the greatest range of choice among values-aligned bond funds for the average investor. Funds in this category tend to fall into impact levels 1 and 2, either avoiding certain investments (do no harm) or applying ESG criteria (benefit stakeholders) to determine which bonds are included in the fund. In this category, you can find funds that vary in terms of focus, quality, risk/return profile, and impact. Let's take a look at Table 6.5 to compare sustainable bond funds.

TABLE 6.5 Sustainable Bond Fund Comparison

Bond Name	Ticker	1–Yr. Return	3–Yr. Return	5–Yr. Return	Fee
Short term					
iShares ESG 1–5 YR ETF	SUSB	5.57%	3.85%	-	0.12%
Intermediate term					
AMG GW&K Core ESG	MBGVX	7.27%	4.74%	3.88%	0.88%
Pax Core Bond Fund	PAXBX	7.09%	4.57%	-	0.71%
Pax High Yield Bond Fund	PAXHX	5.89%	4.86%	5.58%	0.96%
TIAA-CREF Core Impact	TSBRX	6.71%	4.90%	4.18%	0.64%
Long term					
iShares ESG Corp ETF	SUSC	9.50%	6.42%	-	0.18%

Compiled using data from Morningstar as of Sept 18, 2020.

AMG GW&K Core Bond ESG N (MBGVX) is a level 2 fund that incorporates ESG criteria into its investment analysis. The actively managed fund holds approximately 75 bonds and is heavily weighted to investment-grade US corporate and securitized bonds.

TIAA-CREF Core Impact Bond Retail (TSBRX) is another level 2 fund but is much more diversified than MBGVX. This fund holds over 950 investment-grade US government, corporate, and securitized bonds that demonstrate ESG leadership and/or have direct and measurable environmental and social impact.

Pax High Yield Bond Fund (PAXHX) is a very different fund. A portion of the fund is allocated to companies that drive solutions in automotive efficiency, renewable energy, and sustainable communities. So at least part of the fund is approaching level 3 impact (develop solutions). However, non-investment-grade bonds make up the majority of the fund, as it accepts a higher risk to achieve greater returns.

Note: Although they are all included in the same table, these funds are quite different in terms of the sectors they hold, average interest rates, maturity dates, and ratings—all the characteristics we discussed in the earlier bond comparison example. The same holds true for the other tables included in this chapter. If you were evaluating these funds to make an investment decision, you'd want to use online tools to analyze the features of each bond fund so you'd know what it held, your risk, and the potential for return.

If you have more to invest: Many fixed-income and public equity funds come in share classes. Funds within the same grouping can have exactly the same name with the exception of a letter at the end. For example, Neuberger Berman Municipal Impact A and Neuberger Berman Municipal

Impact Inst are basically the same fund. However, one is designed for the retail investor, and the other is created for institutional investors (i.e., pension plans, corporations) and high-net-worth individuals.

Retail funds usually have smaller minimums. Institutional funds, on the other hand, have minimums that can start around $100,000 and go as high as $10 million. In exchange for higher minimums, institutional funds tend to come with the benefit of reduced fees and no loads.

Fund Share Classes

The letters A, B, and C indicate that a fund is intended for the average, or retail, investor. B and C class funds may carry additional fees or loads. I, Inv, or Inst shows the fund is designed for institutional investors.

Adv designates Advisor class funds that can only be purchased through a financial advisor. They may carry additional fees.

There are some sustainable bond funds that have loads at the retail level but not at the institutional level. For example, Calvert Responsible Income I (CTTIX) is available with a $250,000 minimum, while JPMorgan Municipal Income I (HLTAX) and Neuberger Berman Municipal Impact Instl (NMIIX) both have $1 million minimums.

Green Bond Funds

Green bond funds are even more recent market entrants than sustainable bond funds. Of those listed in Table 6.6, only the Green California Tax-Free Income Fund (CFNTX) has a five-year return history. This actively managed fund invests exclusively in investment-grade municipals, providing tax-free interest. The remaining funds and ETFs are intermediate term and hold a mix of government and corporate bonds from around the world.

TABLE 6.6 Green Bond Fund Comparison

Bond Name	Ticker	1–Yr. Return	3–Yr. Return	5–Yr. Return	Fee
Short term					
Green Calif Tax-Free Fund	CFNTX	3.55%	2.55%	2.51%	0.77%
Intermediate term					
iShares Global Green ETF	BGRN	4.67%	-	-	0.20%
TIAA-CREF Green Bond	TGROX	7.35%	-	-	0.80%
VanEck Vectors Green Bond ETF	GRNB	7.59%	2.72%	-	0.20%

Compiled with data from Morningstar as of Sept 18, 2020.

If you have more to invest: You might want to consider the Franklin Municipal Green Bond Adv (FGBKX), which entered the market in 2019. This muni bond fund has a $100,000 minimum. Mirova Global Green Bond Y (MGGYX), Calvert Green Bond I (CGBIX), and AllianzGI Green Bond P (AGBPX) are green bonds that have loads in the retail class but are load-free at the institutional level for minimums of $100,000, $250,000, and $1 million, respectively.

Gender Equity and Social Bond Funds

There's only one fund that I am aware of that specifically targets gender equity. Although it was announced in early 2020, the Artesian Women's Economic Empowerment Bond Fund (WE Fund) was not available at the time of this writing. However, it's expected to be open for investment soon.

For now, the best way to address issues related to women and girls is through social bond funds that deliver affordable housing and support education, improved healthcare, and community development. These interventions have an unusually large and positive impact on women and girls. Some of these social bond funds are compared in Table 6.7.

TABLE 6.7 Gender and Social Bond Fund Comparison

Bond Name	Ticker	1–Yr. Return	3–Yr. Return	5–Yr. Return	Fees
Short term					
Access Capital Community IS	ACATX	4.36%	-	-	0.40%
Intermediate term					
AB Impact Municipal Income	ABIMX	3.63%	5.08%	-	NA
CRA Qualified Investment Retail	CRATZ	4.45%	3.11%	2.46%	0.82%
Long term					
Columbia US Social Bond Inst	CONZX	4.01%	4.26%	3.96%	0.45%

Compiled using data from Morningstar as of Sept 18, 2020.

AB Impact Municipal Income (ABIMX) invests primarily in bonds supporting education, water, healthcare, and mass transit. With more than 80% of the assets invested in municipal bonds, the interest on this fund is mostly tax exempt at the federal level.

CRA Qualified Investment Fund: Retail Shares (CRATZ) is an investment-grade short- to intermediate-term fund that prioritizes affordable housing, minority advancement, and environmental sustainability. Bonds issued by the US government and government agencies make up the majority of the holdings.

If you have more to invest: You might want to consider the institutional class versions of the bonds listed in Table 6.7. For example, the institutional version of CRA Qualified Investment Institutional (Ticker: CRANX) is available for a $100,000 minimum, while Access Capital Community Investment has an institutional class version with a $1 million minimum.

The universe of sustainable, green, social, and thematic bond funds is relatively small. Innovation seems to happen at the bond level first and then moves into funds. With the acceleration we are seeing at the bond level, we hope to see growth in bond funds, too. Nonetheless, there are some options available now for any investor.

Assessing and Mitigating Bond Risks

When you invest in bonds there are four key risks you should be aware of: credit risk, interest rate risk, liquidity risk, and concentration risk. Understanding these risks will help you make more informed bond-investment decisions.

Credit Risk

The most obvious risk when you purchase any type of bond or fixed-income product is credit risk. Since these investments are loans, there's always the possibility the borrower will default.

This risk can be mitigated through the choices you make related to credit quality. Investments composed of AAA quality bonds are far less likely to default than investments in lower-rated bonds. Your trade-off will be in returns. Higher-quality bonds will be safer, but their returns will be lower.

You can assess credit risk by reviewing the credit ratings the bonds received from rating agencies such as S&P, Moody's, and Fitch. Or you can work with a financial advisor who can perform credit risk assessments directly.

Credit risk can change. If the business fundamentals underlying the borrower's ability to repay shift, the bond's credit rating can deteriorate or improve. If a bond's creditworthiness deteriorates, the bond becomes riskier and investors are less inclined to own the bond, so its price goes down. The converse is also true. When credit ratings improve, the bond is considered less risky, making it more attractive to investors, so the value of the bond goes up.

Interest Rate Risk

This risk is tied to fluctuations in the prevailing US interest rate set by the Fed. When you purchase a bond, it has a fixed interest rate (coupon) and maturity date. You'll be paid interest based on the coupon every year as long as you own the bond. That would be fine, assuming all things in the broader economy stayed the same. But that's never the case. Interest rates will fluctuate, and this will affect the value, or price, of your bond. When the prevailing interest rate goes up, the value of your bond goes down. And vice versa.

Assume you own a bond with a 4.0% coupon when the prevailing interest rate is 6.0%. You are—in essence—losing money. If you tried to sell your bond, you'd probably receive less for it than you paid. The fact that there are bonds with 6.0% coupons makes your bond less attractive to buyers. The value of your bond in the market has gone down as has the price that a buyer would be willing to pay for it.

> **Interest Rates & Bond Prices Move in Opposite Directions**
>
> The key to the bond market is to understand that interest rates and bond prices move in opposite directions. Think about this like a child's seesaw. When interest rates go down, the prices of existing bonds go up. Similarly, if interest rates go up, the price you can get for your existing bond will go down. Interest rates and bond prices have an inverse relationship, which means they move in opposite directions.
>
> Created by Luis Prado from Noun Project

Conversely, if the prevailing interest rate were 2.0%, you'd be doing well with your 4.0% bond. Buyers would be attracted to your bond because they could earn 4.0% from it and would probably be willing to pay a higher price to access that return. Thus, as the interest rates went down, the price of your bond would go up.

Given the long time horizon, there is more uncertainty around how interest rates will change over the life of a 30-year bond, which makes it riskier. As a result, longer-term bonds tend to offer higher returns than shorter-term bonds to incentivize investors to assume this added risk.

Since it's possible to buy short (1–5 years), intermediate (5–10 years), and long-term bonds (10+ years), you can diversify this risk by owning bonds with a mix of maturity dates. This strategy allows you to hedge against periods when interest rates increase as well as when they decrease.

Concentration Risk

As you've learned, a well-designed portfolio will allocate money across several asset classes to avoid concentration into a single return driver or exposure. It is also wise to diversify within asset classes. Within fixed income, you can also diversify by:

- **Type:** It's good to own different types of fixed-income investments, such as CDs, individual bonds, bond funds, or ETFs. You can further diversify by purchasing government, municipal, corporate, or asset-backed bonds—or some combination of these.
- **Number:** You can invest in multiple bonds, purchasing several individual bonds or buying a bond fund. The more you diversify, the more you can manage risk in your bond portfolio.
- **Maturity:** You can also own a mix of short-, intermediate-, and long-term bonds. Diversifying across maturities helps manage interest rate risk according to your risk/return goals.

The easiest way to diversify is by buying an aggregate bond fund that holds a range of bond types with different maturity dates. The most difficult approach is building and managing your own bond portfolio.

Liquidity Risk

Liquidity risk relates to your ability to sell your individual bonds whenever you want. Unlike public equities, which you can trade at virtually any time, individual bonds can be more difficult to sell, because there is no centralized exchange like the stock market. The lack of a centralized system also increases the cost of buying and selling bonds. Bond funds and bond ETFs, however, are easier to sell because they're traded on public markets.

Making Fixed Income Investment Decisions

This chapter introduced you to the world of fixed income. While there is more to know about bonds, particularly if you're considering buying and selling them yourself, hopefully you are feeling more confident about them and have insight into values-aligned options in this asset class.

Some of you may be wondering how you will translate this knowledge into investment decisions. Here are a few things to consider. If you're saving your money for a major purchase, you might want to invest in low-risk, fixed-income products that safeguard your assets. For those with less than $50,000 allocated to this asset class, an investment in one or more diversified bond funds could be appropriate. Once you have $50,000 or more for this portion of your portfolio, you might be ready to consider investing in individual bonds, assuming that strategy appeals to you. Most investors at this level are likely to remain invested in bond funds, which are easier to manage and offer increased diversification. Those with larger amounts to invest have more choice, including institutional class funds or working with a financial advisor to build an individual bond portfolio.

To demonstrate how these options play out, let's consider the sample investors we discussed in previous chapters and look at the fixed-income choices they might make, as shown in Table 6.8.

TABLE 6.8 Fixed Income Investment Examples

Jade ■ Fired-up idealist	Jade and her husband will likely need the money they're putting aside for a house in two to three years. As a result, they decided their funds would be safest in cash alternatives or slightly longer-term CDs or notes, like those mentioned at the beginning of this chapter.
Anika ■ Young guardian	Anika has $12,000 that she intends to invest in fixed income. She's planning to split the money between two impact bond funds with varying maturities. One will be intermediate term, and the other will be short- or long-term, depending on prevailing interest rates.
Ava ■ Caretaker and returner	Ava is allocating $300,000 of her assets to fixed income. Although she has enough to consider individual bonds, she wants more diversification. Ava plans to split her money across three funds with different maturities. Ava is conducting research to select the funds that are the best match for her financial return and impact goals. In addition to considering the funds mentioned in this chapter, Ava is also searching the web and talking to her advisor to find additional impact options.
Maria ■ Empire builder	Maria is an accredited investor. She's targeting about 15% of her assets to fixed income. Since she's passionate about uplifting women and girls, Maria has decided to work with her advisor to invest a significant portion of her fixed-income assets in an individual bond portfolio that focuses on affordable housing, education, and other gender-focused initiatives. To increase her diversification, she'll also hold some bond funds.

Take Action

Activating your fixed income doesn't have to be that difficult. As with many of your assets, it starts with knowing what you own.

1. Analyze what you currently own

On our companion website, you will find a template and other tools to help you catalog and analyze your current fixed-income investments in terms of return, maturity, and holdings.

Once completed, consider what you learned from this exercise. Are your fixed-income investments currently diversified, or are they skewed to one type of bond, maturity date, or coupon range? Do you want more diversity? Less diversity? Are there other changes you want to make?

2. Transition one investment into values alignment

Consider starting by picking one investment to shift into value alignment. Think about the type of investment you want to buy to replace it. Would you prefer to replace what you have now "like-for-like" in terms of bond type, maturity date, and so on? Or would you rather use this opportunity to change your allocations?

When you know the type of investment you want to own, you can conduct research to identify the values-aligned products that match your goal.

3. When you're ready, sell your old holdings and buy your new values-aligned investment

Your custodian should save records of your old holdings, but be sure to confirm they will do so before you sell. If they don't offer this service, please remember to save your last statements, cost basis, tax information, and other critical data for your records.

Hopefully, that wasn't too hard, and you're feeling great about what your new investment is supporting. Who knows? You might even be ready to shift another fixed-income asset.

Endnotes

1. https://www.calvertimpactcapital.org/invest.
2. https://www.enterprisecommunity.org/financing-and-development/community-loan-fund/support-our-work/impact-note.
3. https://www.reinvestment.com/.
4. http://bondfunds.com/education/a-brief-history-of-bond-investing/.
5. http://bondfunds.com/education/a-brief-history-of-bond-investing/.

6. https://www.worldbank.org/en/news/feature/2018/11/27/from-evolution-to-revolution-10-years-of-green-bonds.
7. https://www.climatebonds.net/resources/reports/2019-green-bond-market-summary.
8. https://www.climatebonds.net/bond-library.
9. https://www.environmental-finance.com/content/the-green-bond-hub/the-2020s-the-decade-of-sustainable-bonds.html.
10. https://www.globenewswire.com/news-release/2020/09/16/2094804/0/en/Verizon-prices-second-Green-Bond.html.
11. https://financialallianceforwomen.org/news-events/the-growing-power-of-gender-lens-investment/.

CHAPTER 7

Public Equities

Invest in the Stock Market with Confidence

Public equities are stocks or stock funds available for anyone to buy and sell on a public market, or stock exchange, such as the New York Stock Exchange (NYSE) or NASDAQ. For many readers, this may be the most important asset class covered in this book, because it plays a prominent role in most investment portfolios. Although most people have some familiarity with public equities, many of us do not fully understand the stock market, nor do we feel confident when making investment decisions.

Because there's so much to cover on this topic, we have split public equities into two chapters. In this chapter, you'll be introduced to different approaches to investing in this asset class. Some possibilities include picking individual stocks, investing through funds, or working with an advisor to establish a customized account. We'll also cover different methods you can use to diversify your stock holdings to maximize return or minimize risk. In the next chapter, we'll help you find values-aligned investments in this asset class.

The general wisdom about how to invest in the stock market has changed dramatically over the 30-plus years I have owned stock. When I started investing in the late 1980s, the recommended approach was to buy individual stocks in companies that had a widely recognized reputation for quality, reliability, and operational excellence—and hold them. My mother, who was my first investment teacher, adhered to this strategy. At one time, I owned individual stocks in over 30 companies, a few of which don't even exist today.

While many people—including my husband—still invest this way, I do not. As I learned more about investing, I realized there were other approaches I could use that offered more portfolio diversity and took less of my time. What's more, the accepted wisdom about how to invest in the stock market has shifted. There are now many people who believe the smartest strategy is to simply "buy the market," which means owning small amounts of hundreds or even thousands of individual stocks. In addition, we now have online trading platforms, robo-advisors, and amazing web-based research tools that are changing the way people invest. Although having too much choice can sometimes be overwhelming, navigating these options doesn't have to be difficult.

At one time or another, I have used virtually every investment approach described in this chapter. My firsthand experience informed my choices along the way, and I hope it can inform yours as well. Although I have not personally used robo-advisors or online trading platforms, they offer a valuable, low-cost way for many people to get started and participate in the stock market.

The information in this chapter holds true whether you're applying it to a self-managed taxable account or to funds in an employer-sponsored retirement account. Where the funds sit is less important than the types of investments and diversification strategies you choose.

Why Should You Spend Time Learning About Public Equities?

Public equities matter, because they're considered one of the best investment options for anyone who wants to grow their wealth over the long term. They're easy to access and available to accredited and non-accredited investors alike. Historically, returns on public equities have outpaced returns on other traditional asset classes such as cash and fixed income. Most portfolios, including retirement accounts, contain public equities, and in many cases they even dominate the portfolio's composition.

A number of advantages come with owning shares of a public company. First, you have the opportunity to participate in the upside of the company's growth. Second, you may receive regular payments from your stock holdings. Each quarter, when public companies report their net income to shareholders, they can either reinvest those assets in the business or distribute them to their shareholders in the form of dividends.

A third benefit is the right to vote on management decisions. As a shareholder you have the right to advocate for changes you'd like to see the company make in its operations or business practices. Fourth, investments in public equities are extremely liquid, which means you can buy and sell them at any time. And last but not least, this asset class offers a greater depth and breadth of values-aligned options than almost any other asset class.

Of course, there's no guarantee that you'll make money in the stock market, particularly if you're only investing for the short term. The best way to approach public equities is with a long-term view. Over the short term, the stock market can have such significant up-and-down swings that it feels a bit like riding a rollercoaster. But over the long term, public equities are one of the best tools investors have to grow their wealth.

To invest in the stock market, all you need to do is open an account with an investment firm, which then becomes the caretaker, or custodian, of your money. Vanguard, Schwab, and Fidelity are among the most recognizable brick-and-mortar investment firms, while Ellevest, Betterment, and Robinhood are online options that offer varying degrees of trading and advisory services.

Investing in public equities can be as easy as selecting one or two well-diversified funds, or it can be more complex. The approach that works best for you will depend on the amount of time you want to spend, your return expectations, and the amount you plan to invest. When I began investing in stocks, I used a single approach—individual stock picking. Over time, as my knowledge and assets grew, I incorporated multiple strategies. You might find the same thing happens to you.

Trade-Offs in Investment Approach

There is no perfect, one-size-fits-all approach to the stock market, even though you may hear something to the contrary. There are always trade-offs.

When you invest in the stock market, you can take a DIY approach or you can work with a financial advisor online or in person. Regardless of whether you do it yourself or with an advisor, you'll be investing in individual stocks, funds, or some combination of both. Each choice differs in terms of time commitment, potential return, and diversification levels.

Individual Stocks Can Produce Great Returns, but ...

In 1790 when the first stock exchange was established in Philadelphia, the main way to invest was by purchasing stock in individual companies. Unfortunately, this opportunity was primarily available only to the wealthy, and it took almost 150 years for things to change dramatically.

Given its long history, it's not surprising that more has been written about how to buy and sell individual stocks than virtually any other investment topic. Even though it was originally written over 40 years ago, Benjamin Graham's *The Intelligent Investor*—which is considered to be the definitive book on value investing—remains a bestseller.

Value Investing and Values-Aligned Investing

Value investing should not be confused with values-aligned investing. The former refers to picking individual stocks that an investor believes are being underestimated or undervalued by the stock market, while the latter pertains to choosing where you invest based on your values.

Individual stock picking can be a heavy lift, particularly for the beginning investor. Yet, there are still many people who choose to invest this way. They may want direct control over what they own, believe they can outperform the market, or simply enjoy the process. Success requires you to learn about the companies you're investing in and to track their progress regularly.

If you want to invest in individual stocks, you can get started for as little as $100 when you use an online trading platform, such as Robinhood or E*Trade. Stock picking is the preferred choice for some people and the only way they want to invest. For others, it is too burdensome and nerve-racking. Thanks to the innovators and risk takers who have emerged in the last century, we now have other options.

Funds Offer Another Approach

Public equity funds allow investors to own multiple stocks without having to personally make each individual investment decision. One fund can hold hundreds or even thousands of individual stocks, providing an easy way for an investor to acquire a diversified portfolio.

Assume you have $5,000 to invest in US equities. You could buy about three shares of Alphabet (Google's parent company), which was trading for approximately $1,500 per share as of this writing, or you could buy iShares MSCI KLD 400 Social ETF (Ticker: DSI), a socially responsible fund that holds over 400 companies, Alphabet being one of them.

Benchmarks Tell You How Well You're Doing

A benchmark is simply a standard against which similar items can be compared. They're used to measure the performance of an investment. When you invest in the stock of a large corporation, you can use the S&P 500 Index, which tracks 500 of the largest companies on all the major

US stock exchanges, as a benchmark to assess how well your stock is performing vis-à-vis the overall market.

Benchmarks are also used with funds. They can be designed to track broad markets, more narrowly defined market segments, or multiple markets. There are literally thousands of benchmarks. When you invest in a stock fund, it's worth finding out which benchmark is being used because it will tell you a great deal about the types of companies held in the fund. Once you invest, check your investment against its benchmark regularly to track how well it's doing. How often you check is entirely up to you. Some people check their returns daily or weekly and others review their assets just once or twice a year. I used to check monthly, but that became too much of a burden. So now I check my investments quarterly.

Types of Benchmarks

Market Indices

Market indices are benchmarks that track a single broad market or more narrowly defined market segment. The Russell 3000 Index is a very broad market index that follows the performance of 3,000 large- and mid-sized companies across all US stock markets. The NASDAQ 100 Index, on the other hand, focuses on just 100 large companies traded on the NASDAQ stock exchange. Both of these indexes are frequently used as benchmarks.

Blended Benchmarks

Blended benchmarks combine more than one market index into a single benchmark. For example, an investor targeting a 60% global stock and 40% global bond portfolio might pick a benchmark that is 60% MSCI All Country World Index (ACWI) and 40% Citigroup World Government Bond Index.

Absolute Return

benchmarks target an absolute return. For example, if your objective is to earn 5% over inflation, then your benchmark might be 5% + CPI (Consumer Price Index).

Mutual Funds Seek to Beat the Market and Provide Diversity

Around the time of the Great Depression, the stock market was still catering primarily to the rich. Charles Merrill, one of the cofounders of Merrill-Lynch, believed the middle class should be able to prosper from investing in public equities just like the wealthy. He wanted to "bring Wall Street to Main Street" and set out to offer the average American an affordable, easy way to invest in quality stocks. To a large degree, he succeeded. Along the way Merrill upended the way Wall Street did business. He also launched a massive education program to help people understand—and gain confidence in—the stock market.

Merrill singled out women and ran investment courses just for them. In 1949, 800 women lined up around the block waiting to participate in one of Merrill's investment seminars.[1] By the time he died seven years later, members of the middle class were becoming investors, which was a huge departure from what had come before.

Although Merrill played an instrumental role in changing who invested in the stock market, he did not change how they invested. The new investors were still adhering to the original strategy of buying individual stocks—an approach requiring knowledge, effort, and discipline. Changing how people invest required yet another innovation—the mutual fund.

Mutual funds pool the assets of many people into a single financial instrument. Fund managers then invest that money in numerous individual stocks on behalf of the investors. And that is the brilliance of mutual funds. They free investors from having to make stock buy-and-sell decisions themselves.

Although the first modern-day mutual fund launched in the US in 1924, the product did not really take off until the mid-1960s. Before then mutual funds were professionally managed, but many of the fund managers were conservative in their approach, buying in small quantities and holding onto the stocks in their portfolio for years. Enter a new breed of fund managers that included Gerald Tsai, an enigmatic man in his 30s who managed Fidelity's Capital Fund.

Like many of his peers, Tsai did not adhere to the status quo. He had no qualms selling everything in his portfolio in a single year, nor did he flinch at executing large trades. As a result of his skill and the market dynamics in the 1960s, Tsai achieved unprecedented success. In one year, his fund delivered close to a 50% return while the broader market gained only 15%. As a result, Tsai was elevated to rock star status. He appeared in the popular press, and his star power helped ignite a following that shifted the way the average investor thought about the stock market.

Today there are close to 8,000 mutual funds in the market.[2] Like Tsai, today's fund managers pick stocks they believe will outperform the broader market. Because they have a human being making stock selections, these funds are referred to as actively managed. Fees for actively managed mutual funds are typically higher than for other types of stock funds and can be in the range of 0.5% to 1.5% or more. This can have a significant impact on your investment's return. Let's say you invested $5,000 in a mutual fund that provided a gross return of 6.5% over the course of a year. If the fees were 1.5%, your net return would be only 5.0%.

To maximize return, active fund managers tend to buy and sell stocks within their portfolio during the course of the year. This buying and selling is known as turnover, and it's expressed as a percentage of the total assets under management. For example, a fund with 10% turnover means that only 10% of the total stocks in the fund were sold during the course of the year, while a 300% turnover would mean that, in essence, the entire portfolio was bought and sold three times during the year. This matters. If the stocks are in a taxable account and included capital gains when they were sold, you will have to pay taxes on those gains.

Index Funds Offer Simplicity, Diversity, and Market-Rate Returns

An index fund is a special type of mutual fund designed to closely track the performance of a specific part of the stock market. In 1975 John Bogle introduced the first index fund. It tracked the S&P 500 Index and provided a profoundly different way for anyone to invest. His competitors mocked him, called him un-American, and named his fund "Bogle's Folly." But that didn't stop him. Although he started with just $11 million in assets, his fund ultimately achieved great success. Bogle went on to found Vanguard, which is now one of the most successful investment firms in the country and a prominent advocate for index investing.

Multiple Meanings of the Term "Index"

The term "index" has multiple meanings in finance. It can be used as:

- **A benchmark**: "Index" is often used interchangeably with the word "benchmark," but they're actually two different things. An index tracks a specific market or segment, while a benchmark can be composed of one or more indexes.
- **A verb**: "Index" can also be used to describe the process used to create an index, as in indexing is the act of compiling financial data into a single metric.
- **A product**: An index fund is a passively managed mutual fund.

Index funds are not designed to outperform the market. Rather, the intention is for them to stay as close as possible to the index around which they were designed. In this case, the index can become the benchmark against which the performance of the fund is measured. The divergence between the return of an index fund and its associated benchmark is known as tracking error. With index funds, the goal is to minimize tracking error to the point where the fund's performance mimics the index it's following. The tracking error in an index fund tends to be in the 0% to 2% range, while an actively managed fund can have a tracking error of 4% to 7%.[3]

Like all mutual funds, index funds offer investors a diversified portfolio of stocks. However, unlike an actively managed mutual fund where fund managers are making buy-and-sell decisions, an index fund is passively managed. Investment decisions are made automatically and based on a set of rules that govern the fund.

Passive management keeps costs down. Fees on an index fund can be as little as 0.03%, which is only three hundredths of a percent (i.e., three basis points). In this case, if a $5,000 investment resulted in a 6.50% gross return, the net return would be 6.47%. As an investor, you'd capture almost the entire return. There is also very little turnover, making these funds extremely tax efficient. Index funds can hold hundreds, if not thousands, of companies. Because of this you can build significant diversity into your public equities portfolio with just one or two investments. These advantages are important to many investors, as suggested by the growing popularity of index funds.

Basis Points Defined

The term "basis point" is used to describe percentages for amounts that are less than 1%. Each basis point is equal to one one-hundredth of 1%. For example, 50 basis points is the same thing as half a percent, or 0.50%. So 7 basis points equates to seven-hundredths of 1.0%, or 0.07%.

Active versus Passive Fund Management

There's a debate over whether it's better to invest in passively or actively managed funds. The answer varies, depending on your goals as an investor. For many, the issue often comes down to level of control and financial return.

Both sides make salient arguments. Advocates for passive investments point to lower fees and more limited turnover. They also argue that most actively managed funds underperform, or do worse than, their benchmarks over the long term. In their view, investing in a passively managed index fund that holds significant parts of the market is a low-fee, low-maintenance, and automatic diversification strategy.

Some go so far as suggesting that all you need to do is buy one or two index funds—a total stock market fund and a total bond market fund—and never worry about your investments again.

Those on the other side of the debate remind us that active funds can beat the market, and some do so by a significant margin. Because the goal of passive management is to track an index, this side claims that passive funds typically lag the index slightly after fees are deducted. They also believe active managers can protect their clients by investing in high-quality companies that perform better during market downturns. And, finally, they argue active managers can rebalance portfolio allocations based on market movements to keep fund performance consistent.

Thus, when should you use active versus passive? Generally speaking, passive management works well in efficiently priced markets, like the US large-cap, where relevant information is widely available and already factored into pricing, whereas active management can pay off better in less efficient markets where information is not as readily available, as with US small-cap and foreign markets funds. If you want to invest in large-cap, small-cap, and foreign companies, you may want to own both passive and active funds.

Something to keep in mind: The current emphasis on passive funds might be distorting the market. Some predict that important companies may start pulling out of the stock market, or we could experience an index bubble. Even if you're a strong advocate for an index strategy, pay attention to the markets so you can take corrective action should it become necessary.

Public Equity ETFs Mimic Index Funds in Many Ways

Exchange-traded funds, also known as ETFs, first entered the US market in 1993, which is relatively recent compared to the other types of public equity funds. Like an index fund, an ETF in the public equities market holds a group of stocks and tracks the performance of a particular index. Many ETFs are passively managed; however, that is not always the case. So don't assume a fund is passively managed just because it's an ETF.

For our purposes, the primary difference between mutual funds, index funds, and ETFs has to do with the way they're bought and sold. Mutual funds, including index funds, can only be traded at the end of a business day, which is when the price is set. If you "sell" a mutual fund at some point during the day, the price you receive will be the end-of-day price, regardless of the fund's price at the time you placed your sell order. An ETF, on the other hand, acts like an individual stock. It can be bought and sold at any time during the trading day, and its price fluctuates during that time. For the average investor buying an ETF as a long-term investment, this "benefit" probably won't even matter. It primarily affects investors who are playing the market and want to buy and sell during the same trading day to take advantage of price fluctuations in a particular financial product.

A difference that may matter more to you is how these two vehicles handle dividends. Index funds allow dividends to be automatically reinvested in the fund, while ETFs may require a manual process.[4] Unless your custodian offers a commission-free trading option, you may also pay a fee each time you convert your ETF dividends into more shares. So if you plan to make frequent investments in your fund, an index fund might be better for you.

A Note on Reinvestments

As an investor, you have the option of having the dividends and capital gains you receive on your investments automatically reinvested, or you can choose to have those monies moved into a deposit account. You can make this choice by contacting your custodian or picking this option through their online platform.

My mother loved to see her money grow more money, so she was a huge advocate of reinvesting. She wanted all her profits to go right back into the market. Unlike her, I have decided to use my dividends and capital gains as income so I could retire.

Whether you decide to reinvest or not, you will still need to pay taxes on your dividends and capital gains, unless your funds are in retirement or other tax-deferred accounts.

While there are other differences between ETFs and index funds, they're relatively minor. Some say fees on passively managed ETFs are lower than fees on index funds. But this really depends. I've seen both ETFs and index funds with fees, which are also known as expense ratios, as low as 0.03%. There are also claims that ETFs have a lower price of entry, because there are no minimums to speak of. While it's true that some index funds have minimums, many don't. So what you pay to get in and what you pay in fees really depends on the investment you choose.

As a reader of this book, the most important determinant of whether you pick an index fund or an ETF may very well be motivated by how well it aligns with your values, particularly if you're investing for the long term.

Table 7.1 compares different products you can buy in the public equities market. The table is intended to present general differences. With thousands of each of these products in the market, there are no hard-and-fast rules. You can find index funds with higher fees, mutual funds that hold more equities, or any number of other divergences from the figures presented here.

TABLE 7.1 Public Equity Product Comparison

	Active/ Passive	Number of Equities Held	Fees (Expense Ratios)	Purchase Price	Sale Price
Individual stocks	Active, investor selects	Purchased one at a time	None	Stock share price	Set at time of sell order
Mutual funds	Active, fund manager selects	30 to 100 (or more)	0.5%–1.5%	Possible minimum	Set at end of day
Index funds	Passive	100 to thousands	0.03%– 1.0%	Possible minimum	Set at end of day
ETFs	Passive or active	100 to thousands	0.03%– 2.5%	ETF share price	Set at time of sell order

Investing with a Financial Advisor

If you decide that you don't want to go it alone, financial advisors can help you implement any investment strategy. They can help you find the best mutual fund managers, index funds, or ETFs to meet your needs. Some financial advisors will even help you build a personalized portfolio, which is also known as a separately managed account. In this case, your advisor would select individual stocks that align with your values and investment criteria. Minimums for this service tend to be $50,000 to $100,000 or more. The fee you pay for this specialized service could be less than what you are charged for some actively managed mutual funds.

What's the Best Investment Approach for You?

We've covered a lot of ground, so this is a great place to pause and think about your investment options and which approach might work best for you. Table 7.2 will help you get started, as it summarizes the trade-offs between the investment products we have covered so far.

TABLE 7.2 Trade-Offs between Public Equities Investment Products

	Level of Effort	Return	Values Alignment
Individual stocks	High	Depends on investor skills	Full control
Mutual funds	Medium	Seeks to exceed benchmark	Fewer options
Index funds	Low	Seeks to track benchmark	Broad range of options
ETFs	Low	Seeks to track benchmark	Broad range of options

Understanding your priorities will help you identify the investment products that are best suited for you. As you're thinking things over, try to answer some key questions:

- Do you want a simple DIY approach that doesn't require a lot of your time? If so, index funds and ETFs might be the best option. Just realize you might be giving up some return.
- Are you driven to maximize returns or to have a higher degree of control over what is in your portfolio? If so, you could select individual stocks or invest through mutual funds.
- Are you seeking the highest level of impact? If so, you can pick your own stocks, invest in a thematic fund, or work with a financial advisor to develop a separately managed account.
- Are you glad you learned all this information but really don't want to make all the decisions yourself? If so, you can invest through a values-aligned robo-advisor, or you could hire a financial advisor that specializes in impact investing.

Diversifying Your Portfolio

The more you diversify your portfolio, the more opportunity you have to mitigate risk. This is because you're spreading your assets across a number of investments that should react differently under varying market conditions.

We've already discussed one form of diversification, which is the number of stocks included in your portfolio. You can also diversify by company size, growth potential, industry sector, and geography. But you don't have to consider all these factors at once, particularly when you're starting out.

You can select one and add more diversification over time, as you become more knowledgeable and your wealth grows.

Start with Company Size

Whether you're picking individual stocks, investing in funds, or working with a financial advisor, company size is a great way to start thinking about diversification within public equities. A simple metric, called the market cap, is used to describe the size of a company on the stock market. It's calculated by multiplying a company's stock price by the number of shares outstanding. For example, if a company had 25 million shares of stock and the share price were $100, that company would have a market cap of $2.5 billion, making it a mid-cap stock.

Table 7.3 shows the size of companies ranging from mega-cap to nano-cap. You can invest across this spectrum and choose funds that hold companies of the same size or funds that include companies across a range of sizes. In the latter case, you'd be accessing significant market cap diversification with one investment.

TABLE 7.3 Market Cap Size

Market Cap	Approximate Range
Mega-cap	more than $200 billion
Large-cap	$10 billion to $200 billion
Mid-cap	$2 billion to $10 billion
Small-cap	$500 million to $2 billion
Micro-cap	$50 million to $500 million
Nano-cap	less than $50 million

There is a trade-off, however. Smaller-cap stocks tend to offer investors higher growth potential but have higher business risk, whereas larger-cap stocks typically have lower growth rates but often weather market downturns better than smaller-cap stocks. This is why you often hear that larger-cap stocks are less risky than smaller-cap stocks. Unfortunately, this pattern doesn't always hold true.

Since no one can predict exactly what'll happen, having a balance between larger and smaller companies hedges your bets. It provides the opportunity for more return potential while also stabilizing your portfolio during times of economic stress.

Company Size Trade-Offs

Investors who want the stability of larger companies could consider investing in large-cap companies or funds. Those who want more diversity and the potential to balance their portfolios under different market conditions could consider adding mid- and small-cap stocks. You can do this by investing in one total stock market fund, or you could invest in multiple funds—one that provides exposure to large-cap, another to mid-cap, and a third to small-cap companies. Solutions-oriented impact companies tend to be smaller-cap, making this an especially attractive category for values-aligned investors to consider.

Add Growth Potential

Growth potential is tied to cap size, so you're actually making these two decisions simultaneously when you invest in a company or a fund. When you buy an individual stock, the cap size and growth potential are inherent in that company. When you buy a fund, it's possible to purchase a growth, a value, or a blended fund. A blended fund holds a mix of growth and value stocks. You can quickly determine the average cap size and growth potential strategy of a fund by looking at how it appears in the Morningstar Style Box. Figure 7.1 explains how this box works.

Just One Look Holds a Wealth of Information

Just one look at the Morningstar Style Box delivers a snapshot visual of the types of companies in a fund. This fantastic tool depicts the size and growth potential of most of the companies the fund holds.

The vertical axis tracks company size, starting with large-cap at the top. The horizontal axis correlates to growth and shows whether the majority of assets in the fund are considered growth stocks, value stocks, or a blend of both. The fund represented in the example shown here would be a Large-Cap Blend.

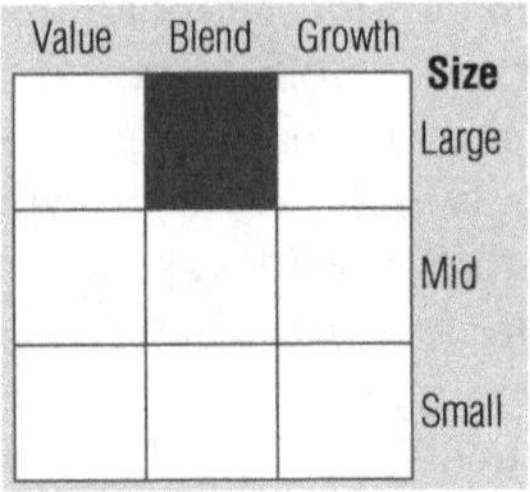

When you search for a fund on the Morningstar website, this style box will be displayed along with other key information about that investment.

FIGURE 7.1 Morningstar Style Box

Growth stocks usually refer to high-quality, successful companies that are expected to grow above the average rate and outperform the market. Value companies are typically more stable, more mature companies that have lower volatility and often pay investors a dividend. Growth stocks tend to be more expensive and often more volatile than value stocks. They also have higher, though less predictable, earnings growth. As a result, they carry the potential for higher return *and* higher risk. In some cases, determining whether a stock should be classified as growth or value is unclear; this classification sometimes involves more art than science.

Growth/Value Trade-Off

- Investors seeking to maximize returns might prefer growth stocks or funds.
- Investors who want to mitigate their risk or capture income from their portfolios could opt for value stocks.
- Those who seek simplicity, moderate range risk, and more diversity could consider a blended fund that includes growth and value companies.
- There are single-cap and multi-cap options in growth, value, and blended funds. This means it is possible to diversify by cap size and growth potential in one fund.

If You're a Bit Overwhelmed

All these choices can be a bit overwhelming. If you've reached your point of information saturation or are pretty clear that you're going to opt for a broad stock fund that captures most of the US market in terms of cap size and growth potential, feel free to skip ahead to the "Putting It All Together" section. You can always come back to the rest of the material, which is most applicable for investors with larger asset bases or specific interests, later. If you're just getting started, you can build a strong portfolio with the information that we've covered so far. Then you can enhance it with the next two strategies over time.

The last two strategies are important for investors who are making individual stock choices, want to target a particular segment of the market, or intend to build more diversity into their portfolio by investing outside the US.

Confirm Industry Sector Diversity

If you want more stability in your portfolio, include a healthy mix of companies from different industries or sectors. This is particularly important for investors who are picking their own stocks. When you purchase a

fund, industry and sector
choices have already been
made and may determine
why you choose one fund
over another.

Table 7.4 shows how
two very different funds—
Vanguard FTSE Social
Index Admiral (VFTAX)
and Invesco QQQ Trust
(QQQ)—allocate assets

TABLE 7.4 Sector Diversification

	VFTAX	QQQ
Technology	28%	45%
Healthcare	15%	7%
Financial services	13%	2%
Consumer cyclical	13%	18%
Communication services	13%	20%
Consumer defensive	7%	5%

Source: Morningstar as of August 18, 2020.

across six different industries. VFTAX tracks the Russell 1000 and is considered a broad-market, well-diversified fund. With the exception of technology, the fund's assets are fairly evenly distributed among a number of
industries. In contrast, over 80% of the assets in QQQ are concentrated in
three industries with technology dominating.

The industries included in VFTAX span all three sectors: cyclical, defensive, and sensitive. This adds another layer of diversification because each
sector responds differently to market conditions. QQQ is not only more
concentrated by industry, it's also more concentrated by sector. These differences influence the volatility and risk-return trade-offs of these two investments. VFTAX should experience less volatility but probably will not match
the return potential of QQQ.

Industry Sectors

Cyclical Sectors

Cyclical sectors include companies that provide products and services
that consumers spend more on during times of economic prosperity.
Examples include clothing and other discretionary consumer products,
airline travel, and automobiles. These industries are correlated to what
is happening in the economy, which tends to be cyclical. They tend to
do very well when the economy is strong but struggle when people are
struggling economically.

Defensive Sectors

Defensive sectors are less correlated to the health of the economy,
because these businesses offer goods and services that are required in
economic upturns and downturns. Companies in defensive industries

tend to behave more steadily through all economic cycles. Examples include healthcare, utilities, and food, all of which are important to people even during difficult economic times.

Sensitive Sectors

Sensitive sectors fall somewhere between cyclical and defensive sectors and include industries such as communication services, information technology, and heavy equipment.

In some cases you may choose to invest in a fund to capitalize on its industry focus. For example, you may purchase shares in Invesco QQQ Trust, because you believe that technology is going to outperform other sectors. Or perhaps you want to use a specific industry, such as real estate, to diversify your portfolio. You can do this by investing in a real estate–focused fund. Or you might increase the impact of your portfolio by adding a fund that invests in renewable energy, timber, or water—all strategies we will discuss in Chapter 10.

Expand through Geography

Investors who are just starting out or who are seeking a simple approach to their portfolios may opt to invest in US companies only. Those who want to mitigate against having all their assets in one economy can consider diversifying by geography.

According to Morgan Stanley's 2020 Geographic Classifications, countries are distributed into the following three geographic regions:[5]

- **Developed markets**: United States, Canada, much of Western Europe, and the strongest economies in Asia;
- **Emerging markets**: Brazil, Russia, India, China, and South Africa—the biggest emerging markets—often referred to as the BRICS; and
- **Frontier markets**: Smaller economies in Eastern Europe as well as countries in Africa and the Middle East.

As the world becomes more globalized and companies increase their operations across many countries, some investors contend where a company is based will become less important as a means of diversifying a portfolio. This perspective is probably more relevant when comparing stocks from developed countries and somewhat less so when considering businesses in emerging or frontier markets. Some argue that the potential for economic growth and stock returns in countries such as Brazil, India, and China will be stronger over the long term than growth in developed countries. For this reason, they believe it's important to have a portion of your portfolio invested outside the US.

Global Funds versus International Funds

International and Global Funds are not the same thing. While both hold stocks from many countries, there's a key difference. Global funds include stocks from the country in which the investor lives, while International funds do not. For US investors, a global fund would offer exposure to companies in the US and other countries in one fund, while an international fund would not include companies based in the US.

Putting It All Together

If you're stock picking, please try to be diligent about ensuring you have a diversified portfolio. The fewer stocks your portfolio holds, the more important this may be. Company size and sector diversity might be the most important criteria for you.

If you're buying funds, consider diversifying first through a combination of company size and growth potential decisions. You can start with just one fund that provides a high level of diversity. This is a great strategy if you're just starting out or you have a smaller asset base. As your experience and wealth grow, you can expand into other sectors and geographies. If you're ready for broader exposure now, you have a number of options.

Table 7.5 describes the decisions the five sample investors introduced earlier in the book might make in terms of their public equities' investments.

TABLE 7.5 Public Equity Investment Examples

Anika	Anika's money is currently in an index fund that holds
■ 27 years old	large- and mid-cap companies as well as a blend of
■ Non-accredited	growth and values stocks. Although this approach is
■ Risk appetite: moderately aggressive	working for her, she plans to replace her current fund with a values-aligned equivalent. Since her assets are in a 401(k), she won't incur taxes when she makes this transition.

Jade
- 32 years old
- Non-accredited
- Risk appetite: moderately conservative

Although Jade and her husband are saving for a house, they've decided to invest some of their money in individual stocks because they enjoy the process and want to pick companies aligned with their environmental goals. They plan to make selections together and will assess both the financials and values-alignment of each company they consider for their portfolio.

Ava
- 46 years old
- Accredited
- Risk appetite: moderate

The investments Ava received through her divorce are all individual stocks, which she doesn't want to manage. She's hiring a financial advisor, who'll help her transition to a mix of values-aligned mutual funds and ETFs. She'll diversify her portfolio by company size, sector, and geography in the process.

Toni
- 73 years old
- Accredited
- Risk appetite: conservative

Toni and her husband need higher returns if they're going to safeguard their daughter's future. As a result, they're transitioning some of their assets to public equities. They plan to invest in a passively managed US large-cap growth fund that will grow over the long term and require minimal management.

Maria
- 51 years old
- Accredited
- Risk appetite: aggressive

Now that she has additional assets, Maria wants a more diversified portfolio. Her current public equities holdings are primarily in US companies. She plans to increase her geographic exposure and is targeting a mix of 55% US, 30% developed, and 10% emerging markets. She's even going to experiment a bit in frontier markets with the remaining 5%.

Take Action

As a first step, and in preparation for the next chapter, you might want to stop for a moment to determine what you currently own.

1. If you haven't downloaded the "What You Have" Workbook from our companion website, you can do so now.

2. Use Morningstar or another online tool to identify the types of equities you own. Are you in individual stocks? Mutual funds? Index funds? ETFs? How much are you paying in fees? What cap sizes do you own? Do you hold growth stocks, value stocks, or a blend? What sectors are you invested in? You can reference the video on our website to learn how to find this information in Morningstar.

3. What did you learn? Are your public equities holdings currently diversified, or are they skewed to one company size, growth potential, industry sector, or geography? Do you want more diversity? Less diversity? Are there other changes you want to make?

Endnotes

1. https://about.bankofamerica.com/en-us/our-story/merrill-wall-street.html#fbid=7aMXOll1Hvh.
2. https://www.statista.com/statistics/255590/number-of-mutual-fund-companies-in-the-united-states/.
3. https://www.styleadvisor.com/resources/statfacts/tracking-error.
4. https://www.fool.com/investing/how-to-invest/etfs/etf-vs-index-fund/.
5. https://www.msci.com/market-classification.

CHAPTER 8

Public Equities
Select Values-Aligned Investments

Women have been leading and are continuing to lead the way in values-aligned investing. There's no better way I can think of to start a discussion of values-aligned public equity investments than by paying homage to some of the trailblazing women who were instrumental in building this field. Together they catalyzed financial markets to think—and act—differently. They launched firms and proved that you can use public equity to grow wealth and build a better world.

One such woman is Joan Bavaria, who has been described as a visionary, a pioneer, an inspiration, and a hero. In 1982, she founded Trillium Asset Management, one of the first socially responsible financial firms. Today Trillium manages close to $3 billion, making it one of the largest investment firms in the US, focused exclusively on values-aligned investing. Starting and building one firm was not enough for Joan. She also founded, cofounded, and inspired a number of other groundbreaking organizations in the social investing space. It's no surprise that Joan is often referred to as the "founding mother of socially responsible investing."[1]

Amy Domini was a contemporary of Joan's and another trailblazer in this arena. In 1990, she launched the Domini 400 Social Index, one of the first socially responsible indexes.[2] It was designed to help investors apply what are now known as ESG criteria to their investment decisions. Amy also founded Domini Impact Investments, another pioneering firm that provides values-aligned fixed income and public equity funds. She continues to serve as the chair of this firm.

In this chapter, we'll explore how you can invest your values through the stock market—an opportunity that would not have been possible without the leadership of Joan, Amy, and other women like them. You'll be introduced to online tools you can use to look inside your current investments, uncovering information about the companies they hold. You'll learn how to find values-aligned products that you can invest in today. We'll also show you how you can harness the power of shareholder advocacy, a process in which stockowners engage directly with corporate executives to drive positive change.

The Current State of Values-Alignment in Public Equities

Within public equities there are literally hundreds of values-aligned financial products. The numbers are growing each year as traditional investment firms, such as BlackRock and Vanguard, jump into the fray. Sustainable funds attracted $20.6 billion in 2019 alone—four times more than the amount in 2018—which held the previous record.[3] You can invest on your own by picking individual stocks or funds, or you can work with a financial advisor to access specialized products.

When you build a portfolio of individual stocks, you decide which level of impact you want to prioritize: do no harm (level 1), benefit all shareholders (level 2), or develop solutions (level 3). You have similar, though more limited, abilities when you invest in stock funds. Although there are options at all levels, the number of level 3 funds available within public equities today is still relatively small. Most funds are designed by eliminating undesirable players or by selecting companies that adhere to ESG best practices.

What Is ESG Scoring and How Does It Work?

An ESG score is used to rate a company's performance against a set of environmental, social, and governance factors. There are currently over 100 ESG rating agencies that create these scores. However, only a handful use rigorous criteria in their evaluations. MSCI ESG, Sustainalytics, and Bloomberg are some of the most recognized agencies. Many ESG fund managers use data from one or more of these leading sources to construct their ESG funds. Other managers use lesser-known agencies or have developed their own scoring criteria. This has led to a lot of divergence between scores.

The high level of variance in the current system is not completely surprising, because ESG scoring is complex. It involves amassing and analyzing non-financial data from literally thousands of sources—all of which has to be condensed into a single score.

Part of the challenge is there are conflicting views about which criteria should be included in a score, the weight or importance each receives, and the sources from which they're derived. A 2019 study by State Street Global Advisors found only a 53% correlation between the

ESG scores from two of the most prominent rating agencies, MSCI ESG and Sustainalytics.

Fortunately, there are a number of people committed to bringing the industry to an accepted standard. Though they are working diligently to that end, it's likely to be some time before they achieve success. As we wait, I believe it's wise to be both pragmatic and patient. While not perfect, there's a lot we can discern from the tools we have today, and they'll only get better as sustainable investing becomes even more commonplace.

Source: State Street Global Advisors. The ESG Data Challenge. March 2019.

Finding Values-Aligned Stocks

When you choose to invest in individual stocks, you can thoughtfully select the companies that are delivering the outcomes you want to see in the world. You can also engage in shareholder advocacy by voting your proxies or joining with other investors to demand changes in corporate behaviors and policies.

When you're considering a stock purchase, you'll most likely research the company's historic returns and growth potential. Evaluating whether the company aligns with your values is just another part of the diligence process. This step comes with a bit of uncertainty because not everyone concurs on the criteria that define a "good" company. As a result, the sources that provide ESG ratings for companies calculate and present their scores differently. Thus, until there are standards, you may have to perform some of your own research and use your best judgment to make your own investment decisions.

Relax: No Decision Is Perfect

One of the things that trips up many investors is the belief that they need to find the perfect solution before they invest. I think this is particularly true in the case of women. However, there's no perfect financial or values-aligned decision. There's always going to be a trade-off.

However, there are a number of things you can do when you're faced with an investment opportunity but are unsure of how it really adds up in terms of your values. You can start by using the tools in this chapter to assess how the company is scored by others. Then, you can perform additional research to uncover any issues or concerns that have been raised about the company.

At some point, though, you'll just need to make a judgment call. But it's your judgment. This is a point where the SDGs can be helpful because they can remind you of your priorities. Once you make your choice, you can find comfort in knowing that the perfect investment and the perfect decision are both illusions. If new information becomes available later, there is no shame in changing your mind. The error is not so much in making a mistake, which will be inevitable at some point, but rather in not taking action.

MSCI ESG, Arabesque S-Ray, Just Capital, and Yahoo Finance offer sustainability scoring on individual companies through their freely available websites. When you're evaluating a stock, you may want to reference a couple of these sources to see how the company fares under each form of scrutiny. Each of these sites contains detailed information on the methodology used to arrive at their scores.

Corporate Social Responsibility (CSR) reports provide another source of information. The GRI Sustainability Database[4] allows you to download CSR reports from nearly 15,000 companies. The documents come directly from the firms themselves, so you might want to keep that in mind when you are reviewing them.

Using this set of tools with other web research can go a long way to giving you visibility into the sustainability and ESG strengths and weaknesses of any company you currently own or are considering as an investment.

Corporate Rating Sources

MSCI ESG

MSCI ESG, one of the premiere ESG rating agencies, provides scores of over 8,500 companies and 680,000 financial products from around the world. Their ratings are presented as grades that range from AAA (leaders) to CCC (laggards). On their site, you can see how a company has ranked over time as well as areas where the business is leading or lacking.

Arabesque S-Ray

Arabesque S-Ray rates over 7,000 global companies daily. It combines more than 200 ESG metrics with analysis from over 30,000 news sources.

Arabesque provides two ratings. One is derived from ESG criteria, and the second applies an additional lens that looks at how each company performs in terms of its human rights, labor, environment, and anti-corruption practices. You can view how scores have changed over time and determine the company's involvement in harmful industries, such as tobacco, defense, and weapons.

Just Capital

Just Capital ranks over 800 companies using a proprietary process. In their methodology, workers' rights receive the highest weighting, followed by customers, communities, environment, and shareholders. Since the environment is not one of their higher priorities, you may want to combine this rating with another source if this issue is one of your key concerns.

Yahoo Finance

Yahoo Finance provides separate environmental, social, and governance scores for corporate entities. It also provides a Controversy score, which depicts the company's involvement in negative ESG incidents, such as using child labor in their supply chain or not responding to an oil spill. The level of controversial incidents can be predictive of the company's true commitment to ESG.

Finding Values-Aligned Stock Funds and ETFs

The great news is there are hundreds of values-aligned stock funds and ETFs. What's more, there are some really good, freely available tools that can help you evaluate the values alignment of these financial products. You can apply these to funds you already hold in your self-managed accounts as well as to funds that are held by your employer, robo-advisor, or any other financial manager. My guess is that when you check, you'll be surprised by what you learn. I certainly was, and it spurred me to action. Once I discovered how badly my investments were performing against my values, I wanted to find better options to replace them as quickly as I could.

But how can you find the fund or funds you want to invest in among hundreds of options? Fortunately, there are ways you can quickly narrow the field. A simple web search for "best ESG funds" or "best sustainable funds," for example, will lead you to a number of sites where others opine on the best investments and provide their analysis. This can be a great way to start. Once you identify a fund this way or get an idea from some other source, you can assess its values alignment using online tools, such as As You Sow, Natural Investments, and Morningstar.

Stock Fund Rating Sources

As You Sow Invest Your Values

As You Sow (AYS) is a nonprofit leader in shareholder advocacy. Their Invest Your Values site is one of my favorite tools. It has the richest content I've seen anywhere and is easy to use. With this tool you can scrutinize over 3,000 of the best-known mutual funds and ETFs to determine where they stand in terms of seven themes: fossil free, deforestation, gender equity, civilian firearms, military weapons, prison industrial complex, and tobacco.

When you enter a fund by name, ticker, or fund family in the site, you're greeted with a wealth of information. To start, each fund is given a grade from A to F for each theme. The site shows you exactly where and how a fund is, or isn't, out of alignment. AYS's site provides a level 1 perspective on whether or not a particular fund is "doing harm" across several vectors.

Natural Investments Heart Rating

Natural Investments is a socially responsible financial advisement firm. To be included on their site, a fund has to have an explicit socially responsible mandate. This requirement has reduced the universe of ESG funds on their site to about 165. Each fund receives a Heart Rating that is based on Natural Investments' unique rating methodology that pushes beyond criteria used in other scoring schemes. For example, as part of its analysis, Natural Investments considers whether fund managers seek positive impact with their cash by holding it in values-aligned financial institutions, such as community banks and credit unions.

Morningstar

Morningstar uses data from Sustainalytics, a recognized source of ESG ratings. The site scores over 21,000 mutual funds and ETFs. When you research a fund by entering its ticker at Morningstar.com, you can find the sustainability ratings under the "Portfolio" tab. Once there, the first thing to notice is whether the fund is designated as a "Sustainable Fund by Prospectus." This indicator lets you know whether or not the fund has a sustainability mandate.

You'll also find an image with one to five globes. This visual shows how the fund ranks in terms of ESG ratings relative to similar funds. Five globes means the fund is in the top 10 percentile among its peers, while one globe shows it among the lowest ranked.

There are also individual environmental, social, and governance ratings as well as a combined score. Scores up to 10 suggest negligible ESG risk while ratings over 40 are considered a severe risk. The individual E, S, and G ratings provide an indication of whether a fund is prioritizing environmental, social, or governance issues.

You can also use these tools to identify new investments. That's what I did. I started my research by looking for funds that matched my investment strategy. For example, I wanted to replace the Vanguard large-cap blend index fund I was holding. I liked the diversity in the fund, the passive management, and low fees. And it fit well with the other public equities funds I was holding. But in terms of impact, it was terrible! The fund received D or F grades from As You Sow in virtually every category.

What I did was run a search for "large-cap" in the fossil-free portion of the AYS Invest Your Values site. Then I sorted the results by the funds that received the highest grades. Very quickly, I reduced the universe to a list of the highest-ranking large-cap funds. Then I used Morningstar to dig into the financials of each fund on my list. From there, I chose a new fund and shifted my money. This process worked really well for me and is explained in more detail in a video on our companion website. You could use a similar process on the Natural Investments site.

Simplify Your Research

In Chapter 6, you were introduced to fund share classes. As you may remember, funds designed for institutional investors often end in I, Inv, or Inst and have minimums of $100,000 or more. If you aren't planning to invest at the higher level, then it may not be worth your time to research institutional class funds. Similarly, if you're planning to invest at higher levels, you might want to start your analysis with class I funds to take advantage of the lower fees.

Special Categories of Stock Funds and ETFs

Within the universe of stock funds and ETFs, there are some special categories I would like to call out because they will appeal to certain types of investors.

Target-Risk and Target-Date Funds

Some of us don't want to think about our money. We want a "set it and forget it" approach where we make one decision and don't worry about it anymore. Target-risk and target-date funds are designed to address this desire. They hold a combination of cash, bonds, and stock in one fund. With target-risk, you can select a fund based on your risk tolerance—conservative, moderate, or growth-oriented—and obtain a diversified portfolio with a single investment. Target-date funds are more complicated investments that automatically reallocate assets in the fund as you age.

The simplicity of these approaches makes them favorites in retirement accounts. Since I'm not a believer in one-step investment strategies, I'm not a big fan of these funds. But if you are, you may be happy to know there are values-aligned versions available. Calvert Investments, Eventide, Green Century, Pax, Praxis, and Walden all offer socially responsible target-risk funds. So you have several options. That isn't the case with target-date funds. At the time of this writing, Nuveen was the only company that had introduced a series of values-aligned target-date funds.

Balanced Thematic Funds

Within public equities there are funds and ETFs that seek broad diversification and are designed with a specific impact theme in mind. These funds are often constructed by avoiding companies that are antithetical to the theme and/or by actively selecting companies that receive high marks related to the theme.

Consider three funds that target gender diversity. Fidelity Women's Leadership (FWOMX), Glenmede Women in Leadership US Equity (GWILX), and Impact Shares YWCA Women's Empwrmt ETF (WOMN) appear to be quite similar at the surface level. They're all large-cap funds with fewer than 175 holdings each, and they are benchmarked against the Russell 1000 on Morningstar. However, these funds are not the same, and those differences are reflected in both their social and financial returns.

Each of the funds has a different approach to delivering gender diversity. Fidelity and Glenmede invest in companies where women hold leadership roles, but they have different metrics. Glenmede looks for 25% of board seats and management positions to be filled by women while Fidelity sets their bar at 33%. Impact Shares, which is a nonprofit aligned with the YWCA, has a very different approach. The fund considers a wide range of issues that affect women in the workplace and donates its advisory fees to the YWCA to advance its work.

The funds are also varied in terms of their financial strategies. Fidelity and Impact Shares are blended funds, holding a mix of growth and value stocks, while Glenmede holds only value stocks. This difference could partially explain Glenmede's underperformance relative to the other funds during the time frame captured in Table 8.1. Impact Shares skews more strongly than the other two funds to mega-cap holdings. These companies have performed exceedingly well in the past year, which could explain this fund's relative overperformance. There are other variations between the funds that could further influence returns.

TABLE 8.1 Gender Fund Comparison

	Ticker	1 Yr.	3 Yr.
Russell 1000 Index		13.40%	11.99%
Fidelity Women's Leadership	FWOMX	13.67%	-
Glenmede Women in Leadership US	GWILX	−1.24%	4.63%
Impact Shares YWVC Women's ETF	WOMN	23.28%	-

Source: Morningstar as of Sept 25, 2020.

The important thing to realize is that it takes a little digging to really understand what's behind a particular stock fund or ETF—on both the social and financial sides. Choosing an investment just because it meets an impact goal leaves important financial considerations on the table and vice versa. Understanding what you're investing in from both perspectives will help you make fully informed decisions.

Note: The Fidelity and Impact Shares gender funds are new. They have little more than a year of history, and both are relatively small with assets under management of just $40 million and $8.6 million, respectively. The short time frame these funds have been in market, combined with their small size, increases their risk. This is particularly true for the Impact Share product, which has less than $10 million in assets. Many professional investors like to see at least a three-year track record and $100 million in assets before they consider investing.

If you're interested in gender diversity, two other funds you could consider are PAX Ellevate Global Women's Leadership, which is available in both retail (PXWEX) and institutional (PXWIX) classes, and SSGA Gender Diversity ETF (SHE).

Sector-Focused Thematic Funds

While still relatively small in number, we're starting to see stock funds that invest in companies developing solutions to key challenges. Many focus on renewable energy, but there are also examples in real estate, water, and other natural resources.

These funds tend to be concentrated in a particular sector, which means they carry more risk than a more balanced, diversified fund. Thus, they may be best positioned as an alternative within your overall portfolio rather than as a primary public equities holding.

The iShares Global Clean Energy ETF (ICLN) tracks an index of companies in the clean energy sector and the Invesco Solar ETF (TAN) follows an index of firms that produce equipment for the solar industry. Both funds have delivered significant returns in recent years, although they didn't hold up as well over a 10-year period. It will be interesting to see how these funds (shown in Table 8.2) perform going forward. Although neither of these funds is benchmarked against the S&P 500 Index, the index is included in the table for comparison purposes only.

TABLE 8.2 Renewable Energy Fund Comparison

	Ticker	1 Yr.	3 Yr.	5 Yr.	10 Yr.
S&P 500 Index		13.40%	11.98%	13.48%	13.49%
iShares Global Clean Energy ETF	ICLN	52.12%	25.54%	15.89%	2.67%
Invesco Solar ETF	TAN	84.52%	40.54%	18.40%	−0.63%

Source: Morningstar as of Sept 25, 2020.

On the Horizon

In the last year, a few, very interesting thematic investments have started to emerge. Although not necessarily the first of their kind, they are pushing boundaries. These opportunities focus on minority empowerment, animal welfare, and social justice. However, it's far too early to tell how well they'll perform over time or if they will even last. At this point, they have track records of about a year and small investment pools. If you're a conservative or moderately conservative investor, these opportunities are probably not right for you, whereas if you're more of a risk-taker or seeking to put your social return before your financial return, you may find some of these products interesting.

An Emergent Social Justice Example

Rachel Robasciotti is another female innovator. She is pushing boundaries and taking a unique approach to values-aligned investing with her company, Adasina Social Capital. Rachel's focus is social justice. The company's forthcoming funds will hold US large-cap, small-cap, and international companies. The funds are being designed through direct engagements with social justice movements. The fund managers are actually bringing the voices of those most affected into the fund design process.

Adasina plans to provide its investors with socially accountable and financially viable investment returns. The fund is still in development but provides a window into what's on the horizon. You can reference Adasina's website for updates and further information.

Some Final Considerations

You have a lot of values-aligned choices within the public equities asset class. In the "Take Action" section, we'll help you navigate your options. Before we move on to talking about some special investments that are available through a financial advisor, there are a few last points to consider.

Active versus Passive Funds

When you're thinking about investing in a fund, you might want to know whether it's actively or passively managed. Here are a few tricks to help you figure that out.

The name of the fund is the first clue. If the name includes the word "index," then it's passively managed. The term "ETF" often indicates a passive fund but not always since some ETFs are actively managed.

If the expense ratio is 0.50% or more, then there is a distinct possibility the fund is actively managed. You can also look at the number of companies the fund holds. Actively managed accounts tend to have fewer

This Fund Might Be Active Because the:

- Name doesn't include "index" or "ETF";
- Expense ratio is more than 0.50%;
- Fund holds fewer than 150 companies;
- Fund has more than two fund managers; or
- Turnover exceeds 15%.

than 150 companies. Another clue is the number of managers involved in the fund. More than two suggests it's actively managed. And finally, the amount of turnover is often higher in actively managed accounts since fund managers are tracking the market and trying to maximize returns. If you want to be absolutely sure, call and ask or review the fund's prospectus.

A Note on Fees

In general, values-aligned funds tend to be a bit more expensive than their traditional counterparts, which is a concern for some investors. While it's possible to see differences in fee structures of 50 basis points or more, you can also find funds with fees that differ by as little as 7 basis points. This is a very small cost differential. However, it's there, and it does matter to people who prioritize fees in their investment decisions. I would suggest, however, that this is not the most important consideration. What really matters are the comparative net returns you receive over time, not the fees you pay. So I try not to get too bogged down when fees differ by less than 1.0%. They aren't the prize for me; returns are. In terms of returns, we're already seeing some values-aligned investments outperforming their traditional counterparts. Impact investors believe this trend will continue because values-aligned investing integrates long-term risks into investment considerations.

In addition, while some values-aligned investments have higher fees today, that probably won't be the case in the future. Part of the fee difference is due to the cost ESG fund providers have to pay to access ESG ratings from rating agencies. As values-aligned investing becomes more commonplace, these fees will likely drop, narrowing the fee differential. Furthermore, since large funds (i.e., those with larger asset bases) tend to have lower expense ratios, we can also expect to see the fees for values-aligned funds drop as the sizes of those funds grow.

Unintentional Concentration

When building a diversified public equities portfolio, watch for unintended concentrations in certain stocks, sectors, and styles. This can happen when you own multiple stock funds that may have overlapping mandates. For example, if you own an All-Cap US Index Fund and a

Global All-Cap Index Fund, both of those funds probably own some of the same companies. To ensure there is limited overlap, check the top-10 holdings in any funds you own or that you are considering purchasing.

Unintentional concentration is sometimes an issue for people who have public equity investments through self-managed accounts and employer retirement funds. Some of us keep those two buckets of money separated in our minds and may not realize they're essentially holding the same stocks—thereby minimizing the diversification of our total asset base and creating unintentional concentration in certain companies.

Investments That Require a Financial Advisor

When you work with some financial advisors, it's possible to access a few specialized investments within public equities that provide a high level of customization and diversification with limited effort on your part. These separately managed accounts (SMAs) hold only your money, unlike stock funds and ETFs, which pool assets from many people. They often have minimums of $50,000 or more and carry additional fees. So they may not be attractive to, or a fit for, everyone.

Actively Managed SMAs

In an actively managed SMA, a financial advisor can make individual stock selections for you based on your values. These accounts can deliver targeted impact and relieve you from having to make investment decisions yourself. You help set the financial and values-aligned criteria and then leave the decision-making and ongoing management of the account to your financial advisor.

Since you own the underlying securities, you can also request that your advisor participate in proxy voting and other shareholder advocacy. When possible, advisors may select the same stocks for many of their clients. This results in a higher total asset allocation to a particular company, which gives the financial advisor more leverage with their advocacy. Shareholder advocacy is a core element of some advisors' business practices.

Another advantage of an SMA is the ability to proactively manage capital gains and losses. It is possible to move non-aligned stock holdings into your SMA and then sell them judiciously to mitigate tax implications. This process, known as tax harvesting, can be an effective way to gradually shift non-aligned assets that contain significant embedded gains into a more aligned portfolio.

Accessing an SMA for $100

Kristin Hull, the Founder and CEO of Nia Impact Capital, wants anyone to be able to invest in a portfolio of values-aligned companies that are targeting multiple SDGs. In 2013 she launched Nia Global Solutions, an all-cap global growth portfolio that invests in companies of any size, anywhere in the world.

Nia actively seeks companies that are developing solutions in at least one of these investment themes: natural and organic food, health-care, education, affordable housing, sustainable planet, and affordable transportation. In addition, portfolio firms must have women in lead-ership positions and be fossil and weapons free. Nia is also actively involved in advocacy and provides regular financial and impact reports to investors.

I became an investor in Nia in 2019, and now it's one of my favorite investments, both socially and financially, as it has been perform-ing well on both fronts. You can invest in Nia Global Solutions for as little as $100 through Newday Impact, an online full-impact invest-ment platform. Folio, a custodian, enables account openings with a $10,000 minimum. And several custodial platforms or brokerage firms, including Fidelity, Schwab, and TD Ameritrade, offer the product with a $100,000 minimum.

Digital Index SMAs

Digital index SMAs are administered by tech-based asset management firms and work somewhat like a passively managed index fund. Like an index fund, these personalized accounts use big data, quantitative analysis, and risk modeling to track a specific benchmark. There is a very significant dif-ference, however. With a digital index SMA, the rules driving investment decisions are set by you, not a fund manager. The result is a customized portfolio based on your personal values, risk tolerance, and tax situation.

Here's how it works. As an investor, you identify the criteria that will guide decisions about what's included in your account. Technology is then applied to make investment selections based on your unique rule set. In some cases, you can get quite granular with your choices. In the end, you have a portfolio that can hold hundreds, if not thousands, of individual stocks—similar to index funds. Like other SMAs, the investment process can also include tax harvesting.

Aperio, Ethic, Parametric, and Just Invest offer this solution. Aperio and Parametric have been in business for at least 20 years while Just Invest and Ethic are relative newcomers. Currently, the only way to invest is through a financial advisor that has a relationship with one of these firms. Minimums tend to be around $250,000. You'll also be paying fees of about 0.50% to the technology company, plus the fee you pay your financial advisor, which is often around 1.0% for accounts under $1 million.

My Investment in Ethic

Jay Lipman, Doug Scott, and Johny Mair cofounded Ethic. They were all under the age of 30 at the time. They believe in a future where all investing is sustainable investing. Their vision includes making their technology available to any investor. However, like many financial start-ups, they're building their business by working first with financial advisors and institutional investors. Ethic integrates multiple sets of traditional and nontraditional data into their leading-edge quantitative models, enabling them to deliver highly precise portfolios.

I met Jay a couple of times, loved Ethic's vision, and decided to invest through my financial advisor. I was given a multipage questionnaire that allowed me to prioritize more than 45 ESG factors. When my rule set was applied to one of my stock funds, I was able to see the companies in it that did not conform to my priorities. We chose the Russell 1000 as my benchmark, and I was told what the tracking error would be if my account became 100% aligned with the criteria established in my questionnaire. At this point, I had the opportunity to revise my ratings until we reached an impact-return scenario that optimized my financial and social return goals. I received a few options with different tax outcomes. I chose one that moved me to full values-alignment over a three-year period.

Caprock, Sepio Capital, and Ellevest's private investment arm are all financial advisors that work with Ethic. Members of each of these firms were collaborators on this book.

Engaging in Shareholder Advocacy

When you own individual stocks or invest in a stock fund, you can bring corporate policies and practices into greater alignment with your values through shareholder advocacy. You can press for changes that you'd like to see a company make in its environmental, social, or governance practices.

Shareholder advocacy has been an important tool for social change since the 1960s. Trillium and Domini, the firms started by pioneers Joan Bavaria and Amy Domini, remain deeply engaged in these practices today.

While you may believe there's nothing you can do, the exact opposite is true. The number of shareholders required to create change is smaller than you might think. As a single individual, you can have significant influence. And you can magnify your impact by teaming up with other like-minded investors. Proposals that garner as little as 6% of shareholder support are difficult for most consumer-facing companies to ignore. Resolutions with 20% or more send a clear message to corporate management that the current company policy is too risky or not supportive of shareholder interests.

Shareholder Advocacy Success Stories

As You Sow has been a shareholder advocacy leader since 1992. The nonprofit focuses on corporations, their supply chains, and the life-cycle impacts of their products. As You Sow holds corporate executives accountable, and they have been successful.

In 2019 alone, As You Sow advanced 93 resolutions that targeted issues related to climate change, pesticides, ocean plastic, forced labor in corporate supply chains, and gender diversity. They successfully resolved more than half their proposals, securing substantive actions or commitments from the companies involved. As You Sow's successes include:

Starbucks will eliminate 3 billion plastic straws each year as a direct result of As You Sow's engagement. Nearly half of the company's shareholders supported a resolution to meet aggressive packaging reuse and recycling goals.

Wendy's, KFC, and Burger King agreed to eliminate chicken raised with medically important antibiotics from their supply chains. This is an imperative, because we're seeing a rise in previously unknown viruses at the same time antibiotics are losing their potency due to overuse and misuse.

Apple, Dell, HP, and Best Buy established e-waste recycling programs that will result in more sustainable disposal of 500,000 tons of excess technology each year.

At one time, I authorized As You Sow to add my proxies to a resolution they were filing with a soda manufacturer. The resolution asked the company to track its supply chain to determine whether a known cancer-causing pesticide was being inadvertently introduced into their products. Although that company did not change, the effort had ripple effects in an unrelated industry—cereal manufacturing—where a corporation did change its policies. Like me, you may also be in a position to engage in shareholder advocacy. There are a number of ways you can get involved.

First, Vote Your Proxies

The easiest way to engage is by voting your proxies. If you're an individual stockholder, you will receive proxy ballots before annual shareholder meetings. These meetings usually take place in the spring, so watch your mail for this information. Then, vote!

If you own shares in a stock fund through a self-managed account, financial advisors, or employer-based retirement plan, you can check their voting record by accessing their N-PX reports on a website maintained by the SEC.[5] Although lengthy, these reports document how a mutual fund company voted on each shareholder resolution.

You also have the right to lobby your advisors and fund managers to request they vote and engage with the companies you own. You can have a discussion with them to communicate how you want your votes handled going forward.

Second, Engage Directly

A more direct engagement approach is calling or writing an investor relations staff member at the company where you want to see change. You may find yourself engaged in a dialogue in which you can express your concerns and desires. You may even be met with open arms and an agreement for rapid change. This does happen. So a call can't hurt.

Many times, though, the staffer will thank you for your opinion and say it will be taken under consideration—then nothing happens. If the response you get does not satisfy your desire for change, you have legal standing to escalate the matter by filing a shareholder resolution. As of this writing, if you own at least $2,000 worth of stock in a publicly traded company for one year before the filing deadline, you can introduce a resolution yourself.

Success requires adherence to a strict set of SEC guidelines and rules, which can be a heavy lift for an individual. And the rules may be changing. Experts counsel those interested in advocacy to not try to go it alone.

Third, Join Existing Efforts

Shareholders have strength in numbers. Fortunately, there's a network of extremely collaborative advocates that have been working on shareholder resolutions for decades. They know all the ins and outs of the process, understand the history behind many issues, and actually appreciate committed investors who want to partner with them. There may be a team of shareholders who are already coordinating an initiative at the company you are concerned about. Should you decide to file a shareholder resolution without checking in with the network, you might inadvertently undermine an engagement process that has been underway for years, possibly even decades, so please check first.

You can quickly determine whether an issue you want advanced is already being addressed by reading *Proxy Preview*.[6] If it is, you can become a co-filer, lending your shares to the broader effort. If not, you can check with one of the advocacy organizations associated with *Proxy Preview* to get their advice on how best to advance your resolution.

Take Action

Hopefully after reading this chapter you're ready to consider moving some of the money you have in public equities into alignment with your values. The steps to identify new investments and make the transition are relatively straightforward.

1. Check the values-alignment of your current assets

Using the tools described in this chapter, research the sustainability scores of the assets that you already own.

What did you learn? Are your current investments supporting the things you care about, or are they working against your goals? If not, are you ready to make some changes?

2. If making changes, decide on your first step

Consider choosing one investment to transition. Perhaps it's the least values-aligned, or maybe it's an investment in a tax-deferred retirement account, or a taxable investment but one with limited capital gains—or even losses.

Think about the characteristics of the investment you want to buy to replace your current holding. Do you want the same type of asset you had before, or do you want to use this opportunity to change any of the attributes of your portfolio? Are you looking for individual stocks? Passive funds? Do you want to move a portion of your assets to a thematic fund?

3. Research your values-aligned options

Using the tools described in this chapter, research your values-aligned options and make some decisions about the investments you want to purchase.

Note: It's wise to know where you want to move your money before you sell existing holdings, because it may take longer than you think to do your research and come to a decision. I've made this mistake, and my money sat in cash while the market went up. So figure things out at your own pace, and then make your changes. You don't need to rush.

4. When you're ready, sell your old holdings and buy your new values-aligned investments

Note: Before you sell, ask your custodian if they'll save records of your old holdings. If they don't, be sure to save copies of your recent statements, cost basis, and tax information.

5. Congratulate yourself on a job well done and think about all the impact your public equity portfolio will create!

6. If you're committed to shareholder advocacy, consider voting your proxies or having a conversation with your fund managers to request their engagement

Endnotes

1. https://www.trilliuminvest.com/about.
2. https://en.wikipedia.org/wiki/MSCI_KLD_400_Social_Index.
3. https://www.morningstar.com/articles/961765/sustainable-fund-flows-in-2019-smash-previous-records.
4. https://database.globalreporting.org/.
5. https://www.sec.gov/edgar/searchedgar/n-px.htm.
6. *Proxy Review* is an annual report that As You Sow, Proxy Impact, and the Sustainable Investments Institute coproduce. https://www.proxypreview.org/.

CHAPTER 9

Private Investments
Explore Private Debt, Private Equity, and Angel Investing

Private investing, particularly angel investing, can be exciting, a great way to build community, and just plain fun! When you make a private investment, you could be supporting a female entrepreneur, the coffee shop around the corner from your home, or an innovative start-up in the US or another country. Each investment is unique in terms of financial return and impact.

This chapter will introduce you to the world of early-stage private debt and private equity. Private investing provides opportunities for portfolio diversification and a very personal investment experience. Whether you're an experienced investor or not, you can learn how to assemble a private investment portfolio you love. You can access training, mentorship and collaboration with likeminded women and engage with amazing entrepreneurs along the way.

This chapter will get you started. We'll explain why you might want to invest this way, what you are buying, how these investments work, and point you to resources you can use to find opportunities that align with your values.

Entire books have been written on the concepts in this chapter, and we realize that we cannot do them justice in this introduction. Our intention is to spark your interest in an investment class in which women have been sorely underrepresented—both as investors and as entrepreneurs.

Private investing is, without a doubt, my favorite part of the investing journey, because I've met incredible entrepreneurs, made new friends, and become part of a community of amazing female co-investors. I love it! And so can you.

Anyone Can Invest in Private Companies

There are two primary approaches to private investing—debt and equity. But there are numerous ways these investments can be structured. In its simplest form, private debt is a loan made to a privately held company, while private equity is buying ownership in a privately held company. You can make these investments company-by-company or by investing in a private debt or private equity fund.

Private investing can be quite risky. As a result, these investments were rarely available to non-accredited investors until quite recently. With the passage of the 2012 JOBS Act, which went into effect in 2016, it became much easier for private companies to open up their investment offerings to non-accredited investors, who can now participate for as little as $100. To safeguard against potential financial ruin, the SEC placed limits on how much these investors can allocate to higher risk investments in any given year.*

Because of the risk, financial experts strongly advise that you invest no more than 10% of your total net worth excluding your primary residence in this asset class, unless you have deep pockets or have a larger appetite for risk. Regardless, you should only invest what you're willing—and able—to lose. It's also wise to only invest in businesses that you understand.

Given the Risks, Why Make Private Investments at All?

Women can make world-changing contributions through private investments. We can use our growing wealth to support the overlooked and underfunded female and minority-led businesses that we'd love to see thrive. We can also support innovative products and services that are designed from the ground up with our needs in mind, as opposed to having to make do with the feminization of male products. The more we invest in entrepreneurs and businesses that support our values, the more we signal that their products, services, and companies matter and that we do, too.

Women involved in private investing are addressing significant challenges such as climate change, healthcare, education, and other pressing social issues. They're supporting products and services that enhance the lives of women and children. And they're learning together, having fun, and meeting amazing entrepreneurs in the process.

---

* As of May 2017, those with annual income or net worth below $107,000 are limited to investing no more than $2,200, or up to 5% of the lesser of their net worth or annual income. Those making at least $107,000 can invest up to 10% or the lesser of either their net worth or annual income.

Address Dramatic Gender and Minority Funding Imbalances

Private businesses, particularly small businesses, matter. They matter to the economy. They matter to our communities. And they matter to women. Small businesses* account for 44% of the US economy and create two-thirds of new jobs in the US.[1] Although women and minorities run more than one-third of the small businesses in the country, they have a disproportionately difficult time raising money. This is true whether they're trying to get a loan from a bank or raising money through private structures. The reason they're having such a hard time is because investors in private companies tend to be white men. Whether intentional or not, this creates a bias against underrepresented entrepreneurs, including women and members of minority communities. As women we can correct this imbalance and change the conversation. Several of the women who contributed to this chapter are doing just that.

Women Redefine Private Investment Models

In 2016 Mara Zepeda, Jennifer Brandel, Aniyia Williams, and Astrid Scholz—four enterprising women—came together to change how start-up businesses are capitalized. Each had created a for-profit company and discovered they were basically nonfundable in the prevailing investment paradigm.

These women collaborated on a revolutionary blog post, "Zebras Fix What Unicorns Break" that was posted on Medium in 2017. In their post they explained that Zebra companies value profit and purpose. They come in many different stripes, represent a diversity of founders and problems they are solving, and are collaborative and feisty.

Zebra companies are all too common. Yet, they're usually ignored by conventional investors. More than 85% of all entrepreneurs in the US fall into the capital gap between bank loans and venture-style equity financing—the two investment models that are typically used to fund start-ups and small business growth.[†]

Because of their post, more than 5,000 individuals and companies are now collaborating with these women through Zebras Unite to create the new financing models, community, and culture that ambitious values-driven companies need to succeed.

---

* The Small Business Administration (SBA) defines a small business by number of employees and/or annual revenue. These figures change depending on the type of business.

† Hwang, V., Desai, S., and Baird, R. (2019). "Access to Capital for Entrepreneurs: Removing Barriers," Ewing Marion Kauffman Foundation: Kansas City.

Invest in Companies That Excite You

Laura Oldanie, a self-proclaimed "reluctant blogger" in the Financially Independent, Retire Early (FIRE) movement, is on a mission to align all her money with her values, and she's using private investing to help her meet her goals. Laura is interested in resilient living and a regenerative future. Through WeFunder, a crowdfunding platform, Laura invested in four companies that resonate with her passions.

Her first investment was a loan to a real estate company that is developing commercial properties to address the needs of underserved communities. Then she made two equity investments. One investee is helping companies buy, sell, or broker recyclable materials. The other focuses on workforce management in the agriculture and food industries. Laura's fourth investment is in a natural food products business. Laura is excited by the regular updates she receives from her investments, which are keeping her engaged and aware of the progress each business is making toward achieving the outcomes she wants to see in the world.

Leverage Your Experience to Help Other Women Succeed

Many women have found that supporting female entrepreneurs can be a lot of fun, particularly when they invest together. Babbie Jacobs is part of Next Wave Impact, a group of women who co-invest in female-led businesses. Babbie realized that, in addition to her financial support, she can also help her investees through mentoring, making critical introductions, and serving as a sounding board. Babbie is delighted to be part of other women's dreams. For Babbie and the women with whom she co-invests there's nothing quite like the excitement and thrill of watching one of their entrepreneurs succeed.

Watch Your Money Grow

Although there are risks, women engaging in private investing can obtain positive market rate financial returns. Financial loss can be mitigated by starting small and risking only what you can afford to lose, learning alongside more seasoned investors, doing your research, and investing in businesses that you understand.

The women who contributed to this chapter have made private investing a hobby, a sideline business, or even their career, because they're excited about the potential impact of the companies they invest in, inspired by the entrepreneurs, and engaged in working together to help these small businesses grow and succeed.

What Are You Buying?

Private investing is a common way that investors support early-stage companies. Although not everyone agrees on the labels, capital requirements, and stages of a company's life cycle, Table 9.1 provides one view of the phases a company might experience if it's planning for growth and scale. As you can see, characteristics and requirements change at each stage. Where you participate as an investor depends on the amount of money you have to invest, your risk appetite, and other criteria.

TABLE 9.1 Company Life Cycle

	Business Characteristics	Amount Raised	Company Value	Investors
Idea Stage	Business concept in development	< $500,000	$1 – $3 million	Bootstrap, crowdfunding, angel investors
Pre-Revenue	Business build out, market entry	$500,000 to $3 million	$3 – $10 million	Crowdfunding, angels, early venture capital, debt
Revenue	Growing traction and proof points	$3 – 12 million	$10 – $30 million	Super angels, venture capital, debt funds
Growth	Business growth, profitability	$10+ million	$30+ million	Venture capital, debt funds
Scale	Business and market expansion	$50+ million	> $100 million	Late-stage venture, institutional investors

Most new businesses will not move through this entire life cycle. In fact, many will reach profitability much earlier than this table suggests. It's not uncommon for a small business to be successful with revenues that are well below $1 million. As long as the company's costs are less than its revenues, the company can make a profit and thrive. However, every new business needs money to get started and to grow to the point of profitability. The amount required depends on the business and the ambitions of the entrepreneur.

Investors have a role to play at every stage of a company's development, regardless of whether the company only needs money during earliest stages or whether they need capital across a longer trajectory. When their capital requirements are relatively small, entrepreneurs turn to family and friends, people in their community, or angel investors. As the need for capital grows, most founders approach venture capitalists, private debt funds, institutional investors, or other well-endowed capital sources.

As an individual investor—unless you have very deep pockets—most likely you'll be financing businesses that are in the idea or pre-revenue stages. Access to later-stage companies is usually only available to accredited investors and is often achieved through participating in a fund. However, this is starting to change, as the 2012 JOBS Act made it possible to use crowdfunding to raise up to $50 million.

Both debt and equity can support a company's growth. Decisions about the type of investment used at each stage have implications for entrepreneurs and investors. The important thing to understand is that an investment in a private company can be structured in an infinite number of ways. We are going to focus on conventional debt, the venture capital equity model, and revenue-based investing. Other options include venture debt, factoring, and recoverable grants.

Private Debt

When you invest in private debt, you're making a loan to a company. In a standard debt structure, a lender provides a borrower with a defined amount of money for a specific period of time. The borrower pays back the loan plus interest in predetermined amounts and intervals. Debt payments are usually made on a quarterly, semiannual, or annual basis. Each loan is governed by a contract between the lender and the borrower that specifies the interest rate, payment schedule, and maturity date (term) of the loan.

Depending on the conditions of the loan, payments can be interest only, or they can include repayment of a portion of the principal. When only interest is paid over the life of the loan, there is a balloon payment at the end of the term in which the principal is due. There are also debt agreements in which no payments are due, even though interest accrues. Known as a grace period, this stretch of time allows the borrower an interval to use the loan capital to build their business and generate revenue before regular loan payments are required. This is extremely helpful from the perspective of many new businesses or businesses that are caught in a difficult situation.

Grace Periods Offer Breathing Room

During the COVID-19 pandemic, some small businesses that were adversely impacted received loans through the CARES relief fund implemented by Congress. Since the purpose of the money was to help recipients rebuild after a difficult business cycle, payments were not due during the first six months of the loan period. However, interest did accrue during that time. This ensured that business owners could use the money they received to regroup, cover staff salaries, and stimulate their revenue before they had to start paying back the money.

Another twist on debt is whether it is secured or unsecured. Debt that is secured is tied to a real or tangible asset that can be sold if the borrower defaults or their business fails. In these cases, there's an opportunity to recover some of the principal and interest due. Debt can also be unsecured, which means it isn't tied to anything tangible. Since there are no assets to recoup the investment, it's more difficult to be paid back when a borrower defaults on unsecured debt.

Returns from private debt vary widely, depending on the loan structure and level of risk. Aggregated data is difficult to find and usually proprietary. A reasonable range can be anything from 3% to 12%. To meet their impact goals, some investors are willing to accept lower below-market rates or even extend interest-free loans.

Private Equity

When you make an equity investment in a privately held company, you're buying an ownership interest in that company. This is the same thing you're doing when you buy stock in a company through the public equities market. The primary difference between private and public equity is that in the public markets it's relatively easy to find a buyer when you're ready to sell your stock. This is not the case with private equity. Buyers are often difficult, or impossible, to find. What's more, there are legal limitations as to when and how a private sale of equity can be carried out. As a result, money invested in private equity can be tied up for a long time, making it unavailable for other purposes.

The venture capital model is one of the most recognized forms of private equity investing. In this model, investors make money by investing at an early stage with the hope that the company will grow very fast and then be sold or go public by transitioning its private shares into public shares that are traded on the NYSE or NASDAQ. In the venture capital model, the first investors are usually individuals known as angels. Active angel investors often form angel groups to consider and evaluate potential investments. Venture capitalists come in at later stages. Any situation that returns the investor's money (usually a sale or initial public offering) is referred to as a liquidity event or exit. Moving from an early-stage investment to an exit usually takes 5 to 10 years, or more. Anything faster is considered a quick exit.

Multiple Meanings of Private Equity

Private equity has two definitions. When written in lowercase (private equity), the term refers to an asset class in which an investor purchases shares of a non-public company. When written in uppercase (Private Equity), it can mean the act of buying fully operating companies and restructuring them.

If the investment was successful, the investor should realize a considerable profit as an outcome of a liquidity event. On average, angel investors seek an annualized return of 12% to 20% or more. In the simplest case, the profit is based on the difference between the value of the company when the investment was made and the value on exit. However, there are a number of variables that can negatively affect the final payback. Since the success of venture capital style private equity investing depends on understanding these details and their implications, prudent angels learn alongside more seasoned investors.

To achieve their return expectations, successful angels invest in a number of companies, because they know many will fail before they reach an exit. In those cases, the investor will lose all, or most, of their money. A standard rule of thumb among angel investors is that 50% of their investments will fail, another two to three will return the original capital plus a bit more, and only a few will provide a significant positive return.[2] In other words, investors expect one or two companies to provide the bulk of their return. For this reason, seasoned angel and venture investors diversify their money across 10 to 15, and oftentimes many more, companies to mitigate their risk.

Although venture capital is a common model for private equity investing, it isn't the only one. Just as there are many ways to structure a private debt investment, there are multiple options within private equity. These alternatives offer shorter periods of illiquidity, regular disbursements, and varying risk-return profiles.

Learning the Hard Way

I learned the hard way about the importance of learning from others and making private equity investments based on more than my excitement about the entrepreneur and her social impact. Following on the heels of my first investment, which was successful, I decided to back a female CEO who was building a business to help women become better managers of their money. This goal was so closely aligned with my values and purpose, that I invested with only a modicum of due diligence. Within weeks of my investment, I discovered there was a competitor in the market who had raised over $30 million and was making rapid advances. With a sinking feeling, I realized the entrepreneur I had backed wouldn't be able to compete. Sure enough, less than six months later, my investee had gone out of business, and I lost all my money.

Although I still love supporting women entrepreneurs and social companies, I am now investing with other women, performing deeper due diligence, and expanding my portfolio to include a broader range of debt and equity structures.

Revenue-Based Investments

Venture capital supports less than 1% of new businesses in the US each year, while loans from financial institutions underwrite only another 17%.[3] That leaves 82% of new companies unfunded. While the amount of companies that receive private debt is unknown, that type of investment is often not a good fit for companies that need capital to build their businesses. This leaves a funding gap that hits women and minority-led businesses hardest.[4] They are often overlooked by conventional investors and have less capital to self-finance their businesses.

To solve this problem, values-aligned investors have begun using innovative financial structures to meet the needs of underfunded start-ups and small businesses. Revenue-based investing, which includes debt and equity options, is one example. It's gaining traction due to the flexibility and benefits this approach provides to entrepreneurs and investors.

Revenue-Based Debt

Revenue-based lending can achieve double-digit annualized returns, causing some investors to view it as an alternative to venture capital. As with most debt, investors receive payments during the term of the loan, which has an expected termination date.

This form of debt is attractive to entrepreneurs who do not want to give up ownership of their companies but do want to provide returns to investors that increase with the success of the business. Because payments are structured as a percentage of revenue, entrepreneurs have a repayment schedule that is not overly burdensome to their businesses. Many revenue-based debt structures have a grace period of 6 to 24 months, which provides even more value and flexibility to founders, particularly in the early stages of their companies' life cycle.

Here's how the most common type of revenue-based debt works: In exchange for capital, a company promises to pay investors a predetermined percentage of revenue on a regular basis, until the original capital and an agreed-upon return is paid.

For example, assume you invest $100,000 in a company that agrees to pay you 5% of gross revenues* each year until you've doubled your money. While structuring the investment, you and the entrepreneur would estimate projected revenue over a period of several years, as shown in Table 9.2.

---

* Revenues can be calculated as gross revenues, which are total revenues before any deductions, or net revenues, which are total revenues less expenses. Many investors prefer to use gross revenues, because there can be disagreements about what expenses should be included in the net revenue calculation.

You would use these forecasts to establish repayment expectations. In our example, the company is expected to generate a total of $4 million in revenues over seven years.

TABLE 9.2 Revenue-Based Debt

Year	Annual Revenues	Annual Payments
1	$200,000	$10,000
2	$400,000	$20,000
3	$480,000	$24,000
4	$640,000	$32,000
5	$720,000	$36,000
6	$760,000	$38,000
7	$800,000	$40,000
Total	**$4,000,000**	**$200,000**

As the investor, you'd be paid 5% of gross revenues each year. Assuming the company hits its revenue projections, at the end of seven years you'll have received $200,000. You invested $100,000 and received two times your money in return. This is considered a 2× return on your investment.[†] That's great! But how can you compare that to the performance of your other investments? How can you translate the doubling of your money into an annual return?

To do that, you need to calculate something called the internal rate of return, or IRR. Getting to this number requires a somewhat complicated calculation. Fortunately, there are online calculators that can do this for you.[‡] In our example the IRR is 17%, a very attractive rate and one that is consistent with many venture capital expectations.

Since things do not always go according to plan, you cannot count on a 17% IRR. Your actual return depends on how long it takes your loan to be repaid. Let's say, your investee did really well and was able to repay you $200,000 in four years instead of seven. In that case, your IRR would be 27%. On the other hand, if the company didn't do as well as expected and took 10 years to pay you back, your IRR would be about 11%.

Details of a revenue-based debt agreement are negotiable. Repayment rates of 3% to 9% of gross revenues are typical, as is an ROI of 2× to 4× for investments in earlier stages and 1.5× to 2× for growth-stage companies. Although the example used annual repayments for simplicity, actual

---

[†] Return on investment, or ROI, is calculated by dividing the total return by your original investment, then multiplying by 100%. In this case, the ROI is 200%, which is more commonly referred to as a 2× return.

[‡] The IRR in this example was calculated using an online IRR calculator. https://www.calculatestuff.com/financial/irr-calculator.

repayments can be set monthly, quarterly, or according to other mutually agreed intervals. Grace periods of 6 to 24 months are not uncommon. The investor and company could agree to suspend payments at the start of the funding term, or at some point during the funding term, to allow for reduced revenues or other business challenges.

A Convert to Revenue-Based Debt

As an early-stage investor, Lisa Frusztajer, a contributor to this chapter, had been all-equity all the time. That's the model she was familiar and comfortable with. In 2016, Lisa met Kim Folsom, who was preparing to launch a revenue-based debt fund. Kim, founder and CEO of Founders First Capital Partners, had a story to tell that few others could. She had secured venture funding for six start-ups, making her, as a Black woman, exceptional in the start-up world. It wasn't just Kim's story that intrigued Lisa, but Kim's perspective on an investment vehicle that Lisa had never heard of: revenue-based financing.

Though intrigued, Lisa was worried that debt could saddle a young company with payments they couldn't afford. She also was skeptical that a revenue-based fund could provide an attractive return. Kim explained to Lisa why she was setting up her fund as revenue-based. The borrowers Kim is funding (people of color, veterans, women) are generally not candidates for funding from mainstream venture firms or banks. Until that bias is rooted out, they need alternative forms of financing, which Kim was offering.

Lisa discovered that Kim's model was more farsighted and less predatory than the classic ones used by start-ups. Because Kim's model doesn't depend on finding an exit to generate a return, it matched Lisa's goals. As a values-aligned investor, Lisa is interested in building strong, sustainable businesses that are good employers and community partners. She also realized revenue-based interest rates are lower and more predictable than usurious credit card debt.

Lisa made a small investment in Kim's proof of concept fund and then followed later with an additional commitment. In 2019, Kim obtained an impressive $100 million in matching funds, enabling her to expand the model.

Revenue-Based Equity

The structure of revenue-based equity is similar to that of revenue-based debt. In fact, Table 9.2 could also be applied to a revenue-based equity investment. In both cases, the investor and the entrepreneur project revenues over a period of years. As long as the company continues to earn revenues, the entrepreneur pays the investor a percentage at regular intervals until an agreed-upon return is achieved.

The primary difference between the two is that with revenue-based debt, the investor is providing a loan to the entrepreneur. As the entrepreneur makes payments, she's paying off the loan. In revenue-based equity, the investor purchases shares in the company. When the business owner makes payments, she's repurchasing equity from the investor. If all goes according to plan, the shares are eventually repurchased in full, investors achieve their expected return, and ownership of the company reverts to the founders.

An advantage of revenue-based equity over revenue-based debt is ownership. If the company is acquired before all the shares are repurchased, the investor can be repaid either at the value that was originally agreed to or at the value placed on the shares by the sale, whichever is higher. This enables revenue-based investors to participate in additional unexpected, but hoped for, financial gain—often referred to as the "upside" of the deal. A revenue-based debt holder, in contrast, would only receive any sums due under the original terms.

Investing for Value and Diversity without Giving Up Return

Village Capital is a venture capital firm that trains and invests in early-stage companies that address global problems through their work in agriculture, energy, or other sectors. They are unique in terms of the types of companies they support as well as their investment approaches. Village Capital experiments with innovative financing and the ways they select the companies they invest in.

The firm doesn't bank on one or two huge winners, as is the case with many venture firms. Rather, they seek to build a diversified portfolio using revenue-based models. Their goal is to generate impact and competitive financial returns for their investors.

Village Capital sources deals across geographies, founder profiles, business types, and investment structures. Their approach has resulted in a portfolio that looks very different than a typical early-stage venture fund: 40% of their capital is invested in companies led by women, 25% in companies founded by people of color, and 20% in non-equity structures. But they are not giving up return. Village Capital seeks a 3x return within a five- to seven-year period from each of their investments.

Summing Up Private Debt and Private Equity

Although standard debt and venture capital equity models are the most common private investment models you're likely to encounter as an investor, a number of alternatives are emerging that benefit both investors and entrepreneurs (see Table 9.3). Companies such as Zebras Unite, Founders First, and Village Capital are helping drive this change. Fortunately, they're not alone.

In her book *Raise Capital on Your Own Terms*, Jenny Kassan describes a range of different private investment structures. Although written for entrepreneurs, her examples shed light on how investors can benefit from these alternatives.

TABLE 9.3 Private Investment Model Comparisons

	Benefits	Challenges
Standard debt model	■ Lower risk than equity ■ Can be secured ■ Clear termination date ■ Often repaid before other liabilities	■ Lower expected returns ■ Assets at risk from default or business failure
Venture equity model	■ Potential for double-digit returns ■ Entire subculture exists to support new investors ■ Easy to co-invest with others	■ Only a fraction of companies are suitable for this type of capital ■ Success often requires multiple rounds of investment and a liquidity event
Revenue-based debt and equity models	■ Can meet the needs of a wide range of currently underserved businesses ■ Offers a breadth of risk-return options to investors and founders	■ Relatively new investment approaches ■ Harder to find opportunities, with fewer funds focused on alternatives available

Getting Started as a Private Investor

You don't have to know every detail about how to structure a deal when you're getting started as a private investor. In fact, most of us don't know much when we begin. Fortunately, there are lots of ways you can learn. At some point, though, you'll just have to dive in and experiment. When you do, it's highly recommended that you collaborate with others and start with small amounts of money that you're comfortable losing.

Crowdfunding platforms are the easiest and least expensive way to get started. Many are available to non-accredited investors. You can choose companies, make your investments, and watch their progress—all through the platform.

Angel groups are a wonderful entry point for accredited investors who want more interaction with entrepreneurs and other investors. These groups make it much easier to find high-quality investment opportunities, which are also known as deals. Since there has been a strong bias against female CEOs in the venture world, women are stepping up to invest in other women through female-focused angel groups.

Private debt and private equity funds can require deeper pockets than crowdfunding or angel investing. For the most part, they're only available to accredited investors, and in some cases, only to qualified investors. A broad range of positive impact and socially responsible private investment funds are available, including a growing number that use revenue-based investing. Table 9.4 compares and contrasts the pros and cons, investment levels, and investor criteria required for crowdfunding, angel groups, and private investment funds.

TABLE 9.4 Private Investment Approaches

	Crowdfunding	Female-Focused Angel Groups	Investment Funds
Description	Online platform, usually early stage	Deal-by-deal, usually early stage	Professionally managed, multiple stages
Benefits	Low entry point	Opportunities for collaboration	Immediate diversification
Investment level	$100 can get you started	$10,000+	$25,000–$100,000+
Challenges	Limited engagement, variable reporting	Engagement options, more time required	Limited engagement, less directed impact
Investor types	Non-accredited and accredited	Primarily accredited	Primarily accredited
Examples	Investibule Republic WeWork	Golden Seeds Next Wave Impact Pipeline Angels	Greenbacker Fledge Elevar Equity

Regardless of your approach, it's wise to invest only in companies that have strong business models, financials, and teams. Ensuring that the fundamentals of the business are in place will help mitigate your risk and maximize your potential return. Also, it's a good practice to diversify your private investment portfolio. Whether you're a non-accredited or accredited investor, you should spread your money across a number of individual investments or funds to reduce risk.

Crowdfunding

While still small relative to other investment approaches, crowdfunding is projected to grow at a rapid rate. By May 2020, more than 525,000 Americans had invested close to $400 million in start-ups and small businesses through these platforms. More than 80% were non-accredited investors, and the average investment size on a per-deal basis was just over $700.[5]

The number of crowdfunding platforms is also growing, but they're not all created equal. Years in business, motivations, and depth of offerings vary, as do the level of vetting that platforms perform on businesses they promote. Since there are a number of options, it's prudent to perform diligence on the platforms and not just on the companies they promote. Some crowdfunding platforms are structured as benefit corporations, B-Corps, or have socially driven missions.

- **Crowdfund Mainstreet** started in 2018 as a benefit corporation. The site services mission-driven entrepreneurs—particularly women and underserved populations.
- **Republic**, which launched in 2016, encourages start-up teams with a diverse mix of race, gender, and geography. You can invest in a Republic company for as little as $10.
- **WeFunder** was founded in 2011 as a benefit corporation. The company is committed to helping keep the American dream of enterprise alive. The firm donates 5% of its annual profits to provide grants, training, and mentorship to start-up founders.

Investibule, a Social Business Aggregator

Launched in 2018, Investibule.co aggregates investment opportunities listed on more than 25 social impact and community-based crowdfunding sites. The Investibule platform makes it easier for anyone to find start-up and small business investment opportunities that meet their values-aligned objectives. Debt, equity, and revenue-based structures are available, as are innovative pre-pay and cryptocurrency options.

Cofounders Amy Cortese and Arno Hesse are leaders in the Loca-vesting and Slow Money movements, respectively. They realized that if they wanted to change who receives capital for their businesses, then they needed to help change who has access to investment opportunities. Through Investibule, Amy and Arno are making social-impact crowdfunding easier and more accessible to all investors.

A 2019 Investibule report tracked 2,000 capital raises via crowdfunding. Investments were made in 717 cities across America, many in areas that professional investors overlook. When you take away the gatekeepers, the results look much different. People of color and women made up a quarter to a third of the campaigns, respectively. But they punched above their weight. Women successfully raised at least their minimum funding target 77% of the time, and people of color 75% of the time. That compares to an overall success rate on the platform of 66%.

Since crowdfunding is relatively new, it's too early to document rates of return. However, anecdotal evidence suggests investors are achieving positive social and financial outcomes.

There are a number of articles, "best of" lists, and other online resources that will help you navigate crowdfunding. Investibule, for example, has a wealth of information on its website. As with all investments, there is risk with any of these strategies. Please do your homework, test the waters before jumping in, and be sure you mitigate your risk by not investing more than you can afford to lose.

Female-Focused Angel Groups

As women become angel investors, we are backing different kinds of entrepreneurs and different kinds of companies than men. Women are funding women! And we are funding businesses that make a difference in our lives. More of us are becoming angels, and that influx appears to be correlated to a nearly 60% rise in the number of female founders who received angel funding between 2011 and 2016.[6]

We're investing through traditional angel models, new learn-by-doing approaches, and by joining—or starting—syndicates. Some groups encourage women to participate by ensuring there are low barriers to entry, opportunities for portfolio diversification, and structured mechanisms to learn. As an investor through one of these options, you can be as involved or hands-off as you choose.

Traditional Angel Group Model

The most typical model for an angel group is a club. Members pay dues that can range from a couple of hundred to several thousand dollars. They meet regularly to listen to entrepreneurs who are seeking capital explain— or pitch—their businesses. If members are interested in a particular company, they can band together to research the company, a process known as due diligence. Members then decide whether they want to invest in the company or not. Individual check sizes are often in the $10,000 to $25,000 range. Depending on the group and the wealth of the members, investments can be even higher.

Some groups that are focused on women have memberships that are exclusively female while others include men. Virtually all of them support female entrepreneurs and a growing number are also targeting minority founders. When you join one of these angel groups, you can learn from other members, many of whom will be more experienced than you. You get to choose where your money goes by investing in only those deals that really excite you. And because you invest alongside other women, your money goes even further.

Astia Angels, Broadway Angels, Golden Seeds, and Plum Alley are among the best-known female-focused angel groups. You can find additional networks through a simple online search for "angel groups for women." The Angel Capital Association also maintains a list of angel groups across the country.

Learn-by-Doing Models

The learn-by-doing model is a relatively new entrant in the angel investment landscape. Pioneered by women like Natalia Oberti Noguera of Pipeline Angels and Alicia Robb of Next Wave Impact, learn-by-doing angel groups function less like clubs and more like funds, although to varying degrees.

PIPELINE ANGELS   Pipeline Angels trains women to become angel investors and focuses on early-stage, social-impact companies founded by women. In this model, a small group comes together as a cohort that learns together. Members of the cohort pay $4,500 for a multi-month training and mentorship program. At the end of the training, the members contribute an additional $5,000 each and co-invest in a start-up they identified and researched during their training. Cohort members can become very close during this process. One group even went on to form a company and write a book to awaken other women to the opportunity of angel investing.

Impact with Wings: A Pipeline Cohort

Suzanne Andrews first heard about angel investing in 2013. She had recently reentered the workforce after being a full-time mother for 13 years and was trying to figure out her path forward. During this time, she heard that women entrepreneurs outperformed men and yet were underfunded. Suzanne wanted to know what it would take to invest in female-led start-ups, because she thought this could be a great way to make money and make the world a better place at the same time. Several people suggested she check out Pipeline Angels, which she joined in late 2014.

Over the course of five months Suzanne's cohort met once a month, for one or two full days. When together, the group went through the process of soliciting applications from founders. They chose some to pitch, asked questions, selected a few for due diligence, and, finally, identified one company to invest in as a group. When they wrote their checks to the company they chose, everyone was elated!

Sitting around the conference table, they asked each other, "Why don't more women do this?" A few months later, six of the members decided to form a company called Wingpact to tell other women about the power of angel investing. They also collaborated on *Impact with Wings*, a book about their Pipeline experience.

Suzanne became increasingly interested in how women could wield their financial resources for more impact. She now works on projects related to finance innovation and is finding ways to flow the world's abundant capital to where it is most needed.

37 ANGELS   Like Pipeline Angels, 37 Angels offers participants a training bootcamp and the opportunity to invest in one company at the end of the process.

THE RISING TIDE PILOT   The Rising Tide pilot used an innovative learn-by-doing model that was so successful, it spawned a number of similar funds over the next few years. In the pilot, 99 women joined together in an investment fund. Each invested $10,000, resulting in a $1 million fund. Ten experienced female angels participated as "lead investors." They did all the hard work: sourcing investment opportunities, leading due diligence, and making investment decisions. The remaining 89 women were limited partners (LPs).

Over the course of a year, the fund invested in 10 companies—most of which were women-led. The lead investors held training sessions and mentored the LPs, who could be involved in as much of the deal flow and diligence process as they wanted. If an LP didn't have the time or interest, that was fine, too. She would still benefit from the financial return on the investment, and she would still be supporting female entrepreneurs. At the end of the year, each investor had a diversified portfolio of private equity investments, many learned to be better angel investors, and some went on to become lead investors in subsequent funds.

NEXT WAVE IMPACT   Alicia Robb, one of the leaders behind The Rising Tide pilot, realized she wanted to do more than support female founders. She also wanted to invest in companies that were having a positive social impact. The fund she spun out of The Rising Tide was called the Next Wave Impact Fund. It followed a similar model. It consisted of 99 female investors (25 of them women of color), nine lead investors, and educational activities. They focused on investing in companies with female founders that were solving real societal problems.

Alicia also shifted the original model to a multi-year investment period with a minimum of $30,000 and a maximum of $300,000. One-third of the total commitment was requested annually over a three-year period. Thus, a woman making a $30,000 commitment to the fund invested $10,000 per year for three years. Next Wave Impact raised $4.5 million this way. Over the next 2.5 years, the fund invested in 16 pre-revenue start-ups. About half of the capital was set aside to reinvest in the portfolio companies that showed the greatest chance of success. These reinvestments are common in private equity and used to maximize an angel investor's return potential.

PORTFOLIA   Portfolia is another series of funds that emerged from The Rising Tide. Trish Costello, Portfolia's founder, was involved in the pilot. With Portfolia, Trish decided to adhere more closely to the original model. Minimum investment amounts for each fund are still $10,000, although you can invest more now. Each fund makes all its investments in a one-year period and provides mentoring and support to the LPs during that time.

At the time of this writing, Portfolia had launched eight funds that focus on women's values and concerns. Fund themes include female-focused consumer products, women's health, active aging, and diversity. So far, Portfolia funds have invested in approximately 40 companies, most of which are female-led. Portfolia plans to continue to open new funds.

Syndicates

Women can invest in private equity through syndicates, which are legal entities that aggregate, or "pool," funds from a group of investors. An advantage of some syndicates is that you can invest as little as $1,000 in a single deal. This creates a lower point of entry than investing alone, allowing an investor into 10 deals for the same amount she would pay to participate in one deal through most angel groups. Whoever manages the relationships, finances, and tax documents for the syndicate takes a fee for performing these services. This is the downside of syndicates, as higher fees can eat into returns.

AngelList, a platform for accredited investors, is one way to find syndication opportunities. 500 Women's Syndicate and Next Wave Impact offer syndicated deals through this platform. Profits from a syndication deal on AngelList are currently split between AngelList (5%), the syndicate manager (15%), and the investors who split the remaining 80% in proportion to their investment in the deal. Profits are calculated after the original investment amount has been returned to investors.

If you want to join a syndicate, you can research the many syndicates available on AngelList, or you can ask a local angel group if they provide syndication opportunities. If you have a group of friends or colleagues interested in investing together, you can even set up a syndicate on your own. There are legal expenses, along with reporting and other regulatory and compliance issues, though. However, these requirements don't have to be onerous. Nonetheless, we suggest you get input and support from experts.

Private Investment Funds

Accredited investors can also invest through private debt and private equity funds. In these structures, investment professionals identify the companies that will receive capital. They perform due diligence and manage the assets on behalf of the investors in the fund. Although specifics vary, in general, debt funds make regular interest payments to investors. Principal is often available after a tie-up period of a few months to several years. Conversely, money invested in equity funds remains illiquid until the fund exits all its investments, which can be 10 years or more.

Minimum investment amounts are often required to access private funds, which can put them out of reach for many investors. Minimums tend to get larger as the size of the fund increases. For example, a private equity fund that is raising $10 million could have minimums in the range of $10,000 to $25,0000. Funds raising $25 million to $50 million might have minimums of $100,000 to $250,000, while funds raising over $200 million could require minimums of $1 million or more. Debt funds often have lower minimums, but these can still be in the range of $25,000 or more.

For those who can opt into these investments, private funds offer the advantage of diversification with minimal effort. As with syndicates, investors pay fees for this benefit. Fund managers are generally paid an annual management fee that is a percentage of the total assets under management and an incentive fee the management team earns when the fund is successful. A 2% annual management fee and a 20% incentive fee are quite common.

While you have discretion over the type of fund you invest in, you don't decide which companies are included. That's the job of the manager. Fortunately, there are many private debt and private equity funds that seek market rate financial return and positive social impact.

Finding Private Investment Funds

Some funds are evergreen, which means they will continually accept capital. The majority, however, go through a capital raise. Once the fund managers have raised the money they plan to invest, the fund is closed to new investors. However, there is always a pipeline of new opportunities.

A good place to start looking for private fund opportunities is with your financial advisor. While not all investment advisors source and perform due diligence on private debt and private equity funds, some do. You can also perform your own research through lists that are available online. Some are curated, which can make your job easier, while others aren't.

ImpactAssets offers the ImpactAssets50. This is an annually updated list of 50 private debt and private equity managers that offer funds with impact themes. Each year, ImpactAssets selects 50 top funds from a wide range of geographies, sectors, and asset classes. Access to this list is free.

Impact Investor Landscape is a search tool for investors who want to back impact companies. It's possible to search for details on almost 80 values-aligned angel groups and impact funds. You can search by sector, geography, life-cycle stage, investment size, and other criteria. The site explains how each fund works as well as the kinds of companies they back.

Once you find a fund that interests you, you can speak to your financial advisor or reach out directly to the staff of the fund. Some funds have investor relations managers on their teams who can field your questions. This way you can learn more about their strategies and get a firsthand sense of their focus, impact goals, and expected financial returns.

Take Action

Entire books have been written on the concepts in this chapter, and we realize we did not fully do them justice. Our intention was to spark your interest in an investment class so you'd be driven to learn more.

To help you on your way, please check out the information and resources we've placed for you on our companion website. We've vetted the content to simplify your process and to point you to some of the most helpful information, regardless of the amount of money you want to invest. So start where you feel comfortable and return to the site whenever you're ready to learn more.

Endnotes

1. https://advocacy.sba.gov/2019/01/30/small-businesses-generate-44-percent-of-u-s-economic-activity/.
2. http://blog.gust.com/the-startup-failure-rate-among-angel-funded-companies/.
3. Hwang, V., Desai, S., and Baird, R. (2019). "Access to Capital for Entrepreneurs: Removing Barriers," Ewing Marion Kauffman Foundation: Kansas City.
4. https://www.kauffman.org/currents/2018/07/3-trends-that-prevent-entrepreneurs-from-accessing-capital.
5. Crowdfund Capital Advisors. Industry Review: Regulation Crowdfunding Finishes Its Fourth Fiscal Year with Some Impressive Results. 2020. https://crowdfundcapitaladvisors.com/regulation-crowdfunding-turns-four-cca-report-analyzes-the-data/.
6. https://www.forbes.com/sites/geristengel/2017/06/21/wanted-more-startups-and-more-savvy-angel-investors/#44a0b6757d9e.

CHAPTER 10

Alternative Investments
Achieve Deeper Diversification and Impact

Alternatives encompass all the investments that do not fit in the conventional asset classes of cash, fixed income, and public equities. Even private investments, which we covered in the last chapter, are usually considered to be alternatives. Currency, gold, real estate, natural resources, art—virtually anything you can buy and sell—can be an alternative.

People invest in these assets for a variety of reasons. They may be pursuing portfolio diversification, a hedge against inflation, opportunities to grow wealth, or a personal interest. Here's a breakdown of each:

- Portfolio diversification is a commonly cited reason for investing in alternatives because these assets are not usually correlated with stock and bond markets. Happily, there are a number of values-aligned alternatives you can invest in to achieve this goal.
- Tangible assets such as gold, art, or real estate are often used as a hedge against inflation or economic setbacks. Investments in foreign, or even crypto, currencies can serve a similar function. My husband owns both gold and cryptocurrency, while I hold neither.
- Many people view real estate as a means of generating wealth, particularly in markets that have historically experienced rising property values over the long term. I was weaned on real estate and count on it as part of my income during retirement.
- Sometimes, we have specialized knowledge we want to capitalize on and invest accordingly. Or we're so interested in a subject that we decide to learn. That's what happened with some people I know who are investing in sustainable agriculture.

How much of your money you allocate to alternatives depends on your goals. If you're interested in this asset class primarily as a means of diversifying your portfolio, many advisors recommend placing no more than 10% of your investable assets here. Those with more wealth might consider a larger allocation. If you're looking at real estate or using specialized knowledge to build your wealth, you may have a significant percentage allocated to those alternatives, particularly if you consider them a side business.

Alternatives Come in Many Forms

As you'll learn in this chapter, you can take a nontraditional approach to your investing using fixed income, public equity, private debt, or private equity instruments. You also can invest in alternatives by purchasing tangible assets or physical property. Since each option comes with its own risk-return trade-off, you'll need to assess each investment individually.

This chapter will introduce you to several values-aligned alternative investments. You'll learn what's possible within this asset class and walk away with some options you can invest in right away.

REITs' Cross-Impact Categories

The first alternative investment we're going to look at is a real estate investment trust or REIT. This is a company that finances, owns, and/or operates income-generating real estate or natural resources. REITs collect rent or generate income from the properties they hold and pass those profits to investors through regular dividends. Some REITs are publicly available while others are private. Public REITs function a lot like mutual funds. They're traded on the stock market, which makes them a fairly liquid investment.

Although REITs can invest in any type of real estate, most specialize and typically hold properties in a single real estate category. Although most REITs are not values-aligned, some are. Examples include REITs that invest in senior health, renewable energy, farmland, timber, and climate change.

People invest in REITs because they're looking for the dividend income and capital appreciation associated with owning real estate coupled with the ease of investing in publicly traded stock. As you will see in Table 10.1, returns on REITs can be as variable as the real estate holdings they own.

Like any stock offering that focuses on a single sector, these investments can be risky. When you invest in a REIT, you're also putting your trust in a real estate management company. Before investing, make sure you know something about the integrity of the company and the people behind it—from both a financial and an impact perspective.

TABLE 10.1 Real Estate Investment Trusts

	Ticker	3-Yr. Return	5-Yr. Return	10-Yr. Return	Other
Digital Realty Trust	DLR	7.84%	21.63%	11.26%	Owns and operates data centers; the company has a long-term goal of powering its entire portfolio with renewable energy
Hannon Armstrong	HASI	23.33%	19.95%	-	Invests in climate change solutions; every investment they make has to lower or mitigate climate change
Prologis	PLD	17.73%	24.11%	16.36%	Invests in distribution centers and warehouses; considered to be a sustainability champion by cutting greenhouse gases and expanding use of solar and LED
Welltower	WELL	−2.99%	3.79%	6.88%	Has an emphasis on senior care; finances senior housing, assisted living, memory care communities, and medical facilities
Weyerhaeuser	WY	−1.59%	4.63%	8.91%	One of the largest private owners of timberland and mills; sustainability of their lands and community development are stated goals

Source: Morningstar as of Sept 11, 2020.

Renewable Energy

You don't have to look far to see the negative impacts that pollution and climate change are having on our environment. Support of clean and alternative sources of energy is accelerating and their use is growing. Hydro-, wind, solar, and geothermal power are all forms of renewable energy. In 2019, their use in the US exceeded that of coal for the first time in 130 years.[1] Their importance is reflected in the stock market as well. Returns on several clean energy funds were more than double the S&P 500 Index in 2019. Although nothing is guaranteed, if this trend persists, we could continue to see significant returns into the future.

Anyone Can Invest in Renewable Energy

The easiest way to support renewable energy is by banking with the Clean Energy Credit Union, which was introduced in the cash chapter. It's also possible to invest in renewable energy though the public equities market where there are currently 10 to 12 renewable energy ETFs. You were introduced to a few of these funds in Chapter 8, and can find a more comprehensive list in Table 10.2. The one-year return data is included for comparison purposes only. If any of these ETFs interest you, please use Morningstar or other online tools to get a full picture of the investment's performance and to assess its historic risk-and-return profiles.

TABLE 10.2 Renewable Energy ETFs

	Ticker	2019 Return	Fees	Other
S&P 500 Index		**31.49%**		
ALPS Clean Energy ETF	ACES	51.67%	0.65%	Invests at least 80% of its assets in US and Canadian companies involved in the clean energy sector, such as renewables and clean tech
First Trust ISE Global Wind Energy ETF	FAN	31.18%	0.62%	Invests at least 90% of its assets in US and global companies around the world working actively in the wind energy industry
First Trust NASDAQ Clean Edge Smart Grid Infrastructure ETF	GRID	42.83%	0.70%	Invests at least 90% of assets in US and global hardware and software companies involved in creating a smart energy grid infrastructure
Invesco Cleantech ETF	PZD	36.45%	0.65%	Invests at least 90% of its assets in US and global companies involved in cleantech; at least 50% of revenues must come from these activities

	Ticker	2019 Return	Fees	Other
Invesco Global Clean Energy ETF	PBD	40.01%	0.75%	Invests at least 90% of its assets in US and global companies that generate and use clean energy or that advance renewable energy
Invesco Solar ETF	TAN	66.53%	0.71%	Invests at least 90% in companies in developed markets that generate a significant portion of their revenue from some aspect of the solar industry
Invesco WilderHill Clean Energy ETF	PBW	62.57%	0.07%	Invests at least 90% in US and global companies advancing cleaner energy and conservation
SPDR S&P Kensho Clean Power ETF	CNRG	63.25%	0.45%	Invests at least 80% of assets in US and global companies driving clean power innovation through their products and services

Compiled with data from Morningstar as of Aug 11, 2020.

Backing Renewables with Private Debt and Private Equity

My research and personal experience have uncovered limited private debt investments in renewable energy. On occasion, private debt funds become available, enabling investors, most often accredited, to participate. Once the amount the fund managers set out to raise has been obtained, the fund closes and is no longer available for investment.

Wunder Capital and Greenbacker Renewable Energy Corporation have offered renewable energy debt funds in the past. Although the funds are now closed, it's likely these companies will offer new funds in the future. If you're interested, hop on their websites. You can also tap into email lists, industry associations, and impact investment clubs to stay informed.

As an accredited investor, you also have the opportunity to invest directly in alternative and renewable energy start-ups or venture funds. In my opinion, making investment decisions at this level requires significant levels of due diligence, specialized interest, or expertise—most likely all three. There are some angel groups that focus primarily on environment issues, such as E8 Angels in Seattle and Clean Venture Group in Cambridge. You can also check AngelList for other private equity investors interested in this sector.

Private Debt That Fuels Renewables

Greenbacker Renewable Energy Company

Greenbacker invests in and operates businesses in the clean energy sector. The company measures its impact through kilowatt hours of clean energy produced, green jobs supported, and metric tons of carbon abated and uses the SDGs to benchmark its progress. You can read Greenbacker's impact report on their website. Previous minimums have been $25,000 with one-year lock-ups and expected returns in the range of 6.5%. Investors need to be accredited and usually access these funds through their financial advisor. Opportunities were available at the time of writing.

Wunder Capital

Wunder Capital provides loans to finance commercial solar products. The most recent funds projected returns of 6.0% to 7.5% with tie-ups between 5 and 10 years. Wunder Capital's website has information on their investments, impact, and financial return dating back to 2016. Even though minimums have been as low as $1,000, investors needed to be accredited. You can sign up on Wunder's website to be notified when new investment opportunities become available.

Residential and Commercial Real Estate

What types of real estate investments have a positive impact? This is a question that Eve Picker asks every person she interviews on her Impact Real Estate Investing podcast, and each guest has a different answer. This is not surprising, because there are several societal and environmental issues that can be addressed through real estate. In this section, we'll focus on a few of the most recognized interventions, because they offer a diversity of investment opportunities. Specifically, we'll look at affordable housing, community development, and green building.

On the social side, affordable housing is an increasingly critical issue as our cities grow and real estate prices rise. Lower-income people are forced out of their homes—sometimes to suburbs that are hours from their places of work or, in the worst-case scenario, onto the streets. Socioeconomic inequities and discrimination in property ownership have devastated some of our neighborhoods. Revitalizing these areas through community development and ownership not only changes the place, it can also change outcomes for people who live there.

On the environmental side, our homes and offices are major contributors to climate change. Building construction and operations account for 40% of global energy use, 30% of energy-related greenhouse gas emissions, approximately 12% of water use, and nearly 40% of waste.[2] A green building movement emerged in the 1960s and 1970s to reduce the negative impact of the way we live and work. Progress is being made in some parts of the world. The European Union, for example, passed regulations that require all new buildings to be net zero starting in 2021.[3] A net zero building produces at least as much energy as it uses over the course of a year. Sadly, the US is trailing other countries in the move toward green construction. However, as an impact investor, you can address these challenges with your capital whether you're accredited or not.

Getting Started in Impact Real Estate Investing

The easiest way to get involved in impact real estate is by investing in community loan funds or notes. These are basically fixed income assets that target homelessness and lack of affordable housing. Another easy entry point are REITs that were designed around green building and sustainability.

From Simple to Complex

1. Community loan funds or notes;
2. REITs;
3. Crowdfunding platforms;
4. Private debt;
5. Community ownership;
6. Private equity and venture funds; and
7. Personal property ownership.

Some of these options were mentioned in Table 10.1. There is also a real estate crowdfunding platform that anyone can invest in for as little as $100.

Private debt and private equity provide additional options. There are also start-ups and venture funds that focus exclusively on impact real estate and the broader industry. Investment amounts, risks, and return potentials vary widely.

The most time-consuming, but potentially most rewarding, way to be involved in impact real estate investing is to use your capital to buy single- or multi-family residences or commercial properties that you develop to achieve your personal impact goals.

With the exception of community notes, minimums and risk-return profiles on a real estate investment are as varied as the deal itself. Real estate also carries additional risk. Projects can go belly-up for a number of completely legitimate reasons, including delays in development, declines in property values, and errors in assumptions related to costs and revenue. There are also unscrupulous players in the market, so please do your due diligence before you buy.

Community Notes That Support Affordable Housing

Community notes and loan funds allow you to invest in a portfolio of loans that help low-income households buy homes. These are fixed income vehicles. As such, they have relatively low risk-and-return profiles.

Affordable Housing: Fixed Income Options

Calvert Community Investment Note

About 20% of the loans provided are directed to affordable housing. The minimum to invest is $20. Returns vary from 0.5% to 3.5%, depending on the term of the note.

Hope Impact Fund

Offered through Affordable Homes of South Texas (AHSTI), this note provides mortgages to low-income families at no interest, making a home purchase possible for many who would otherwise be excluded from ownership. The minimum is $100. Returns currently vary from 2.0% for a one-year term investment to 4.0% for a 10-year term investment. Check AHSTI's website for the most current information.

Enterprise Community Impact Note

This product is available through the Enterprise Community Loan Fund, a CDFI that focuses on affordable housing and community development. There is a $25,000 minimum, and returns range from 0.50% to 3.0% for terms of 1 to 10 years.

REITs

Some REITs that invest in multi-family housing and commercial real estate have made commitments to implement ESG and/or green building practices. Digital Realty Trust (DLR) and Equinix (EQIX) are examples of REITs striving to achieve 100% renewable energy usage across their portfolios. Vert Global Sustainable Real Estate Fund (VGSRX) and HIP Investor are funds that hold multiple sustainable REITs.

A Diversified Sustainable REIT Fund

HIP Investor, a provider of corporate, bond, and fund ratings since 2006, offers six impact-focused investments, one of which is the HIP Sustainable Real Estate REIT ESG strategy.

This HIP investment holds a portfolio of 40 to 50 real estate and REIT stocks, so it provides a broad exposure to the real estate asset class. To be included in the fund, companies and real estate trusts must implement sustainable real estate practices, such as operating buildings that are energy efficient and that provide occupants access to clean air and water. Sustainable buildings can result in lower tenant turnover, contribute to healthier living, and ostensibly produce higher returns.

The HIP Sustainable Real Estate ESG strategy allows investors to diversify their real estate holdings through a single fund. It's possible to invest in this product for as little as $100 on the Newday Impact Investing platform (newdayimpact.com), directly through HIPinvestor.com with a minimum of $30,000 or through a financial advisor.

Crowdfunded Affordable Housing and Community Development Projects

When you invest in real estate through a crowdfunding platform, you're investing in a specific building or real estate development. Although there are a number of platforms that allow you to invest for as little as $500, there is only one I know of that is specifically designed for impact—Small Change. It's also one of the few real estate platforms open to non-accredited investors.

Impact Real Estate Crowdfunding

Small Change was founded in 2016 by Eve Picker, an Australian-born architect, urban designer, and real estate developer. By her own admission, Eve is obsessed with cities. Much of her career has been devoted to supporting development opportunities that others overlook because they're in underserved neighborhoods or difficult to finance through traditional models. For more than 25 years, Eve put her passion to work in Pittsburgh. Now she's helping developers in other cities around the US.

Small Change promotes projects that will have positive transformational impacts in their communities and provide a solid financial return to investors. Impact can range from access to affordable housing to community development to green buildings. The company's primary goal is to list real estate deals that investors can get excited about for their financial and social return.

To date, Small Change has helped raise funds for real estate projects in nine major US cities. Each deal is different, with liquidity tie-ups from a few months to 10 years and annualized returns that ranged from 7.5% to 20%. While the volume of deals on the Small Change platform is relatively small at this time, Eve is working hard to grow the volume.

Private Debt Offers Unlimited Impact Real Estate Opportunities

Opportunities to use private debt in support of impact real estate deals emerge frequently. However, you have to be tracking the market, involved in impact real estate discussions, or aligned with a financial advisor who actively seeks these opportunities to know about them.

AFFORDABLE HOUSING. The development of affordable housing for lower-income people, seniors, and other at-risk populations is critically important, and developers are looking at a range of innovations to meet this growing need. In a well-established model, a real estate developer raises debt in the form of a note or bond to construct an apartment complex, senior living center, or other multi-family building for underserved populations. Investors underwrite the debt, enabling the developer to purchase property and construct the building. During the term of the note, investors are paid an annual dividend, and the principal is returned once the building is completed and sold. Terms can be less than 10 years.

There are a number of real estate developers around the country that offer this type of investment opportunity. The economics differ with each investment. Many housing developments that offer units at rents below market rate can fail to deliver attractive returns to investors. Given the severity of the housing problem, some investors are willing to accept concessionary returns to achieve their social impact goals. Promissory notes that pay 2% to 3% interest over a 5- to 10-year time horizon are not uncommon for affordable housing developments.

COMMUNITY DEVELOPMENT. Community development initiatives bring new investment into existing underserved neighborhoods. Successful projects improve the quality of life for inhabitants, stimulate economic revitalization, and support the local housing market. Financing can come from a mix of sources, including public or private subsidies, tax credits, debt financing, and even private equity.

Community ownership is a form of community development. It can address socioeconomic inequalities in housing and property ownership. In some models, residential and commercial buildings are purchased by a for-profit or nonprofit in "trust" for a community. Investors provide capital for either a downpayment or the entire purchase price of a property and receive regular payments during the term of their loan.

Meanwhile, the building residents or other community stakeholders gradually purchase complete ownership in the property. The new owners can sell their shares and realize a profit. In some cases, the profit is tied to conditions established beforehand to ensure rents remain affordable for lower-income residents or business owners.

Community Ownership of Commercial Property

Plaza 122 is a mid-century retail center in Portland, Oregon, that is home to about 30 businesses. What makes this project particularly compelling is that neighbors can opt into ownership of a retail center for as little as $10 per month.

The story began when Mercy Corps, an international humanitarian aid organization, partnered with a private investor to purchase the complex. Mercy Corps initially invested roughly $100,000 while the investor brought in an additional $230,000. These funds were used as the downpayment on the shopping center, which was valued at $1.2 million. Once purchased, ownership was transferred to the Community Investment Trust, which was established for this purpose. Rent from the businesses covers the mortgage, taxes, insurance, management, and other expenses related to the property.

Community members were invited to become investors in the Community Investment Trust and, hence, co-owners of Plaza 122. Each investor makes payments of $10 to $100 per month. They also receive dividends from the profit made on the building, which has averaged 9% annually in the three years since its launch. The private investor who advanced the $230,000 is realizing a 4% annual return on her loan and the principal is gradually being repaid.

Over 150 residents are currently investors. Half are first-time property owners. The majority are people of color. The co-owners are now members of a community. On occasion, they join together to make improvements to the property. Mercy Corps is now working with other cities to implement similar models.

While these opportunities exist, you have to either be paying attention in your local community or be willing to kickstart an initiative yourself.

GREEN BUILDING.   Green buildings are properties that are designed, built, and maintained using environmentally responsible materials and resource-efficient processes. They can be new construction, renovations, or remodels. In addition to their positive environmental impact, green buildings make good economic sense because they result in higher property values, are healthier, and have lower maintenance and operating costs. Any of us can go green in our homes. There are also opportunities to invest in developers or development projects that do just that.

My Green Building Investment

Green Canopy is a pioneering for-profit homebuilder based in Seattle that deliberately set out to combat the effects of climate change by developing deeply sustainable residential housing. The company constructs new homes in Seattle and Portland. Green Canopy strives to integrate high-quality, healthy materials and efficient design into each of their properties, and they continue to push the envelope. They now offer "net-zero" homes and are expanding into affordable housing.

Investors have been able to participate in Green Canopy's mission and success. The company first engaged accredited investors by offering three debt instruments, each of which paid approximately 11% in annualized returns with less than a 5-year lock-up. Green Canopy pivoted to equity on their fourth fund. They believe this structure creates greater resilience for investors because homes can be rented or sold, generating income regardless of market conditions.

I invested in Green Canopy's second debt instrument because the investment provided an easy way for me to support innovative building practices in a city where I lived at the time. That investment turned out so well, I invested again in their third debt fund. Once again, all my money was paid back on time, in full. And I made close to 11% each year. Both of these investments were great for me because I did extremely well financially and socially.

Private Equity Underwrites Innovative Start-Ups

Start-ups are popping up all over the residential and commercial real estate industry. And some are developing solutions to challenges we face in the way we currently live and work. They are innovating building construction and management, addressing inefficiencies and inequities in existing models, and reimagining the way cities and communities develop. Some use technology to disrupt previous models or to design new solutions. While not all of these enterprises would be considered values-aligned, some definitely are.

As an investor, you can support individual start-ups as an angel investor, or you can invest in an impact real estate fund. If either of these options interest you, one of the best places to start is by reading Daniel Wu, a privacy lawyer and writer who is passionate about affordable housing and transport. In 2019, Dan evaluated over 200 innovative housing start-ups. He looked at everything from construction to property management, from affordability to access. Dan's analysis included start-up businesses, venture funds, and market trends. In his work, Dan provides names and descriptions of many of the companies and funds he researched. You can find his writing on Medium and TechCrunch.

An UrbanTech Fund

The Urban Innovation Fund is a venture capital firm launched in 2016 by two women, Clara Brenner and Julie Lein. They invest in start-ups that use technology to shape the future of cities. The two women are looking for innovative solutions to transportation, housing, education, and other challenges that plague rapidly growing urban areas. They want to make sure cities remain livable and have engaging environments. Their fund also targets underserved entrepreneurs. As a result, its portfolio companies have a make-up that is unlike most VC firms: 70% of their investments have a woman or person of color on the founding team, and 78% have a woman or person of color on the board.

Although the Urban Innovation Fund is still relatively young, the founders' goals are ambitious. They aim to be the largest deployer of capital for urban innovation start-ups, investing over $250 million over the next decade. At the time of this writing, their third fund was open to accredited investors.

Individual Property Ownership

Assuming you have, or can raise, the capital, you could choose to purchase or build a residential or commercial property that you intend to make green or use to create more equity in the housing or commercial real estate markets. You can also stretch your money by partnering with others through tenants-in-common agreements, special-purpose vehicles, or other legal structures. The possibilities are limited only by your resourcefulness and imagination.

One of the simplest examples I know is building an accessory dwelling unit (ADU) to increase housing density. Better known as granny flats, ADUs are small residential units located on the same lot as a stand-alone single-family home. If you have the money, space, and local zoning regulations that allow for it, you can add an ADU to your existing home, backyard, or rental property. These units help alleviate the housing crisis if they enable people to live in neighborhoods they could not otherwise afford.

Sustainable Agriculture

Many of our current agricultural processes are depleting the soil, polluting the land and waterways, and negatively affecting farm workers. Sustainable food and agriculture seek to reverse these trends by applying farming and production methods that can meet society's food needs while ensuring a healthy environment, socioeconomic equality, and economic profitability. These objectives extend from farming to food production to consumption and include sustainable, organic, and regenerative practices.

Investments in sustainable food and agriculture can provide positive financial, social, and environmental returns. Unfortunately, there are only a few investment opportunities accessible to non-accredited investors. But that doesn't mean those with lower asset bases are without recourse. If this is an important issue for you, a first step could be divesting from businesses that harm the land. A simple web search can help with that.

Opportunities for Any Investor

Non-accredited investors can also create positive impact by banking with CDFIs and credit unions that lend to small farms or sustainable companies in the food industry. For example, Maine Harvest Federal Credit Union uses all of its assets to support food systems in its community. Craft3 in the Pacific Northwest, the Natural Capital Investment Fund in Appalachia, and the Cooperative Fund in New England are other financial institutions that support sustainable agriculture. Accredited individuals can also use fixed-income assets to invest directly in the loan funds of these financial institutions.

Gladstone Land (LAND) is the first publicly traded REIT that invests in farmland. More than 35% of its acreage is either organic farmland or in transition to become organic. Another option for any investor is a non-traded REIT, which unlike most REITs, cannot be sold on public markets. Thus, it's more akin to a private investment and should be treated as such in your considerations. There's also a crowdfunding platform focused exclusively on sustainable food and agriculture that's available to any investor for a minimum of $100.

Iroquois Valley Farms Offers a Sustainable Farmland REIT

Iroquois Valley Farms is a benefit corporation and a B-Corp. The company transitions traditional farmland into organic farmland, which it then rents to organic and regenerative farmers through long-term leases or mortgages.

At the time of this writing, non-accredited investors could purchase shares in the Iroquois REIT with a $10,115 minimum and a five-year lock-up. The REIT was available as an alternative investment from Fidelity, Schwab, and TD Ameritrade. Accredited investors also have the option of investing in Iroquois' Soil Restoration Notes. This investment has a $50,000 minimum, a five-year lock-up, and pays an annual return of 2.75%.

Steward Farm Trust Is Crowdfarming

Steward Farm Trust refers to itself as a "crowdfarming" platform that allows anyone to invest in sustainable food and agriculture for as little as $100. Since the company is still relatively new, the number of deals available on the site is fairly limited. Returns are projected to range from 6% to 8%.

Additional Options for Accredited Investors

Accredited investors have additional options because they can invest in food-based start-ups or venture funds using private debt and private equity vehicles—most of which are not available to non-accredited investors. They're also more likely to be able to purchase ownership in sustainably managed farms or farmlands. Once again, this level of investing requires specialized knowledge. Any approach you take within this sector should be thoroughly researched for its financial, social, and environmental returns.

Agri-Food Venture Funds

AgFunder

AgFunder is a venture capital firm that invests in agri-foodtech. They support companies that are innovating in plant-based protein, precision farming, and satellite imaging. Their portfolio includes companies driving change in food and agriculture systems. In 2020, AgFunder raised money for their GROW Impact Fund. The investment is only for accredited investors and has a minimum of $25,000.

Salmon Innovation Fund

Salmon Innovation Fund invests in early stage companies working to rebuild or protect dwindling salmon and steelhead stocks in the Pacific Northwest. Unlike many funds, this firm introduces investment opportunities, one at a time, through syndicates. Although investors have to be accredited, minimums are in the $5,000 to $10,000 range, making these opportunities accessible to a wider range of investors.

If the idea of investing in farmland, sustainable food, and agriculture interests you—and you can participate as an accredited investor—then you might want to engage with likeminded individuals who can help you learn. You can connect with a Slow Money chapter or follow the work of the Global Alliance for the Future of Food.

Sustainable Food and Agriculture Clubs

The Slow Money Institute is a nonprofit that catalyzes the flow of capital into local food systems. The organization achieves its goal by encouraging the formation of clubs that invest in farmers and other food-related businesses. Founded in 2010, the movement currently has 27 chapters around the country, each of which is structured and run independently. To date, these groups have invested more than $73 million in over 750 small local enterprises.

No Small Potatoes, a chapter based in Maine, provides uncollateralized loans of up to $5,000 to farmers, fisheries, and other small food companies in the state. Loans are used to assist with marketing, distribution, and other initiatives. Members make an initial investment of $5,000, and additional capital is provided in $1,000 increments.

The SOIL Network is located in Northern California. This group of investors meet with entrepreneurs and then explore potential investments as a team. The Austin Foodshed Investors, Slow Money Kentucky, and the Let's Eat Investment Club based in Nebraska are other groups in the Slow Money movement.

Sustainable Forestry

Forests cover 31% of our land and harbor most of our terrestrial biodiversity.[4] This critical resource is dwindling. Agriculture appears to be the primary cause of deforestation, with just four commodities—beef, soy, palm oil, and wood products—driving the greatest losses.[5] Timber harvesting and development also play a role. While there are conflicting views about the speed of decline, there seems to be agreement that we need to do something about the rate at which forests are being eradicated.[6]

Individuals and institutions that invest in forests are hoping to harvest timber sustainably, conserve land for future generations, and maintain biodiversity. Revenues from these investments can be generated through land appreciation, timber sales, carbon offsets, and land leasing. However, these assets are also subject to unusual risks, such as natural disasters, the politicization of regulations, and long periods—perhaps decades—of illiquidity. As a result, investors should be committed and very patient.

Limited Investment Opportunities

To date, support has come primarily from philanthropy, as well as institutions and high-net-worth individuals with millions or tens of millions to invest in these assets. Although there are timber ETFs and REITs, most of these investments are extractive rather than conservation focused. Thus, values-aligned investment options in timber and forestry conservation remain limited for most of us.

Private investment funds and land purchases are the most common tools used for timber and forest conservation. While the Global Impact Investing Network (GIIN) showed that values-aligned timber funds outperformed conventional timber funds during the period from 1997 to 2014, with a pooled return of 5.9% for the former and 3.3% for the latter,[7] there are a limited number of opportunities. When they're available, funds generally require investors to be accredited. These funds also have high minimums and are only available to investors while the fund is being raised.

Lyme Timber, Ecotrust Forest Management, Conservation Management, and The Forestland Group are all firms that have offered investment opportunities in sustainable timber and forests. These are all closed funds with a limited window of time to invest. Minimums are in the neighborhood of $250,000 or more, putting these investments out of reach for most people.

The ImpactAssets 50 is one resource you can use to search for current opportunities.

Water

Clean drinking water is a basic need of every human being and animal on the planet. Yet water systems around the world are in stress. Globally, 4 billion people experience water scarcity at least one month a year, and the situation is expected to get worse as temperatures rise.[8] Even more striking, a child dies from water-related illnesses every two minutes.[9] In the US, nearly half of our rivers and streams and more than 30% of our lakes are unfit for swimming, fishing, or drinking.[10] Sadly, women, children, and people of color are often the hardest hit by these challenges. Investing in water can be good for our wallets and the planet.

Water is a much more complex space than I realized. It goes well beyond water conservation, pollution cleanup, or desalination. A knowledge-sharing platform called The Water Network lists almost 10,000 different organizations working with water. AngelList has almost 700 start-ups within the water space engaged in everything from designing more sustainable water bottles to companies developing smarter water management systems for cities. Your money can be invested to increase efficiencies in water management, remove plastics from our oceans, or ensure water usage remains affordable for all people.

Anyone Can Invest in Water

For years, I've wanted to invest in water but didn't think I had enough money, and I didn't know how. I thought this sector was only accessible through philanthropy and to those who could invest large sums of money—much like sustainable forestry. While researching this chapter, however, I discovered some water investments that anyone can participate in. For example, WaterWorks recently launched a crowdfunding site that allows investments in water for as little as $500.

One of the easiest ways to invest in water is through the public equities market. Table 10.3 lists the two water-related mutual funds and five ETFs that are currently available. The mutual funds have minimums of $1,000, higher fees, and turnovers in the 30% to 40% range. All the funds have a high sustainability mandate and earned high grades from As You Sow. Although these funds are not benchmarked against the S&P 500 Index, the index is included in the table for comparison purposes.

Investors can also support water projects at the local level through municipal bonds, which are an increasingly popular way to finance improvements in municipal water systems. Repayments of these bonds are often tied to usage fees, which provides a certain level of security for these investments. Since water delivery is considered an essential service, these are also considered to be more conservative options within the municipal bond market.

TABLE 10.3 Water Mutual Funds and ETFs

	Ticker	2019 Return	Description
S&P 500 Index		**31.49%**	
Allianz Global Water Fund	AWTAX	32.77%	Invests globally in companies offering solutions to water resource management and access to clean water
Calvert Global Water Fund	CFWAX	28.02%	Invests globally in water-related companies operating in alignment with the Calvert Principles for Responsible Investment
First Trust Water ETF	FIW	37.37%	Tracks the ISE Clean Edge Water Index, which is comprised of US companies involved in potable and wastewater industries
Invesco Global Water ETF	PIO	35.58%	Tracks Nasdaq OMX Global Water Index, which includes companies designing products that conserve and purify water
Invesco S&P Global Water ETF	CGW	34.04%	Tracks S&P Global Water Index, which includes companies involved in water utilities, infrastructure, equipment, instruments, and materials
Invesco Water Resources ETF	PHO	37.57%	Tracks Nasdaq OMX Global Water Index, which includes companies designing products that conserve and purify water
Tortoise Water Fund ETF	TBLU	38.74%	Uses a proprietary index comprised of companies around the globe in the water industry, particularly public water distribution.

Source: Morningstar as of Jul 17, 2020.

Accredited investors have numerous opportunities to support start-up businesses in the water sector. However, it requires research and participation in angel or environmental groups to find them. One place to get started is talking to angel groups that are focused on environmental issues, as many of them include water in their mandates. You could also look into Imagine H_2O and BREW Accelerator—two accelerators that work with start-up companies in the water space.

My Angel Investments in Water

Through my involvement with Next Wave Impact, I am invested in two water-related companies founded by women: StormSensor and Aquacycl.

Until I co-led due diligence on StormSensor, I didn't know that storm water is the leading cause of water pollution in our cities. Nor did I understand how expensive and difficult it is to track floodwaters. StormSensor has developed solutions that will lower the cost and increase the efficiency of tracking storm and wastewater running beneath our city streets. In the process, StormSensor is disrupting a pretty staid male-dominated industry.

Aquacycl's mission is to ensure all people have access to clean water and sanitation. The two female PhDs who cofounded this company have developed a low-cost, simple, and rapidly deployable wastewater treatment system that can work anywhere in the world. The company's technology can transform the polluted wastewater discharged through manufacturing and other processes into irrigation-quality water. Their solution is being tested in the US with swine farmers, chocolate producers, and soft drink companies and will ultimately be deployed globally.

Venture funds with an exclusive focus on water are few and far between. Some that have been recommended to me include Cimbria Capital, MazarineVentures, Helios Capital Ventures, and XPV Water Partners. You could also consider firms that focus on cleantech and include water under that umbrella.

Some Thoughts on Due Diligence

Due diligence is the research you undertake to identify risks and validate information about a potential investment. By the time you have reached this point in the book, you've already learned a number of skills that you can apply to the investments described in this chapter.

For example, if you're moving cash to a financial institution that's supporting affordable housing, make sure your funds will be insured up to $250,000. If you're making a fixed-income investment, get information about the historical returns and default rates. Public equity investments are volatile, but you've learned how to use Morningstar and other tools to look at fees, turnover, and historic returns. Private debt and private equity opportunities require the same type of diligence that we spoke about in the previous chapter on private investments.

Direct investments in real estate, land, sustainable agriculture, or a natural resource are unique. Risks are based on market and business conditions related to each category of investment and can differ from place to place. Successful investing in these assets requires specialized, and often localized, knowledge. To get started, you might want to:

- Look for opportunities that are making a difference in the impact areas important to you;
- Invest in projects in, or near, your community so you can assess the risks and potential return more easily; and
- Assume that return projections are aspirational—understand what needs to happen for you to start generating return on your investment as well as what could affect full repayment.

Take Action

Have some fun with this group of investments. You don't have to risk a lot. As you learned, there are several options available for as little as $100. Try a few different investments, experiment, and track the impact. You might even consider bringing together a group of women to consider options, perform research, undertake diligence, and perhaps even invest together. Learning more about nontraditional investments that create a deeper impact can be a great reason to start an investment circle.

1. Pick one cause that resonates with you; then think about the level of investment that feels comfortable to you.

2. Consider the options mentioned in this chapter and do some research to see if any other opportunities pique your interest. Be sure to study the risks and returns relative to other investments in the asset category you have chosen.

3. If you are interested in a private debt or private equity investment, you can ask your advisor to identify additional opportunities or to help you with due diligence. Or, even better, you can connect with other people who are interested in the same topic and learn from them. The process is a lot more fun that way, and you may be surprised at whom you meet.

4. Once you have picked an investment, done your homework, and feel good about both the financial and social return, pull the trigger and invest.

Endnotes

1. https://www.eia.gov/todayinenergy/detail.php?id=43895.
2. https://greenmoney.com/the-case-for-investing-in-sustainable-buildings/.
3. https://ec.europa.eu/energy/content/nzeb-24_en.
4. http://www.fao.org/state-of-forests/2020/en/.
5. https://www.ucsusa.org/resources/whats-driving-deforestation.
6. https://e360.yale.edu/features/conflicting-data-how-fast-is-the-worlds-losing-its-forests.
7. GIIN and Cambridge Associates. "The Financial Performance of Real Assets Impact Investments: Introducing the Timber, Real Estate and Infrastructure Impact Benchmarks." 2017.
8. https://www.unwater.org/water-facts/scarcity/.
9. https://water.org/our-impact/water-crisis/.
10. https://www.nrdc.org/stories/water-pollution-everything-you-need-know.

CHAPTER 11

Maximize Your Philanthropy
Finish with Grants and Concessionary Investing

Y ou don't have to be Melinda Gates or Oprah Winfrey to make a significant difference with your charitable giving. Everyday charity, which
comes from passionate and committed individuals giving their time, talent,
and money to causes they care about, accounts for more than two-thirds of
all donations made in the United States each year.[1] Even though the average annual contribution at the household level is just about $2,500, our
combined donations outstrip giving by the mega-billion-dollar foundations
and corporations.[2]

What's more, research by the Women's Philanthropy Institute shows that
women, across all categories of age, race, and ethnicity, are more philanthropic than men. We are also interested in collaborative giving and participate this way at much higher rates than men do.[3] Women are also becoming
major donors.[4] The growth in our philanthropic power stems from the same
trend that has been discussed throughout this book—the simple fact that
more and more women have their own money to spend—and give.

However, many of us don't think of ourselves as philanthropists. Rather,
we approach our donations in an ad-hoc, unplanned manner. We send
money in response to a global crisis, make a grant when a friend asks, or
think about our donations toward the end of the year when the big campaigns kick in. This approach is considered charity. Charitable acts tend
to be more emotional, immediate responses to an urgent situation or personal request.

On the other hand, philanthropy refers to a considered deliberate
approach to giving that is built on a desire for longer-term outcomes.
Table 11.1 shows the key differences between charitable and philanthropic giving. While both are beneficial, approaching our giving with a

philanthropic mindset allows us to do more with our charitable donations. Philanthropists have learned that more strategic and collaborative giving results in greater impact and more personal fulfillment.

TABLE 11.1 Charitable vs. Philanthropic Giving

	Charitable Giving	Philanthropic Giving
Approach	Contributions based on immediate priorities and emergent needs	Long-term giving plan directed toward causes that matter deeply to you
Result	Ad-hoc, reactive, contribution amounts vary from year to year	Strategic, more consistent annual contributions, deeper impact
Modality	Individual	Collaborative, share knowledge and research, pool financial resources
Engagement	Limited, unless significant donor	Increased opportunities for tracking outcomes and closer grantee relationships
Administration	Personal tracking and management	Efficient, one-click, repeat giving, managed tracking, records for accountant
Taxes	Deductible once itemization limits have been met	Flexible approaches to maximize tax deductions

There are three valuable tools you can use to maximize the impact of your donations and shift from charitable giving to strategic philanthropy. First, you can develop a personal giving plan. Second, you can join a giving circle, an increasingly popular way that women are coming together to learn, pool their assets, and make joint grant-making decisions. Third, you can open a values-aligned donor-advised fund (DAF), a financial tool that provides tax advantages and flexibility around how and when you make contributions to it.

Develop a Personal Giving Plan

Let's start with the idea of creating a personal giving plan. This involves figuring out what problem you want to solve, which organizations are doing the best work, and how you want to give. In the "Take Action" section of this chapter, there is a simple five-step process to help you create a straightforward plan. Table 11.2 gives an example of a plan that I created for my annual giving.

TABLE 11.2 Sample Annual Giving Plan

Problem	▪ Homelessness in local community
Pathway	▪ Direct service and volunteering
Actions	▪ Donate $1,500 each year to a shelter in our community that focuses primarily on youth facing homelessness and human trafficking
	▪ Donate $1,200 each year to a local food bank
Cadence	▪ Monthly donations automatically paid through credit card
	▪ Volunteer 4–6 times per year at food bank
Outcomes	▪ Deeper understanding of the problem and possible solutions
	▪ Experienced commitment and personal relationships

Not surprisingly, the first step in the process is determining what you value. If you went through the exercises in Chapter 2, then you should already have some idea of the causes that matter to you and how you want to have a positive impact on the world. The results of that exercise can apply to both your investments and your philanthropy. Other steps in the process include determining the qualities you want to see in the nonprofits you want to support, researching and rating prospective grantees, and summarizing your decisions in a giving plan.

Unless you're planning to make substantial donations, it's relatively easy to create a giving plan on your own. Some people, however, prefer to have assistance. There are advisors that specialize in helping individuals, corporations, and foundations structure their philanthropic goals. These advisors help their clients reduce the amount of time they spend in the process, bring creative approaches based on experience, and help wealthier clients avoid pitfalls.

Join a Giving Circle

Another option you have is to join a giving circle. This is actually a wonderful way to create community, learn more about issues that matter to you, and magnify your contribution. Jenny Berg, the former president of a circle with several hundred participants in Cincinnati, happily makes her $1,000 donation to the group each year. When it comes time to participate in the annual meeting where members vote on where to allocate their pooled funds, her contribution has been matched by hundreds of other members, which amplified her impact 400 times. Prior to attending the meeting, Jenny likes to tell people, "I'm going to be making $400,000 in grants this afternoon."

The Power of Giving Circles

A giving circle is simply a group of people who come together for philanthropic purposes. A circle can be as small as a few people or as large as several hundred. It can include friends, family members, coworkers, or any other likeminded individuals who meet as often as monthly or as infrequently as once a year. Group members pool philanthropic funds, which can range from a few dollars to millions of dollars, and collectively agree on how those assets will be allocated.

Giving circles in the United States have proliferated from just a handful in the early 2000s to over 1,600 today.[5] Combined, these groups include more than 150,000 people and have collectively raised more than $1.29 billion over a recent 20-year period. You won't be surprised to learn that a majority are comprised of women. In fact, a few years ago, 70 percent of all giving circle participants in the US were women, and nearly half of the groups were identified as women-only.[6]

Joining a giving circle is a particularly attractive approach to philanthropy for women who value the camaraderie of community, are unsure about where they want to target their donations, or would like their contributions to have greater impact. This form of collaborative giving democratizes and diversifies philanthropy because anyone—particularly women and donors of color—can engage as a philanthropist and do so in a safe, respectful manner that results in close connections with peers and community. Some of the women interviewed for this chapter talked about how moving their experiences have been and how they became more deeply engaged over time. First, they joined a circle, then they got involved in a committee, and one was so enamored with a grantee that she now serves on its board.

How Giving Circles Work

Many giving circles support nonprofit organizations in their local communities, while others align with specific priorities such as social justice or women's issues. Educational events are included in many giving circle structures. These help members learn together about the issues that will be supported by the group's grants. In some cases, members meet with potential grantees as part of their decision-making process. One group interviewed for this chapter brings their children to their annual meeting and leaves the final grant decisions to them!

There is enormous flexibility in how a giving circle can be organized. You can join an existing circle that aligns with your priorities, build a new chapter within a network structure that already exists, or choose to start a circle from scratch. Even though there are several models, there are no specific rules. Each group can decide individually how it wants to operate.

Making Children Part of the Process

The Impact East Bay Circle was founded by a group of women with children. They knew they could only commit to forming the circle if they included their children, so the women built the kids into the circle's giving process. Each grant finalist provides a five-minute, kid-friendly presentation during the group's annual decision-making meeting. The children attend and are each given a dollar bill. At the end of the presentations, the children use their dollars to vote for their favorite grantee. As a result, the children feel like they're a part of the act of giving in their own community. In addition to voting, older children learn speaking and leadership skills by making presentations about the Impact Circle in their local schools. The cofounders say their approach "brings philanthropy conversations to the dinner table."

The Impact100 Council is an example of a network. Their model has been replicated around the United States and Australia. The network boasts over 50 chapters and combined giving of more than $67 million since its inception in 2001. Part of Impact100's success is the "open source" approach they've taken with their framework. All the information and materials required to start a circle are available for free download on the Impact100 Council's website.[7] Each new chapter can modify the model to meet their own needs. It also can rely on the Impact100 Council and other circles for support and guidance. This collaborative approach allows all Impact100 groups to flourish as they share templates, web pages, and success stories.

For example, the Impact100 Redwood Circle was cofounded by five women who held the group's initial meetings in their homes. These women brought in friends from bridge clubs, Mahjong tables, and local hiking groups. Within four years, the group had grown to over 200 members, who each contribute $1,000 a year. The Impact100 Redwood Circle's goal is to create a significant and lasting difference in the lives of those in their community, and the members believe they are succeeding.

The Diversity of Giving Circles

Central Valley Giving Circle

The Central Valley Giving Circle is a member of the Latino Giving Circle Network, which is the largest network of Latino philanthropists in the US. The network has more than 20 giving circles across California, each of which is centered on the values of love, culture, and justice. America Hernandez joined the Central Valley Giving Circle to live out those values. She cherishes the opportunity to make a difference in her backyard by participating in collective philanthropy with her mentors, heroes, and neighbors. For her, it's a special place like no other, because everything they do is rooted in their *corazón* (heart). The Latino culture is filled with love and generosity, and through their giving circle, members are sharing those gifts with the world.

Asian Women's Giving Circle

Hali Lee, the founder of Asian Women's Giving Circle, started her group based on the tradition of geh in Korea. Over the past 15 years, the Asian Women's Giving Circle has raised and distributed over $1 million to Asian American Pacific Islander women and girls who use arts and culture to bring about equitable social change in their New York City communities. In pooling their resources to fund projects led by Asian American women artists and community groups, circle members take risks by investing in emerging and cutting-edge changemakers, and they stay rooted in their community. For them, funding is a form of activism.

Greenville Women Giving

Based in South Carolina, this circle was founded in 2006 as an initiative of the Community Foundation of Greenville. It grew very quickly to become one of the largest giving circles in the country and has over 575 members, each of whom makes a three-year commitment to give $1,200 annually. Of that, $1,000 goes into a pooled grantmaking fund, while the remaining $200 covers the cost of operations and educational events. Grants support local initiatives in the arts, education, environment, health, and human services.

Open a Donor-Advised Fund

Regardless of whether you choose to go it alone or take a more collaborative approach through a giving circle, Donor Advised Funds (DAFs) provide an invaluable tool for any philanthropy plan. They're easy to use, provide important tax advantages, and enable greater flexibility in how you invest your charitable dollars. The most innovative "Impact First" DAF providers are taking an active role in offering a range of values-aligned investment options that include the ability to use your charitable funds to support experiments, social businesses, and other enterprises that straddle the for-profit and nonprofit line.

How DAFs Work

A DAF is a financial instrument that is offered by a specialized public charity (see Figure 11.1). It allows you to make charitable contributions, receive immediate tax deductions, and recommend grants over time. Developed initially for the wealthy, DAFs are becoming more viable for a greater number of people—even those with more limited budgets. Because assets can sit in a DAF for years, they're sometimes referred to as foundations for the rest of us.

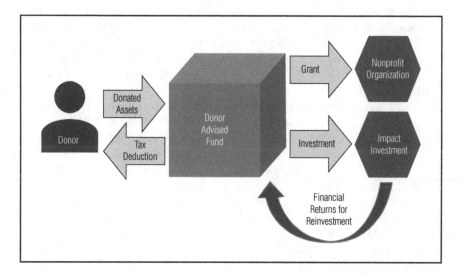

FIGURE 11.1 How Donor-Advised Funds Work

Source: Cornerstone Capital Group. Mobilizing Donor Advised Funds for Impact Investing. Nov. 2018.

When you contribute to a DAF, you're essentially making a donation to a charitable organization and receiving an immediate tax deduction for the full amount of your gift. It's important to understand that money contributed to a DAF will never be available to you again for your personal use or gain. All funds in a DAF are earmarked for charitable purposes. However, the money in your DAF can be held indefinitely until you're ready to give it away through grants. In fact, unlike a foundation, which has federally mandated laws to give away at least 5% of the assets each year, DAFs have no "drawdown" requirements. This has led to a great deal of controversy.

While assets are sitting in your DAF, they're usually invested to maximize return. In a typical DAF, this money would go into fixed-income and public equity investments. Any financial returns that are made on these investments are returned to the DAF to be granted or reinvested. Neither the funds you put into the DAF nor the returns can come back to you. If the investments in your DAF return more in value than you're giving away each year, the asset base in your DAF can grow. This is further fueling the debate about DAFs.

A Growing Controversy over Foundations and Donor-Advised Funds

While foundations are required under IRS rules to give away 5% or more of their money each year to support charitable causes, in most cases, the remaining 95% of its assets are invested to maximize return. But the investments that are made through the principal are often at odds with the foundation's purported charitable intentions. This has caused a number of people to start demanding more accountability from foundations.

A DAF can be even more problematic because unlike a foundation, there are no payout requirements for DAFs. The National Philanthropic Trust reports the average payout across all DAFs in a given year is about 20%, which is far greater than the foundation requirement. However, this still leaves a lot of money out of circulation and out of the hands of the charities that are in such desperate need.*

As the popularity and size of DAFs have grown over the past decade, a controversy about the lack of payout requirements has gained attention and is becoming louder. On the plus side, some argue that DAFs make it easier for individuals to earmark money toward philanthropy, thus increasing dollar flows. They also point out this source of capital can underwrite important innovations and businesses that would not otherwise receive the capital they need to prosper and grow. Others contend that DAFs are financial repositories for wealthy people who are seeking tax write-offs even though they don't plan to make grants. They point to Fidelity Charitable, Schwab Charitable, and the Silicon Valley Community Foundation, all of which are DAFs, as some of the fastest-growing charitable organizations in the country. There are also concerns that DAF providers, which benefit from the fees on the DAF assets under management (AUM), do little to encourage their clients to spend down the principal funds in their DAFs. Another concern relates to anonymity. Since the source of a grant doesn't need to be identified, there is potential risk that dark money could flow through these vehicles, even though there are restrictions and grants can't be used for lobbying or other political activities.

---

* National Philanthropic Trust. 2018 Donor Advised Fund Report.

> We believe there is merit on both sides of the DAF debate. However, we also believe that funds in DAFs should not be allowed to sit idle for years. This money should be spent, and we advocate that DAF owners actively grant and invest. DAFs should be fulfilling their full potential and should support philanthropy, as intended. Like many other structures, a DAF by itself is neither good nor bad. It's how it's used that increases or diminishes its value.

Benefits of a DAF

Why would you donate to a DAF, rather than making grants directly to the charity or charities you want to support? This is an important question since many DAFs tend to require a first-time contribution of $2,500 to $5,000 or more and charge fees that can be as high as 1.0% of assets under management. Benefits include the ability to plan ahead, realize tax advantages, and take financial risks to support innovations that could result in deep impact.

PLANNING AND MANAGEMENT   DAFs allow you to budget and plan for your philanthropy rather than making ad-hoc, end-of-year decisions. Once you've established your DAF and paid in the initial contribution, you can make donations on a routine or irregular basis. Funds can be released with the click of a button to your selected charities.

Consider a DAF when:

- You want to plan and budget your giving over a period of more than one year;
- You seek easy and efficient management of your annual giving;
- Your income fluctuates year to year, but you want to give annually;
- You receive an influx of money through an asset sale, inheritance, or other largess;
- You want to maximize your tax deductions;
- You want to donate stock or other non-cash assets;
- You involve other family members in your philanthropy and/or choose to set up a succession plan; or
- You want your grant funds to support high-risk innovation, systemic change, or to underwrite unsustainable ventures that have deep and positive impact.

The DAF will maintain detailed records of your contributions over time, so you can easily see where your money is going and track year-on-year giving patterns. Staff at the DAF can even help you make investment choices about the funds that remain in the DAF each year. Depending on the sophistication of the DAF and the amount you've invested, you may even get individualized support. In addition, DAFs will track your investment performance, send you reports, and provide you with the documents you need at tax time.

UNEVEN INCOME   DAFs are particularly valuable if you have an uneven or inconsistent income flow. This is because you can make a larger donation to your DAF in the years when you are flush, gaining all the tax advantages, and then grant the funds out over time, keeping your giving consistent, whether you earn a lot or a little.

You will receive similar benefits if you make a large, multi-year donation at the time you receive an unexpected cash windfall though real estate sales, inheritance, or stock vetting. If you want to share some of your largess with others, you can make a contribution to your DAF and use that donation to offset the capital gains associated with your windfall. Then you can grant the money out over time. Beth Stelluto, a primary contributor to this chapter, chose to contribute 10 years of her projected charitable giving into her DAF all at once. In addition to making grants every year, Beth is using her principal to support high-risk ventures that are deeply aligned with her values.

TAX MAXIMIZATION   The Tax Cuts and JOBS Act of 2017, which went into effect in 2018, fundamentally changed the way most people manage their taxes. As a result of the law, charitable donations are only deductible if you itemize. This was not the case in prior years. What's more, standard deductions almost doubled from $6,500 for single filers and $12,700 for married couples filing jointly to $12,000 for single filers and $24,000 for married couples. Thus, you need a lot more standard deductions, of which charitable giving is a portion, to reduce your taxable income.

By front-loading charitable contributions into your DAF, you can reach the standard-deduction minimums in a year when you would not have been able to do so otherwise. For example, assume you are single and plan to donate $5,000 per year for the foreseeable future. In year 1, you could open a DAF with $10,000 and receive the entire tax benefit in that year. This would get you a lot closer to the standard deduction of $12,000 in that year. Then, the following year, you wouldn't itemize. However, you'd still have assets left to donate. In year 3, you could itemize again. This "bunching" allows you to reach the standard deduction in a given year and set aside money to give at consistent levels in subsequent years.

NONCASH DONATIONS   In addition to cash, you can make donations to your DAF of stock, real estate, pre-IPO shares, and even bitcoin, depending on the capabilities of your provider. These additional options have their own tax advantages.

Stock is one of the most common alternatives to cash contributions, because donating appreciated stock results in a bigger donation to your DAF or charity, and it provides a larger tax advantage to you than you'd receive if you'd sold the stock first. Let's see how that works.

Looking at Table 11.3, suppose you sold $100,000 worth of stock to make a charitable donation. Assume the cost basis of the stock—its cost when you purchased it—was $60,000. That means you've made a profit of $40,000. Further assume a federal income tax rate of 24% and a federal long-term capital gains rate of 15%. Now you're ready to either sell the stock and donate the proceeds or simply donate that stock to your DAF. What would be your tax outcome in each case and how much benefit would your DAF realize? According to Fidelity Charitable's tax calculator,[8] you'd save $7,440 in taxes if you donated the stock directly to your DAF or another charity, and the charity would receive an additional $16,000 in value.

TABLE 11.3 Stock Donation Example

	Sell Stock, Then Donate to Charity	Donate Stock Directly to Charity
Stock value	$100,000	$100,000
Long term cap gains tax paid	$6,000	$0
Amount donated to charity	$94,000	$100,000
Tax savings	$16,560	$24,000

Donating appreciated stock is a great strategy if you're already planning to make a charitable contribution. It's particularly beneficial in a year when you want to maximize your deductions. I started my DAF with a stock transfer during a period when I was selling some of my non-values-aligned stock funds to transition those assets to values-aligned holdings.

FAMILY INVOLVEMENT   Just as one group of women in a giving circle involved their children in the process, the DAF structure provides an opportunity for family members to think about, discuss, and jointly make decisions about grant or investment recipients. Some families get together annually to discuss their current year's giving record, using reports from their DAF. They agree on future gifts and goals and then provide instructions to their DAF managers to carry out. By enabling them to participate in decision-making, this approach can be an engaging way to instill the value of giving in children and can be a valuable family experience.

DAFs are also a great option for donating at the time of death. Assets in the DAF can be transferred to family members, nonprofits, or other beneficiaries upon your death. The recipient can continue giving based on your predetermined objectives, or you can empower them to make their own grant decisions going forward. I did this with my own will. In the past, my will designated specific charities that would receive money upon my death. Every time my charities of choice changed, I had to change my will. This was laborious and expensive. Finally, I revised my will to donate a percentage of my assets to my DAF. Upon my death, ownership and management of my DAF will pass to my niece, who will then be able to give the funds away at her discretion.

INVESTMENT OPTIONS   Because this book is dedicated to helping you get as much of your money aligned with your values as possible, the principal in your DAF should also be doing as much good for the world as the rest of your investments. This is entirely possible, depending on which DAF provider you choose. The level of values-aligned investment options varies considerably from provider to provider. In the worst-case scenario, you'll be offered the same types of nonaligned cash, bond, and mutual fund options that you're choosing to move away from with the rest of your portfolio. In the best-case scenario, you'll be able to invest in values-aligned options of all types, including private investments and alternatives.

With some DAF providers, you can use your principal to provide loan guarantees, offer subsidies, underwrite unproven business models, or accept below-market-rate returns to advance initiatives with deep and positive impact. Funds in DAFs can also be instrumental in affecting systemic change. Beth Stelluto and I are using our DAFs to support innovations that are deemed too high-risk for investors seeking market-rate returns.

Using DAFs to Support High-Risk Ventures

An angel group that Beth Stelluto belonged to was considering an investment in an innovative filtration system that provided clean water to impoverished people in emerging markets. Beth was on the due diligence team and became enamored with the company. Because the company was at a very early stage, the investment was deemed too risky, and the angel group chose to pass on the opportunity. Beth was quite disappointed because she had come to love the company's mission and wanted to support them, and she did—through her DAF.

I made a similar choice when I was asked to invest in a fund that was supporting values-based start-up entrepreneurs in developing countries. The investment was risky due to the small size of the businesses and their widely dispersed locations. In addition, the fund was going to be experimenting with revenue-based lending. That was more risk than I wanted to take on with my primary assets. However, I loved what this fund was doing, and I realized that if it were successful, it could be a proof point for a new type of financial product, so I invested through my DAF.

Beth and I also used our DAFs to co-invest in a clothing company that was built on the ideals of sustainability and female empowerment. The company would like to eventually transition to a cooperative model that enables the fair-trade farmers and seamstresses in their supply chain to have ownership in the business. This vision makes the company higher risk than investments Beth and I make with our other assets. But our DAFs provided a perfect, no-risk opportunity to support this high-impact business.

Primary Types of DAFs

Most sources refer to three different types of DAF providers: Community Foundations, National Charities, and Affinity Group Foundations. Each of these categories has their own origin stories, attributes, and qualities. We're also including a fourth group that we'll call Impact First. Members of this group were designed from the ground up to maximize their clients' ability to invest their DAF assets in a range of values-aligned financial instruments.

COMMUNITY FOUNDATIONS The very first DAF was established in 1931 through the New York Community Trust, a community foundation that is still operational today. Community foundations are charities that tend to focus on improving the lives of people within their locales. Many offer DAFs as a means to fund their work and provide an easy way for donors to support their local community. A growing number recognize the need to help their DAF clients make innovative, location-based impact investments with their principal assets. Hundreds of community foundations operate in urban and rural locations around the country. If you choose a community foundation DAF, you may be asked to allocate a portion of your donations to causes the foundation supports.

NATIONAL CHARITIES   For decades after their founding, DAFs remained a largely underutilized philanthropic instrument. That changed in the mid-1990s when DAFs began to grow in visibility and popularity. At that time, several financial investment firms, such as Fidelity, Schwab, and Vanguard, created subsidiaries that could function as DAFs. Set up as national charities, the DAFs run by these financial institutions have become some of the largest charities in the country. DAFs associated with financial service providers typically offer low minimums, low administration fees, and a range of traditional investment choices. Some of these DAFs are starting to offer values-aligned options to their clients.

AFFINITY GROUP FOUNDATIONS   Affinity group foundations are formed around a religion, a membership group such as a university, or an issue that draws people together. The National Christian Foundation, Cornell University, and the Sierra Club are all examples. Not surprisingly, these DAFs promote philanthropic goals that are aligned with their sponsoring organizations. Like community foundations, they may restrict the types of grants you can make. A West Coast university, for example, requires that 50% of funds donated to their DAFs be allocated to the university. An affinity group can be a good choice if you plan to make regular donations to the causes their DAFs champion.

IMPACT-FIRST DAFS   A new type of DAF provider that takes a broader view of philanthropy has been emerging. The underlying belief of these pioneering organizations is that the principal within a DAF should be doing as much good for the world as the grants it makes. Therefore, these organizations actively curate and evaluate values-aligned investment opportunities across asset classes. As a client of this type of DAF, virtually all of the investment options available to you will be steeped in social and/or environmental impact. The emergence of these innovative approaches is helping to drive more traditional DAF providers to offer more values-aligned investment options as well.

Table 11.4 compares the key attributes of these four different types of DAFs, considering minimum contributions, administrative fees, and investment options.

TABLE 11.4 DAF Provider Comparison

	Community Foundation	National Charity	Affinity Group Foundation	Impact First
Example	Greater Cincinnati Foundation	Fidelity Charitable	Sierra Club Foundation	ImpactAssets
Minimum Contribution	None	$5,000	$100,000	$5,000
Administrative Fees	Greater of $400 or 1.1%	Greater of $100 or 0.6%	1.0%	1.0%, then sliding scale
Investment Options	Limited choice, limited values-aligned options	Moderate choice, limited values-aligned options	100% fossil-free and mission-aligned portfolio	Broad choice, 100% values-aligned
Level of Control	Full control	Full control	Limited control	Full control
Primary Benefit	Emphasis on local	Lower admin fees	Single-purpose mission	Options for 100% alignment
Drawbacks	Limited options	Limited support	Often high minimums	$10,000+ min for innovative options

Four Pioneering Impact-First DAFs

RSF Social Finance, Impact Assets, Tides Foundation, and the Triskeles Foundation are four pioneering impact-first DAFs that are pushing the boundaries on the types of investments that can be made with DAF assets. Each of the impact-first DAF providers profiled here has a different approach to the way in which they work with their clients. However, they're all striving to ensure that all the assets held in their DAF accounts are invested in ways that are advancing positive social and environmental outcomes. They're also helping their clients use their DAF funds to invest in innovative ways.

RSF SOCIAL FINANCE   RSF believes that assets in their DAFs have an important role to play in seeding new ideas, building community, and taking outsized risks to achieve deep social and environmental returns. The DAF offers two values-aligned investments, neither of which prioritizes market rate returns. The Liquidity Portfolio makes loans to environmental banks, microfinance institutions, small-scale agriculture lenders, solar providers, and other social and environmental innovators. The Food System Transformation Fund supports enterprises building local and regional food systems. There is a $5,000 minimum to open a DAF with RSF.

IMPACTASSETS   ImpactAssets is a trendsetter because their DAF offers a broader and deeper array of values-aligned investments than any other provider we've seen. Few other DAFs come close to the span of opportunities in terms of values alignment and personal involvement. ImpactAssets offers everything from complete values-aligned portfolios that you could choose with one click to customized private debt, private equity, and alternative investments. Beth Stelluto and I both have our DAFs at ImpactAssets. We used their customized option for the investments mentioned earlier. Every year, the company also publishes the ImpactAssets 50, a curated list of some of the top values-aligned private fund managers. The 50 firms selected each year are a representative sample, showcasing managers who invest across a variety of geographies, sustainable development goals, and asset classes. Like RSF, ImpactAssets has a minimum contribution of $5,000.

TIDES FOUNDATION   The Tides Foundation's DAF seeks to push boundaries and catalyze real, lasting change with every dollar invested. The foundation has a participatory model that targets higher-net-worth philanthropists who can meet its $100,000 minimum. If this is within your comfort zone and you choose to donate through Tides, you'll be assigned your own philanthropy advisor. Tides advisors work closely with their clients to hone their grant-making and investment strategies. Then they assist in implementing those plans. The foundation also helps clients develop communities of interest, through which Tides' clients connect to each other for inspiration, support, and collaboration.

TRISKELES FOUNDATION Like the Tides Foundation, the Triskeles Foundation is best suited to individuals who have large DAF asset bases, complex grant and investment needs, or the desire for professional support to develop and implement a robust grant-making and principal asset investment plan. The organization works closely with each of its clients to develop their plan. Once completed, the client is partnered with an outside investment advisor to implement the plan and oversee the DAF going forward. Since both Triskeles and the investment advisor charge fees, this is a particularly expensive approach. Fees can be as high as 1.3% to 1.8% per year.

Take Action

In this chapter, we introduced three ways you can maximize your philanthropy. You can develop a personal giving plan, join a giving circle, or open a DAF. You might even choose to take more than one action. Since each has a different set of steps, we decided to address each option separately. When you know which approach or approaches you'd like to take with your philanthropic dollars, please proceed to that section. And thank you for considering philanthropy as part of your total investment strategy.

Develop a Personal Giving Plan

On our companion website, download the following templates to use while developing your plan:

- Personal giving plan worksheet
- Potential grantee worksheet
- Your personal giving plan

1. Determine main aspects of your plan

Starting with the "Personal Giving Plan Worksheet," determine the main aspects of your plan. Elements include the social and environmental problems you want to address, the geographic locations where you'd like to focus, and the amounts you plan to donate each year. You'll also be considering the frequency of your giving and how you'll measure success.

Use this worksheet to structure your thinking before you start identifying the organizations you want to support. If you aren't sure which issues matter the most to you, give yourself permission to take your time. There's no rush. And there's nothing that says you have to get it right the first time. Reaching a level of certainty about what matters to you is a process. It's totally natural to change your mind as you work through these documents.

2. Identify grantee qualities

Once you've completed the "Personal Giving Plan Worksheet," pull out the "Potential Grantee Worksheet." Start by thinking about the qualities you want your grantees to embody. Do you value transparency? Strong financials? Gender and racial diversity in the leadership or throughout the organization? Regular updates and reporting on progress? Make your list, prioritize the top five qualities, and add them to your worksheet.

3. Create your short list

Now it's time to do your research. If you already have some grantees in mind, skip to step 5. However, if you aren't sure which organizations to support or you'd like to add to your list, go online and research large and small nonprofits that work on the problems you want to address in the locations you'd like to focus on. You might consider inviting some friends, family members, or giving circles to help you conduct research and narrow your list.

Create a short list of the top three to five organizations that piqued your interest and enter them in the spreadsheet provided in the "Potential Grantee Worksheet."

4. Dig deeper into prospects

Deepen your understanding of the organizations on your short list by researching their websites, looking for more information about teams, services, partners, and impact. As you go through this process, use your worksheet to enter a rating for each organization.

Further validate your short list by searching through the online databases of GuideStar, Charity Navigator, and Give.org. These websites and others like them provide detailed information and ratings on thousands of nonprofit organizations. They also offer reams of useful information about charitable giving.

Check to see whether the charities that interest you are listed on these sites. The amount of information presented will differ on a charity-by-charity basis, but these are wonderful resources, nonetheless. Particularly useful, when available, are financials and links to tax returns, as these documents can show the percentage of assets used for overhead, how much money is sitting unused, and the charity's annual spend rate.

At the end of this process, you should have a good idea about which organizations you want to support. If all of your choices fell off your list as a result of the due diligence you just performed, return to step 3.

5. Complete your personal giving plan

Once you feel good about the work you completed in both of your worksheets, summarize the results in the document titled "Your Personal Giving Plan." Then write your checks or wire money.

After you've made your donations, refer back to your plan once or twice a year to ensure it still meets your needs and priorities. Also, make sure that you're seeing progress. Don't donate blindly year after year without checking on the organization's impact and results at least once a year.

Join a Giving Circle

There are basically three approaches you can take to getting involved with a giving circle. You can find an existing circle that aligns with your values, engage with a network of giving circles, or start your own circle. Here's how.

1. Find an existing circle that aligns with your values

You can look for a giving circle in your local community by conducting an online search for "Women's Giving Circle" and the name of your town or county. If you choose this route, be sure you know what the group stands for before you join, as some giving circles can have very targeted goals. I found this out the hard way when I paid $5,000 to join a giving circle only to discover the group focused exclusively on a set of social issues that were a low priority for me.

2. Engage with an existing network

There are over a dozen giving circle networks that support hundreds of local circles. Through them, you can find an existing circle accepting new members or learn about the giving circle model in general and how you can get involved. Links to some of the leading women-focused giving circle networks are available on our companion website.

3. Start your own circle

Connecting with a giving circle network is the easiest way to start a new circle and receive support. At *activateyourmoney.net*, you'll find links to networks that can guide you through the process of starting your own circle. Even if you don't want to be part of these networks, you can still access and download their materials free of charge.

Open a Donor-Advised Fund

On our companion website, you'll also find a document with the questions to ask DAF providers plus a spreadsheet to record your findings. Download both of these forms.

1. Find a new DAF provider

To simplify the process, first identify the category or categories of DAFs that resonate with you. Are you more inspired by having your DAF with an Impact First provider, Affinity Group Foundation, Community Foundation, or National Charity?

- If you want to invest your DAF assets with an Impact First provider, contact one of the organizations mentioned in this chapter or do additional research on this type of DAF.
- Perhaps you have a specific charitable organization that you want to support, like your university, a religious organization, or an emergency relief organization. If so, call them to see if they offer a DAF or if they are aware of other organizations with a similar mission that may have a DAF.
- Finding a Community Foundation in your area just requires a little research. You can simply conduct an online search for "Community Foundation" followed by the name of your city or town, and you're likely to get at least one hit. Another option is to use the Community Foundation Locator on the Council of Foundations website.[9]
- If a National Charity is your preference, ask your financial custodian if they offer a DAF. Many do.

2. Work with your existing provider

If your DAF provider doesn't offer values-aligned options and you want more flexibility, a good place to start is encouraging them to make more options available. If that fails to achieve the results you desire, then it might be time to start looking for another provider.

3. Transition from your current DAF

If you decide you want to move your funds to a more values-aligned provider, you'll need to start by talking to both your new and old DAF providers to understand their requirements for transferring securities.

While it's easy to open your new DAF and transfer any cash assets, moving existing investments may be a bit more complicated. You need to either sell existing securities first and then transfer the funds as cash, or sign transfer agreements for each investment you want to move. These agreements would be between you, your old DAF provider, and your new DAF provider.

Depending on the holdings in your current DAF, selling assets that do not align with your values may be the easiest option. Because you're transferring assets between two charitable organizations, there shouldn't be any tax implications, even if the securities you sell hold gains. Your new DAF provider will undoubtedly help you make these decisions.

Endnotes

1. https://www.charitynavigator.org/index.cfm?bay=content.view&cpid=42.
2. Lily Family School of Philanthropy Article by Andy Ware, July 12, 2018. https://blog.philanthropy.iupui.edu/2018/07/12/fewer-americans-are-giving-money-to-charity-but-total-donations-are-at-record-levels-anyway/ and https://www.nptrust.org/philanthropic-resources/charitable-giving-statistics/.
3. Women's Philanthropy Institute. (2015). How and why women give: Current and future directions for research on women's philanthropy. Indianapolis, IN: Indiana University Lilly Family School of Philanthropy.
4. Johnson Center. 11 Trends for Philanthropy for 2019. Dorothy A. Johnson Center for Philanthropy at Grand Valley State University. 2019.
5. Bearman, J., Carboni, J., Eikenberry, A., and Franklin, J. (2017). The landscape of giving Circles/collective giving groups in the US, 2016. Indianapolis, IN: Women's Philanthropy Institute at the Indiana University Lilly Family School of Philanthropy and the Charles Stewart Mott Foundation.
6. Bearman, J., Carboni, J., Eikenberry, A., and Franklin, J. (2017). The landscape of giving Circles/collective giving groups in the US, 2016. Indianapolis, IN: Women's Philanthropy Institute at the Indiana University Lilly Family School of Philanthropy and the Charles Stewart Mott Foundation.
7. https://impact100council.org/.
8. https://www.fidelitycharitable.org/tools/securities-donation-calculator.html.
9. https://www.cof.org/community-foundation-locator.

Building a Community of Support

You may find that you are more successful as an investor when you have a community of support around you. Many of the contributors to this book have found that investing is a lot more fun in the company of other women with whom you can learn, share stories, and, in some cases, even co-invest.

Part 3 will show you how you can work with financial advisors, friends, and employers to strengthen your investing muscles. We love the idea of shifting discussions of money from being taboo to something that empowers you and builds your confidence. And that can happen as you build trust with family, friends, and select advisors.

The first chapter in this part of the book describes different categories of financial advisors, the services each provides, the fees they charge, and the level of support investors should expect from them. You will be guided to resources that can help you find a values-aligned advisor. Since many Americans invest through retirement accounts, we have also dedicated a chapter to this subject. It will help you understand how you can direct the assets in your retirement plans into values-aligned investment options. We close Part 3, and the book, with information about how you can join an existing investment club—or start one of your own. Several of the contributors in *Activate Your Money* have benefited from these communities.

CHAPTER 12

Professional Support
Find Values-Aligned Financial Advisors

A key step in growing your money and aligning it with your values is finding the right support. A great financial advisor can serve as a trusted educator, thought partner, and valued confidant. Selecting an advisor who can meet you where you are—at your level of knowledge, confidence, and wealth—is an important choice. An advisor who is tuned into your needs will be able to integrate your hopes, fears, and life goals into a financial plan and investment strategy that will give you peace of mind. They'll also help you find ways to invest your values across your entire portfolio.

A good advisor should be able to build your confidence and make you more comfortable with risk. They should help you get to the point where you trust that you're financially stable and on the road to financial fulfillment. Wouldn't it be great to be in a position where you knew that in your bones? You should be able to count on your advisor to be transparent, respond fully to your questions, and provide you with regular updates on both the financial and impact aspects of your portfolio.

You have the right to believe that you and your money are being well cared for by your financial advisor. You also have the right to feel empowered by them and to enjoy working with them. You shouldn't settle for less.

When Should You Hire a Financial Advisor?

The point at which you move your assets into greater alignment with your values is a perfect time to reevaluate an existing relationship or to consider hiring a new values-aligned investment advisor. For example, you may want to consider hiring a financial advisor when:

- You feel a bit overwhelmed and could use some help getting started with a financial plan, asset allocation strategy, or kick-starting your move to values-alignment;
- You're looking for an informed partner who can point you to interesting investments or perform the diligence required to understand risk/return trade-offs; or
- You don't want to do it yourself and prefer to have someone else make investment decisions and manage your assets for you.

A financial advisor can act as a neutral third party who can place events in perspective for you, whether that's instilling confidence in your plan or helping you manage your emotions during times of uncertainty and instability. You might be surprised at how helpful this can be, particularly in times of market turmoil.

How Much Money Do You Need to Hire a Financial Advisor?

To some degree, this depends on your goals. If you're seeking help with financial planning, you can hire a fee-for-service advisor who can address questions related to budgets, debt reduction, and retirement planning. In this case, there are no minimums. Garrett Planning Network and XY Planning Network are some resources you can explore for these services.

Because they rely on computers rather than human advisors to create and manage portfolios, robo-advisors provide an easy, low-cost entry point for limited services. Several of these platforms offer preselected portfolio options at investment minimums as low as $100 and fees that tend to be in the range of 0.25% to 0.50% of assets.

Investment or brokerage firms such as Vanguard and Fidelity offer their clients limited investment advice free of charge. You can access a higher tier of financial support at some of these firms when you invest at least $50,000 and pay a fee of approximately 0.30%. Advice from these sources, while helpful, may prioritize the firm's financial products and is less likely to include a full range of values-aligned options. I keep some of my money with Vanguard and do appreciate their insight, but I make my own investment decisions, manage the assets myself, and do not pay their advisory fees.

Independent investment advisors that offer a broad array of services tend to have minimums in the range of $100,000 to $500,000 or more. According to a rule of thumb, you should consider hiring a full-service investment advisor if you have over $500,000 in investable assets. You will likely pay a fee of about 1.0% of the total assets being managed for these services for amounts up to $1 million with the potential of a sliding scale thereafter.

What Services Can Financial Advisors Provide?

The term "financial advisor" is a bit of a catch-all phrase that describes individuals who offer a range of services—not all of which will be right for you. Generally, advisors who focus on financial planning can support you with budgeting, risk management, and basic investing. They can also help you prepare for major purchases, such as buying your first home. Investment advisors assist with a broader array of investment services, including asset allocation, investment selection, due diligence, and ongoing portfolio management. Wealth managers go even further by helping you set long-term philanthropic and legacy goals. They can also coordinate or manage a broader team of professionals, such as estate lawyers and tax attorneys. Since there are no hard-and-fast rules, a specific advisor's services may incorporate aspects from any of the generalized categories shown in Table 12.1.

TABLE 12.1 Financial Advisor Service Comparison

Financial Planning	Investment Advice	Wealth Management
■ Budgets and cash flow ■ Debt and risk management ■ Major purchase advice ■ Retirement projections ■ Foundational investment plan	■ Asset allocation strategy ■ Investment due diligence ■ Implements values-aligned strategies ■ Buys and sells securities ■ Rebalances portfolio ■ Provides regular financial and impact reports	■ Support for trusts and wills ■ Philanthropy and legacy planning ■ Collaborates with other professionals (lawyers, CPAs) ■ Tax mitigation strategies

To increase your likelihood of a successful relationship with an advisor, you might want to spend a bit of time thinking about the types of services you want before you start your search. I wish I had done that. Over the course of 10 years, I've had four different impact advisors. While I don't recommend you switch that often, I did learn from the experience and will be sharing some of that with you in this chapter.

You're Hiring an Advisor *and* a Firm

One of the first things I learned in my own journey is that it's not just about the advisor. It's also about their firm. When I decided to shift my money into alignment with my values, I hired my first financial advisor. I selected him specifically because of his reputation as a leading thinker in impact investing. When I signed on with his firm, my new advisor recommended that I sell a significant portion of my stock so we could reinvest my assets with more impact. Super-eager to move in this direction, I did that. Unfortunately, that was a big mistake!

Although my advisor had experience with impact investing, the firm he worked for did not. As it turned out, my advisor had other priorities and did not have the time to work with me as promised. I was passed onto a junior advisor with virtually no impact experience. My advisor kept promising that he would have time for me soon. So my money sat in cash while I waited. After nine months of watching the stock market tick up, I realized his "soon" was never going to happen, so I pulled my money and moved on to my second advisor.

Chances are that at some point in your relationship, your advisor will leave their firm or move into another role. When this happens, your account will most likely be shifted to another advisor. So it's important that you feel comfortable with both the advisor you are selecting and their firm.

Seven Attributes of a Values-Aligned Advisor

When you're deciding to stay with your current advisor or to hire a new one, there are seven attributes that will help you determine whether they—and their firm—have your best interests at heart. These attributes will help you determine if they're committed to values-aligned investing and whether they adhere to an investment philosophy that resonates with you or not. These attributes are as follows.

Attribute 1: Values-Alignment is a Tenet of Their Investment Philosophy

When I was younger, I thought all financial advisors believed pretty much the same thing. I was in my early 30s the first time I talked to a finance expert. Since I didn't have enough money to warrant an advisor of my own, I spoke to my mother's advisor. He met with me, on occasion, as a favor to her. At the time, I pretty much believed whatever he told me.

Since then, I've learned that advisors have their own investment philosophies as well as their own beliefs about asset allocations, preferred investment vehicles, and impact. Recognizing an advisor's point of view and biases is critical in choosing someone who's going to be a good match for you. In fact, I think it's one of the most important elements of a strong advisor-client relationship. A deep commitment to achieve both financial and social return should be a core tenet of an impact advisor's investment approach.

One way to uncover an advisor's philosophy is to gain some understanding of your own. You might want to spend some time examining your own beliefs about investing. For example, are you wary of the stock market, or do you embrace it? Do you have an opinion about the relative value of active versus passive funds? Do you have strong beliefs about specific impacts you want to make with your money? Are you excited by the thought of investing in private deals and other alternatives, or does the idea scare you? And do you want philanthropy to be integrated into your investment landscape?

If you don't know the answers to these questions or have an investment philosophy of your own yet, don't worry. These are questions you can revisit as you learn. They'll become clearer over time. You can use the process of interviewing prospective advisors as an opportunity to listen to different perspectives, gain more knowledge, and further your own views.

Attribute 2: They Are a Fiduciary

Almost half of Americans believe that all financial advisors are legally obligated to act in their client's best interest.[1] However, that isn't true. Different types of advisors have varying levels of obligation to you. Advisors that are fiduciaries have a legal and ethical responsibility to prioritize your interests over their own or their firms'. Regardless of the type of advisor you select, confirm they are a fiduciary.

Registered Investment Advisors (RIAs), one of the most highly regulated types of financial advisors, are bound by law to be fiduciaries. And most, if not all, robo-advisors are registered as RIAs.

Attribute 3: They Don't Receive Commissions

Broker-dealers are another type of financial advisor. Also referred to as brokers or stockbrokers, they can provide investment advice to clients just like RIAs. However, they also promote and sell financial products they receive a commission on. In June 2020, the Securities and Exchange Commission

(SEC) enforced new reforms that require brokers to perform in the best interest of their clients. This new requirement brings brokers closer to the fiduciary role of RIAs. Today, if a broker offers you an investment they receive a commission on, they have to disclose the commission they will be paid as well as any conflict of interest.

An advisor can be both an RIA and a broker-dealer. Before you hire an advisor, ask whether they are affiliated with a broker-dealer or could receive commissions as a result of their relationship with you. If an advisor can receive commissions, spend some time considering why they would be preferable to an advisor who only works on your behalf.

Attribute 4: They Offer the Core and Values-Aligned Financial Services You Want

In addition to their core services, a values-aligned advisor should also be able to discuss the selection criteria or impact lenses they will apply to their investment decisions. They should be able to talk to you about how they'll report on the impact your investments are having and be able to show you sample reports. You should also learn the extent to which they engage in shareholder advocacy as well as what will happen to your proxies.

Attribute 5: They Are Open to a Nondiscretionary Relationship

In a discretionary relationship, you give your advisor the legal ability to buy and sell investments on your behalf without asking you first. In a nondiscretionary relationship, your advisor will suggest investments to you, but you have to approve those recommendations before securities are purchased.

While a nondiscretionary approach provides you with more control, it will take more of your time. It requires you to be more educated about asset allocations, portfolio strategies, and investment options. If you're willing to commit the time, a nondiscretionary relationship can provide a wonderful opportunity for learning, especially if you choose a financial advisor that takes your education seriously and considers it a part of their job. At this point, most of my assets are self-managed or nondiscretionary. However, I have given discretionary power to the manager of a separately managed public equities account I'm invested in because she trades more frequently than I want to be involved and I trust her decisions.

While you may provide discretion to your advisor to buy and sell securities on your behalf, they should not have the ability to withdraw your money from your accounts. So when you are interviewing an advisor, confirm that your money will be held with a third-party custodian, such as Fidelity, Vanguard, or Schwab.

Attribute 6: Their Fees Are Fair and Follow Industry Standards

You should pay either a flat fee for service or a percentage of the assets an advisor is managing on your behalf. Percentage fees tend to be deducted directly from your account and are often on a sliding scale: The higher the investment, the lower the fee. An advisor might charge 1.25% to manage assets of $500,000 or less, then drop to 1.0% for assets of $501,000 or more, dropping again to 0.090% after the first million invested, and so on.

Don't assume the only fees you are paying are the fees you pay your financial advisor. Most likely you'll pay additional fees for any funds, private investments, or other assets your advisor is managing. These fees can be quite low, as is the case of index funds (0.15% or less), or quite high (1.5% or more) in the case of actively managed accounts or private investments. It's good to know all the fees you pay on your investments because what you don't know could hurt your returns.

What Katie Didn't Know Was Sinking Her Returns

My friend Katie was not happy with her investment advisor. She felt he wasn't doing anything for her. Plus, she was losing money. So Katie decided to fire him and take control of her own assets. While that was a good step, she didn't really know what she was doing and called me for help. We got online together and looked at the holdings in her brokerage account. Unbeknownst to Katie, about half her money was invested in non-investment-grade bond funds—one of which had a 3.0% fee. That information went a long way to explaining why Katie was not getting a meaningful return. However, her former advisor probably was. From what we could discern, he was being paid a portion of the 3% fee each year.

Attribute 7: Their Approach to Working with You Is Clear

The last attribute relates to the process an advisor will use to work with you. An advisor should be able to explain how they will develop their relationship with you as well as share a complete roster of their services, including what you can expect in the earlier phases of your engagement as well as what happens over time. When searching for an impact advisor, be sure to get clarity on their approach by asking questions such as:

- How will they start?
- What are the terms of engagement?
- How will your investments be selected?
- What lenses will they use?

- What types of reports will they provide and how often will you receive them?
- Will you get impact reports?
- What can you expect in terms of regular communication?
- Are they involved in shareholder advocacy?

Do You Have a Gender Preference?

Since women tend to have different investment priorities, you might want to consider whether you would prefer to work with a male or female advisor. Research has shown that women are more likely than men to focus on their family's financial goals over absolute investment performance. Many of us would also like to understand the bigger picture, rather than just the technical details. Since we tend to personalize our finances, it can be helpful to talk about our money with someone who understands our perspective and has had similar experiences. As a result, some women feel more comfortable with a female advisor.

Of the four financial advisors I have worked with, two were women. I have enjoyed my relationships with my female advisors and continue to work with women today.

Seven Foundational Questions

These seven attributes can be turned into a set of questions that you can ask any advisor to help you decide if you want to continue working with them or hire them. Since the questions about investment philosophy and relationship style are the most complex, they're last in this list. If you aren't happy with the answers you receive to the earlier questions, you can end the conversation before getting into the meatier topics.

1. Are you a fiduciary?
2. Are you paid through commissions?
3. What services do you offer?
4. Will you have discretionary power over my assets?
5. What are your fees?
6. What is your firm's investment philosophy?
7. How will you work with me?

A Values Advisor Litmus Test

As sustainable investing becomes more mainstream, you'll find that a growing number of financial advisors claim expertise. But when you dig a little, you find that sustainable investing is not central to their business. While these firms may suggest investments in ESG stock funds, their ability to help you with a broad range of impact investments is often limited, as is their deeper knowledge of the field. If an advisor tells you that values-aligned investing is not profitable in most asset classes or just too hard to achieve, keep looking.

An advisor for whom values-aligned investing is essential to their business should be able to speak to you about it in detail—across asset classes. They'll recognize references to industry organizations like B-Corp, US|SIF, Confluence Philanthropy, Toniic, or GIIN—and may even be members of one or more. They should be able to point you to investment opportunities in virtually any asset class. And if they cannot help you directly, they should be able to point you to resources that can. Many will be involved, at some level, in shareholder advocacy. The following seven questions can provide insight into the depth of an advisor's knowledge with values-aligned investing.

A Litmus Test for Values Alignment

1. How long have you been integrating impact into your investment approach?
2. Is your firm a B-Corp or a legal benefit corporation?
3. Are you members of US|SIF, GIIN, Confluence Philanthropy, or any other impact association or membership group?
4. What are examples of investments that you would suggest for the fixed income and public equities portions of my portfolio?
5. Will you have opportunities for me to invest in values-aligned private debt, private equity, or other alternative investments through your firm? What are the usual minimums?
6. Can you explain what your firm does in terms of proxy voting and shareholder advocacy?
7. How will you measure and report on the social impact of my investments?

Finding My Second Values-Aligned Advisor

After leaving my first impact advisor, I went back to the drawing board and interviewed a few advisory firms that specialized in values-aligned investing. This time, I interviewed the head of the firm as well as the person who would be my personal advisor. When I settled on a firm, our philosophies seemed aligned, and I liked some of their ideas about where they would move my money. There was also an opportunity for my stock to be used for shareholder advocacy. And they passed all the basic hurdles: They were fiduciaries, took no commissions, and charged industry standard fees. I hired them. True to their word, my assets were moved into fixed-income and public equity investments that were as socially responsible as possible at the time, and I was getting a solid return. I was happy for a while.

Bring Impact into Your Advisor Relationships

Regardless of where you are in your journey with financial advisors, there are values-aligned options for you. Robo-advisors can be a great low-cost option if you're new to investing, have limited resources, or have a simple asset allocation plan. Investment firms, such as Vanguard and Fidelity, provide another relatively inexpensive way to get advisory support, although they're less likely to offer deep values-aligned assistance. Assuming you already have an advisor, if you really love them, you may be able to work together to bring values alignment into your portfolio. However, if you aren't that happy with your current advisor, you may be ready to move on.

The point at which you shift to an impact-investment strategy can be the perfect time to switch advisors or hire a new one. Whatever your situation, you can explore ways to move forward to a more fulfilling relationship with an investment advisor that will help you grow your wealth and change the world.

Values-Aligned Robo-Advisors

Due to their ease of use and low fees, the appeal of robo-advisors is increasing, particularly among younger generations. As Table 12.2 suggests, these

TABLE 12.2 Robo-Advisors: Are They for You?

Strengths	Weaknesses
■ Low fees and low minimums ■ Investment selection based on information gathered about you and your financial objectives ■ Provide automated portfolio management, including investment selection and rebalancing ■ High levels of transparency and reporting	■ Best for new investors and simple portfolios ■ Investments may be limited to passive stock and bond funds and ETFs ■ Provide basic financial support only and minimum portfolio diversification ■ Limited human engagement and advice

firms have strengths and weaknesses that you should consider to determine if they're right for you.

Some well-known robo-advisors, such as Folio, Betterment, and Wealthsimple, provide values-aligned financial products on their platforms. Newday Impact, OpenInvest, and EarthFolio go even further. As shown in Table 12.3, these robo-advisors were designed with values alignment as a core part of their investment strategies.

TABLE 12.3 100% Values-Aligned Robo-Advisors

Company	Fees and Minimums	Investment Strategy
Newday Impact	$100 minimum; 0.75% annual fee	Certified B-Corp. Investors have a choice of impact themes, including climate action, sustainable agriculture, animal welfare, and fresh water; 5% of revenues donated to nonprofit partners. *Option to invest in portfolios from HIP and Nia Global Solutions*
OpenInvest	$100 minimum; 0.50% annual fee	Public-benefit corporation. Investors have a choice of more than 15 impact themes; you can also invest in individual stocks and use an app to vote your proxies on your phone. *Option to invest in portfolios from HIP*
EarthFolio	$25,000 minimum; 0.50% annual fee	Member of US|SIF. Investors choose among a group of funds that are classified as sustainable or responsible in their prospectus. Provides easy access to financial and impact reports. Managed by Blue Marble Investments, an impact advisory firm that has been around for more than 20 years.

A Female-Focused Robo-Advisor

Ellevest is a very unique investment platform. The platform was built from the ground up by women for women. Their algorithms take women's longer life expectancy, earlier peak annual earnings, and increased time out of the workforce into consideration. Their site also includes an online "magazine" filled with information targeting women's financial concerns and needs. In addition to online portfolio management, which you would expect from any robo-advisor, Ellevest offers financial advice through a digital offering and in-person support from a team of female professionals.

The company was founded in 2014 by Sallie Krawcheck. Once considered the most powerful woman on Wall Street, she recognized the investing industry had traditionally been "by men, for men," and she wanted to change that. With Ellevest, Sallie set out to help women realize that if they are going to achieve financial success, they need to be investing.

The Ellevest platform makes investing easy and possible for as little as $1 per month, so any woman can participate. The site offers women the opportunity to use their money to make an impact on the issues that affect them and their children the most. The company's private wealth philosophy includes getting more money into the hands of, and in support of, women. The female-centric focus and range of services that Ellevest provides makes it a standout choice for women.

Working with Your Current Advisor

Just because you aren't working with your current advisor to integrate values into your investments doesn't mean they aren't prepared to help you or that they aren't willing to learn. If you love your advisor but are now ready to build positive impact into your portfolio, it's worth checking in to see if that's an area where your advisor would be willing to work with you.

You might be pleasantly surprised and find they're ready to help. This happens sometimes because advisors can be reluctant to introduce the topic of impact investing. Instead, they choose to wait until their clients initiate the conversation. If this is what happens to you, congratulations!

Another possibility is that your advisor doesn't know much about values-aligned investing but is willing to learn. In this case, you have a number of options.

As a first step, consider sharing this book with them. You could also introduce them to industry forums, membership organizations, and educational websites that can help them build their expertise.

Your advisor could also partner with impact providers, such as Aperio, C-Note, Ethic, HIP Investors, Nia Capital, Just Invest, and OpenInvest, that have investment products or platforms that your advisor can leverage to access more values-aligned opportunities for you. There are even a few consultants who can work with advisors to help them bring ESG and other impact-oriented financial products to their clients.

Perhaps when you spoke to them, your advisor warned you against investing with your values. Perhaps they said you'd have to give up financial return to achieve positive impact. If that was the case, ask them why they believe that. Question their beliefs to see if there is room for compromise. If you ultimately realize that your advisor can't—or won't—help you become values-aligned, then you may want to consider moving on.

Finding My Third Advisor

There could be a number of reasons you decide to move on from a current advisor. Perhaps you just never clicked with them. Or maybe you aren't seeing a lot of enthusiasm when you mention your values-alignment goals. Or possibly, like me, you've simply outgrown their abilities or interests.

As I gained confidence with investing, I was ready to take more risk and wanted to start investing in private equity and alternatives to diversify my portfolio further and achieve greater impact. I was excited by the possibility of engaging my money in new ways, and I wanted to support some of the amazing female entrepreneurs and positive social change businesses I was hearing about. Unfortunately, my second advisor wasn't engaged in this type of investing and had no plans to move in that direction. If I wanted to pursue investments beyond stocks and bonds, I was going to have to find them myself. Since I didn't have the time or experience to do that, my search began for yet another advisor. To be fair, my second advisor had been the right pick at the time, but I grew, and they didn't. So I needed to move on.

Moving On from an Advisor

Letting anyone you work with go, for whatever reason, is often difficult. The hardest part is preparing ourselves mentally. We can feel uncomfortable, possibly even guilty, when we have to dismiss someone. This is particularly true with longstanding relationships. It's even more challenging if you feel conflicted or unsure of your decision.

I've found that one of the best ways to prepare myself for a difficult conversation is to be extremely clear about why I am making my decision. It helps me to write down my reasons. I include the things that I need, or want, that my current relationship is unable to deliver. I recommit to the goals I set, the decisions that I made, and the reasons I am ready to step away. I used this technique when I realized I needed to fire my old CPA. Gaining clarity made the process so much easier. My old accountant understood—and agreed with—my rationale. As a result, we had a very amicable parting.

Realize in advance that your advisor may counter with arguments about why you shouldn't leave, or they might offer to do better. When that happens, be prepared to stand your ground. Regardless of the feedback you receive, listen respectfully and stick to your decision. Thank your old advisor for their service, let them know what you'll need from them during the transition period, and move on. Be prepared to pay any final management fees to your old advisor, some of whom charge in arrears.

If you're leaving your advisor because they aren't able to help you align your money with your values, please let them know. If advisors start to realize they are losing clients because of their inability to offer values-aligned services, they'll be more motivated to educate themselves about the field and to pressure their firms to support them in offering these services.

Finding a New Values-Aligned Advisor

When you're ready to hire an advisor with deep impact knowledge, look for a firm that has integrated sustainable investing into its investment philosophy from the start. Why settle for less?

There are a growing number of firms that meet this bar. Examples include Abacus Partners, Robascotti & Philipson, Veris Wealth Partners, and Zevin Asset Management, all of which have been providing values-aligned investment services since their founding. Other contributors such as Cornerstone Capital Group, Figure 8 Investment Strategies, Nia Impact Capital, Promethos Capital, Syntrinsic Investment Counsel, and Uplift Investing are newer entrants, but sustainable investing is also core to their models. What's more, all of these firms are either run by women or have women in prominent positions.

Almost every financial advisor who contributed to this book is steeped in impact investing. You can find more information about them on the "Meet Our Guides" tab of our companion website. You can also find values-aligned financial planners and investment advisors in the Financial Services Directory on the US|SIF website.[2] Another resource is the B-Corp directory, which lists companies that have built their commitment to sustainable and equitable business practices into their bylaws. As of this writing, there are almost 70 investment advisors listed as B-Corps.[3] You can search by city and state to find an advisor near you.

A Matchmaking Tool on the Horizon

A curated list of impact investment advisors is also available through ValuesAdvisor, a nonprofit organization that was started by Lisa Renstrom. When she was leading a divestment campaign, Lisa learned that investors who wanted to shift their assets to more aligned investments were unable to do so because their financial advisors expressed skepticism or were not aware of the range of sustainable investments that were available. But she knew something better was possible.

The need and demand for advisors who were both supportive and knowledgeable about values-aligned investing sparked the creation of ValuesAdvisor, a web-based tool that allows investors to search for highly qualified impact advisors. To be included in the ValuesAdvisor platform, advisors must be put forward by a member of a ValuesAdvisor partner and meet the following five criteria:

1. Financial advisory services are a core business of the lead advisor/team.
2. The lead advisor/team has 25% or more of their current assets under management in values-aligned investing. Or the advisor/team shows a dedicated, significant, long-term commitment to the growth of the sustainable field through thought leadership.
3. The lead advisor/team has offered values-aligned investment options for at least three years.
4. The lead advisor/team must reference sustainable investing or values alignment in the description of the lead advisor or firm's website.
5. The lead advisor/team must demonstrate significant knowledge of the sustainable investing field, as determined at the sole discretion of the ValuesAdvisor team.

ValuesAdvisor is maintaining the integrity of their platform by not accepting funding from the impact advisory community. No personal information is required to access the platform, and the site does not save any user data.

Create a Successful Relationship

Once you select an investment advisor, you'll want to build a trust-based relationship that can last for many years. You will lay the foundation of that relationship at your very first meeting and build upon it over time. Success is dependent not only on your advisor, but also on how you show up and communicate your needs and concerns. A trusting relationship requires both parties to be fully engaged.

Your First Meeting with a New Advisor

To be as helpful as possible, your advisor will need to know about your current financial situation, your aspirations, and the challenges you're facing. If your money is comingled with a spouse or partner, it would be a good idea for the two of you to have conversations about your financial aspirations before meeting with your new advisor. It's also a good idea for both of you to be present at any meetings so you can be equally informed, share perspectives, and discuss options.

In addition to your dreams and aspirations, you should also bring financial information with you to your first meeting. The most important pieces of information are your cash flow and an accounting of what you already own. Make this as thorough as possible. A cash flow document should show from where and how much money is coming in and going out each year. If some of your expenses are particularly large, you might want to highlight them.

Even if your advisor will be overseeing only a portion of your assets, it will be helpful for them to have a view of your entire financial picture so they can understand how the portion of your assets they'll be managing fits into your broader financial landscape.

At the end of a successful first meeting, you should understand how your relationship with your new advisor will unfold over the next three to six months as well as the steps your advisor will be taking to bring your investments in alignment with your financial and social goals. You should have discussed a written document that articulates the services your advisor will be providing, how they will be building impact into your portfolio, the reports you receive, and the frequency of meetings you can expect. This is a document you can reference, as needed, going forward.

The First Six Months

Expect to spend a significant amount of time with your advisor as they develop an investment and transition plan that will move your existing assets into a new value-based portfolio. Be sure you allocate enough time to be a reliable and engaged partner. Your advisor won't be able to develop the best plan for you without your input, thoughts, and consent.

You can also use this time to get to know your advisor and deepen your trust. Fostering trust requires an initial investment of time for the advisor and the investor. If you don't put in the time required to prepare and meet with your advisor, then you may not have a high degree of trust around their decisions. Trust is a two-way street that requires active and considered participation from all parties.

Ongoing Relationship

After you and your advisor have established a plan and transitioned your portfolio, you should fall into a pattern of routine engagements that consist of receiving regular financial and impact reports and having regular meetings.

It's very easy, in our busy lives, to let opportunities for regular updates fall to the bottom of the to-do list, particularly if paying attention to your money has traditionally been something you tried to ignore. However, each time you don't open the reports from your advisor, you're missing an opportunity to build your confidence. Every time you ignore a request for a meeting or you don't reach out to your advisor when you have a question, you're bypassing a chance to grow your knowledge. Instead, use these opportunities to learn, build your confidence, and take responsibility for your money.

It can take as little as 15 to 20 minutes to review monthly financial statements, and a bit more if they only come quarterly. Isn't staying abreast of your financial life worth that much time once a month or quarter?

Reading Your Financial and Impact Reports

Although your advisor is there to support and advise you, you have a responsibility to understand the details of your investments, including their financial and social return. In your financial report, be sure you're looking at returns net of fees and that your advisor is showing you how each investment is performing against its benchmark. In your impact report you should be able to see the results your investments are having and be informed of any shareholder advocacy efforts.

Don't be surprised if your advisor refers to the SDGs when they report on your impact. This practice is becoming more commonplace. As an example, Figure 8 Investment Strategies targets six SDGs, including health, reduced inequalities, and climate action. Their impact report articulates what their clients hold in support of each goal and what is changing as a result. Some advisors, such as Veris Wealth Partners, produce impact reports that are publicly available and can be downloaded from the web, while others provide updates through regular communications.

If anything in your reports makes you uncomfortable or you don't understand, ask. Reports are another learning tool and can add to the level of transparency and trust you have with your advisor.

Get in Front of Tax Consequences

Before the end of the year, it's helpful to get an update from your advisor on any dividends and capital gains your portfolio has generated in your taxable accounts. While it's true that tax gains can occur even in the last days of the year and you cannot know exactly what will happen in advance, you can get an indicative estimate in the October/November time frame. This gives you time to implement any tax mitigation strategies, such as accruing losses to offset gains and making philanthropic donations before December 31.

If you're really concerned about the tax implications of your portfolio, you might want to talk to your advisor earlier in the year to set a capital gain limit according to which your advisor can manage your portfolio throughout the year. This way there will be fewer surprises at the end of the year.

The End of My Advisory Story—For Now

Over time, I learned from my earlier mistakes. My third financial advisor worked for a firm that was built on values-aligned investing. When I shifted to them, I was hiring both an advisor and the firm. One of their core strengths is private investing. They do a great job performing due diligence on private debt, private equity, and alternative investments—the services lacking with my second advisor.

About two years after hiring them, my third advisor left the firm and went into a different line of business. Remember when I mentioned this might happen? Since I picked the firm as much as the individual advisor, I wasn't overly concerned when I was assigned to another advisor. As it turns out, I really like her! She's a smart, savvy woman who provides good advice, serves as a thought partner, and can be very helpful when I'm considering new investments.

In addition, I still have assets with Vanguard and call them when I have specific questions about some aspect of investing. Although I do not have a dedicated financial advisor there, I almost always get an informed response to my questions. This provides a second source of information and perspective.

My financial advisor journey has been a circuitous one, but I think I have finally arrived at a point where I feel comfortable and supported. My hope is that this chapter has provided you with enough information that you can reach that state more quickly, regardless of your current situation.

Take Action

Are you ready to own your relationship with your financial advisor? The specific actions you take will depend on your current situation.

1. Reacquaint yourself with your current advisor

If you have an advisor but aren't completely satisfied with them or unsure about key aspects of their investment philosophy, give them a call and ask them the seven foundational questions.

2. Help your current advisor become more values aligned

If you have an advisor you are happy with but would like them to do more for you in terms of impact, take the actions described under "Working with Your Current Advisor."

3. Find a values-aligned advisor

If you are ready to find a new advisor, you can start by doing the research mentioned in "Finding a New Values-Aligned Advisor." Narrow your list to the top three candidates, and then interview them. You can use the questions provided, or if you want a more comprehensive list, download the questionnaire on our companion website. You can modify it in whatever way works for you.

If possible, meet your candidates in person. If that isn't an option, consider meeting them online. There is nothing quite like looking someone in the eyes when you are asking them pointed questions.

When you're ready, hire your new advisor. Bask in the glory of knowing that you've made a huge step toward achieving your financial goals and building a values-aligned portfolio.

4. Move on from your current advisor

If you're ready to move on from your existing advisor, find a new values-aligned financial advisor first. Then, when you're ready, return to the steps in the "Moving On from an Advisor" section.

5. Set yourself and your advisor up for success

Whether you stay with a current advisor or decide to find a new one, try to follow the advice in the "Create a Successful Relationship" section.

Endnotes

1. https://view.ceros.com/personal-capital/2019-financial-trust-survey-mobile/p/1.
2. https://www.ussif.org/AF_MemberDirectory.asp.
3. https://bcorporation.net/directory.

CHAPTER 13

Retirement Accounts
Build Values into IRAs and Employer Plans

The belief that we can depend solely on Social Security or a pension plan in our retirement is beginning to sound a bit unrealistic, particularly to younger generations. Whether we like it or not, it's on us to plan and save for our retirement. And we can't start too soon.

Even though we know that we should, many people are not saving enough for their retirement. When I was young, I certainly didn't heed the recommendation of advisors who suggested we maximize our retirement contributions from an early age. At that time, I didn't understand my options. Over the years, I have contributed to traditional IRAs, SEP IRAs, Roth IRAs, 401(k)s, and 403(b)s.

If I'd been smarter from the beginning, I probably would have invested in retirement accounts earlier. And if they'd been available, I would have probably used Roth IRAs during my younger years when my income was relatively low. When they were introduced in 1997, I shifted some of my IRA assets to a Roth, but I really didn't know what I was doing, and there was no one to help me. In hindsight, if I'd been more on top of my money then, I probably would have transferred even more assets.

Whenever I had an employer that was willing to add their money to my 401(k) contributions, I tried to invest enough to receive the entire match. In my view, that was free money that I could grow over time. I also saved money in nonretirement accounts, so I could have capital available as a safety net and to grow my wealth by purchasing real estate and other assets that I did not believe I could access with the funds in my retirement accounts.

In this chapter we're going to look at retirement plans—those you set up yourself as well as those offered by employers. We'll discuss your options and help you figure out how to move assets in your retirement accounts into alignment with your values. Your choices will vary depending on whether you're self-employed, a contractor, or have an employer-sponsored retirement plan. You might be surprised to learn that you have more flexibility than you thought was possible.

Making the Most of Your Retirement Accounts

Even though many of us recognize the power of saving regularly, investing, and taking advantage of compound growth, retirement accounts are still underutilized in this country. This is particularly important for women, because we earn less, save less for retirement, and invest less aggressively than men. As a result, we have significantly smaller retirement balances—about 30% less.[1] To complicate matters, our money needs to last longer, since we outlive men by seven years on average.

Although 59% of Americans have access to an employer-sponsored retirement account, only 32% invest in one.[2] Obstacles—such as debt, other savings priorities, or a lack of confidence in investing—can discourage participation. Another obstacle is lack of will, which I experienced in my own youth and am now seeing in some of the younger women around me. These obstacles have an impact. Friends and acquaintances my age are beginning to realize they may not have enough saved and invested to live out their final years the way they'd expected. That's not the place you want to find yourself in your 50s or 60s.

Chances are you've heard about traditional IRAs, Roth IRAs, and 401(k)s. But you may not be aware there are several more options, particularly if you're self-employed or running your own business. There are also two relatively unknown retirement accounts that provide incredible flexibility in terms of how you can invest your money. These accounts—SDIRAs and Solo 401(k)s—can be appealing to investors who are interested in pushing the boundaries of what is possible.

Retirement Account Models

At a high level, there are basically two retirement account models: pre-tax and post-tax, the primary difference being when funds entering and exiting the accounts are taxed.

Pre-Tax and Post-Tax Retirement Accounts

Money placed into a pre-tax retirement account is not taxed in the year your contribution is made. The funds grow tax-free and are taxed at the time you withdraw them, hopefully after the age of 59½. These accounts can offer advantages when you want to reduce your taxable income.

Money invested in a post-tax retirement account has already been taxed. From the time your money enters this type of account, both the principal and your gains can grow, and neither are taxed again—even when the funds are withdrawn after retirement. These accounts can be beneficial when you have a long time horizon for capital growth or if you believe your tax-rate will be higher at retirement.

The decision to invest with pre- or post-tax money depends on your age, your earning potential now and in the future, as well as whether you think the tax rate will be higher or lower when you retire. The correct choice is far from clear and can change over time. While there's no crystal ball to predict your particular situation, there are tools and a lot of information online to help you understand the pros and cons of your choices. It can also be helpful to talk to an accountant or other financial professional.

Types of Retirement Accounts

There are several commonly recognized types of retirement accounts: traditional IRAs, Roth IRAs, and employer-sponsored plans, which include 401(k), 403(b), and 457 accounts. There are also lesser-known plans such as SEP IRAs, Simple IRAs, SDIRAs, and Solo 401(k)s. The differences between them in terms of eligibility, maximum contributions, tax consequences, and age of withdrawal are summarized in Table 13.1. The data in the table is offered as guidance only. Please consult with your accountant or other professional advisors for the most current information as well as how it applies to your situation.

Traditional IRAs and Roth IRAs are the most well-known individual retirement accounts. Traditional IRAs are pre-tax accounts while Roth IRAs are post-tax. Once established, you can make contributions to these accounts every year up to the maximum allowed by law. Since maximums often change annually, you'll need to stay current on those numbers.

There are also additional amounts you can save if you're over 50 years old. For example, in 2020, someone 50 or older could contribute up to $7,000 to their IRA or Roth IRA, as opposed to the $6,000 limit for younger people.

TABLE 13.1 Retirement Account Summary

Individual Retirement Accounts		Employer-Sponsored Accounts	
Type	**Characteristics**	**Type**	**Characteristics**
IRA	■ Pre-tax contribution, taxed at withdrawal ■ $6,000 annual contribution, +$1,000 if >50 years old ■ At age 72, must start withdrawing	**401(k), 403(b), and 457 Plans**	■ Pre- and post-tax options ■ $19,500 annual contribution ■ +$6,500 if >50 years ■ At age 72, must start withdrawing ■ Roll-over options available
Roth IRA	■ Post-tax contribution, not taxed at withdrawal ■ $6,000 annual contribution, +$1,000 if >50 years old ■ Fully tax-free after 59 ½ and 5 year waiting period	**SEP IRA**	■ Pre-tax contribution, taxed at withdrawal ■ Lesser of $57,000 or 25% of compensation ■ At age 72, must start withdrawing
SDIRA	■ Pre-tax contribution ■ $6,000 annual contribution, ■ +$1,000 if >50 years old ■ At age 72, must start withdrawing	**Simple IRA**	■ Pre-tax contribution, taxed at withdrawal ■ $13,500 annual contribution ■ +$3,000 if > 50 years old ■ At age 72, must start withdrawing
		Solo 401(k)	■ Pre- and post-tax options ■ Lesser of $57,000 or 25% of compensation ■ At age 72, must start withdrawing

Employer-sponsored retirement accounts are often available in both pre-tax and post-tax forms; 401(k)s are provided by private companies, while nonprofit organizations and government agencies might offer 403(b)s or 457s. Since these plans are often quite similar, for simplicity's sake, we'll refer to all of these options as 401(k)s for the remainder of the chapter.

In any given year, you can invest in your employer's plan as well as a traditional IRA or Roth IRA, as long as you do not exceed the maximums.

A Simplified Employee Pension, or SEP IRA, is a less-discussed, though quite important, option. It's a retirement plan offered by employers for the benefit of their employees or themselves. A SEP IRA can be extremely valuable for the self-employed because the maximum contribution is multiple times higher than what is allowed through a traditional IRA or a Roth IRA. When you contribute as an employee and an employer, you can save almost 10 times more through a SEP IRA.

Simple IRAs, which stands for Savings Incentive Match Plan for Employees Individual Retirement Account, are retirement plans for businesses with fewer than 100 employees. Those who are self-employed or sole proprietors can also set up a Simple IRA. In these cases, you can contribute as an employee and an employer.

Still relatively unknown, self-directed IRAs (SDIRAs) and Solo 401(k)s are unique in the way they are set up and managed as well as in terms of the benefits they offer. These accounts require more effort and oversight than other retirement options, and there are serious consequences if you break the rules—even if you do so inadvertently. The investment flexibility you have with these accounts, though, is fantastic. With them, you can use your retirement funds to invest in assets such as private debt, private equity, real estate, and other alternatives that aren't available through traditional retirement accounts. Since these accounts come with unique upside and downside potential, they're best suited for investors who are willing to take on the additional responsibility and risks associated with the accounts and the alternative investments they hold.

Rolling Over Retirement Accounts

When you leave a job, you have several options when it comes to rolling over your retirement account. Sometimes, you can leave your 401(k) where it is, or you can transfer it to a new employer or to a traditional IRA. This is known as a rollover, and it allows you to move your funds from one type of retirement account to another with no tax consequences. As a values-aligned investor, you may want to roll 401(k) assets into an individual retirement account to access a broader range of impact investments. You can also use a rollover to combine certain types of retirement accounts.

Bringing Values-Aligned Investments into Your Retirement Accounts

You can set up a traditional IRA, Roth IRA, and SEP IRA account through robo-advisors and investment firms such as Fidelity, Schwab, and Vanguard. Once established, you can invest your money in any financial product your custodian has available on its trading platform. The asset classes that are usually available are cash, fixed income, and public equity. Most investment firms will offer you a broad range of values-aligned options within these categories. Robo-advisors may have a more limited pool of choices, so if you can't find the investments you want on the platform you are using, you might consider moving your assets to another firm.

While you should have significant values-aligned options in your individual retirement accounts, you'll likely be much more limited within your 401(k) accounts—many of which have no values-aligned options at all. We'll discuss how you can work with your employer to provide more choices in those accounts later in this chapter.

Self-Directed IRAs and Solo 401(k)s

If you want to invest some of the money in your individual accounts in private debt, private equity, or other alternatives, you won't be able to do so through most retirement accounts. However, you do have this flexibility through self-directed IRAs (SDIRAs) and Solo 401(k)s. These options are unfamiliar to most people. In fact, only 4% of investors in this country have self-directed IRAs.[3] These accounts will be most attractive to investors who want significant control over their retirement assets and who want to use these funds to invest in nontraditional opportunities. Before moving forward with them, it's best to learn more about them and to speak with other investors who have direct experience with these accounts.

An SDIRA can be opened by anyone eligible for a traditional IRA or Roth IRA. Although the contribution limits and withdrawal requirements are similar to what you'd find with traditional IRAs, SDIRAs are quite different in many other ways.

Solo 401(k)s are "one-participant" 401(k)s and were designed for business owners with no employees. According to the IRS, you cannot contribute to a Solo 401(k) if you have full-time employees. Since nearly 40% of working adults get some of their income from self-employment jobs, Solo 401(k)s are a viable option for many people.[4] You even can open a Solo 401(k) if you have another job, the catch being only your self-employment income can be used in determining your Solo 401(k) contribution amounts.

The Most Important Thing to Know about SDIRAs and Solo 401(k)s

Money in SDIRAs and Solo 401(k)s can be held in a wide range of alternative investments and have piqued the interest of investors—even non-accredited investors—who want to use their retirement accounts in this way. However, and this is very important, there are a number of restrictions on these accounts, including a few types of investments that are absolutely prohibited. SDIRAs and Solo 401(k)s cannot invest in:

- Collectibles, such as art, wine, and coins;
- Life insurance;
- Stock in an S Corporation; or
- Prohibited transactions with disqualified persons.

The most complicated ban is prohibited transactions with disqualified persons. Disqualified persons include members of your family. People like your spouse, parents, grandparents, children, children's spouses, and other relatives. This prohibition is intended to keep you from investing retirement assets in anything that would directly benefit you or a disqualified person. For example, suppose you bought a cabin in the mountains that you rent out for most of the year. That's fine. But if once in a while you or a family member spends a day or two enjoying the cabin, that would be prohibited, because you're obtaining a direct benefit from the investment.

Not adhering to these rules can be extremely costly since there are financial repercussions for not abiding by the above restrictions. If the IRS determines one of these accounts includes a prohibited investment, the account could lose its tax-protected status, and you could end up paying fees that consume the majority of your holdings.

Setting Up and Managing an SDIRA

Unlike any other IRAs, you cannot simply set up an SDIRA with an investment firm and manage the account on your own. You have to work with a qualified provider that can administer your account. However, it's important to understand that these providers cannot offer you any investment advice.

SDIRA Provider Attributes

- Free tutorials;
- Responsive, knowledgeable customer support team;
- Competitive fee structure (types and amounts);
- Investments available;
- Referrals.

Should you pursue an SDIRA, look for a reliable, reputable, and experienced provider. Many offer free in-person and online tutorials. Taking advantage of these educational opportunities is one way to screen providers before opening a SDIRA. Another thing you want to do is test their customer service to see if they respond quickly and have knowledgeable, professional staff. Be sure to compare fees, too. Most providers charge several fees: one to set up your account, another for annual account maintenance, and others for each transaction they manage on your behalf. Providers may also charge extra for financial transactions they don't feel qualified to administer. Some have limited types of assets available on their platform, which will restrict what you can invest in through them. It might be helpful to know the kind of investments you want to make with your SDIRA before talking to prospective providers. Other SDIRA account holders can provide insight and recommendations. Fortunately, there are communities of investors using SDIRAs and Solo 401(k)s that are happy to help.

Setting Up and Managing a Solo 401(k)

Unlike an SDIRA, Solo 401(k)s don't require a provider. Once established, they can be completely self-managed. Theoretically, you should be able to open a Solo 401(k) at any bank, credit union, or investment firm. However, many banks are unfamiliar with this form of retirement account, which means you could run into a few brick walls trying to find an informed financial institution. The resources on our companion website can help you find financial institutions that are known to offer this support.

To establish your Solo 401(k), you'll need an investment plan that is approved by the IRS. This sounds more onerous than it is. There are books that can guide you through the process. And there are companies specializing in Solo 401(k)s that can help you create your plan. If the funds in your Solo 401(k) exceed $250,000, you'll also have to fill out an annual report for the IRS. Although I haven't done this, I have been told this form is relatively straightforward and easy to complete.

If you are interested in learning more about SDIRAs or Solo 401(k)s, visit TheNextEgg.org, a community of investors who are helping each other use SDIRAs and Solo 401(k)s to invest in their local communities. The book *Put Your Money Where Your Life Is: How to Invest Locally Using Self-Directed IRAs and Solo 401(k)s* provides additional information.

Activating Your Employer Accounts

If you use an IRA, SEP IRA, Roth IRA, SDIRA, or Solo 401(k), you have a lot of options to ensure your retirement assets align with your values. This is most likely not the case if you have an employer-sponsored 401(k), 403(b), or 457.

The majority of 401(k) plans require you to choose your preferred investments from a limited list of financial products. The average plan provides 8 to 12 options that include cash, fixed income, and public equities. With the growing popularity of values-aligned investing, you might expect that many 401(k) plans would include values-aligned choices. Unfortunately, only a small percentage do, creating a disconnect between what's available and what people want.

The World Business Council for Sustainable Development (WBCSD) reports that only 8.4% of 401(k) plan providers include socially responsible funds.[5] This research was corroborated when Vanguard studied 1,900 plans they keep records for. Their result was almost identical, with only 9% of retirement plans including values-aligned options.[6]

This is the case even though most people want their 401(k) plans to include values-aligned options. A recent study showed that 61% of respondents say they would increase their 401(k) contributions if socially responsible options were available, and 66% who do not participate in their employer-sponsored plans say they'd be more likely to do so if they knew their money was supporting the things they care about.[7]

Values-Alignment Drives 401(k) Investments

Stok, a small real estate firm dedicated to regenerative and sustainable buildings, experienced a remarkable uptake of their 401(k) plan when they incorporated values-aligned investment options. Before this shift, only 14% of employees were taking advantage of the plan. When the company researched the problem, they found their employees weren't interested in investing in business models that were "destroying the future." In partnership with HIP Investor, Stok replaced some of its existing 401(k) investment options with funds that had better ESG scores and historically higher financial performance than the funds they replaced. Within two years, 95% of employees were invested in Stok's 401(k) plan. Given that Stok is a certified B Corporation, the new plan aligns with Stok's business mission and purpose.

Source: https://www.asyousow.org/blog/2017/11/27/why-are-401k-plans-not-aligned-with-sustainability-goals.

What's the Problem?

The administrators of retirement accounts cite several reasons they aren't incorporating ESG or other values-aligned investment approaches in the funds they manage. The most pervasive arguments are centered on the belief that employees don't care, values-aligned investments lose money, and they have a fiduciary responsibility to maximize returns, which precludes them from including values-aligned options.

If you reached this point in the book, then you know the first two claims are not really valid. The vast majority of women and millennials *do* want to invest with their values, and they want the option to do so with the assets in their retirement funds. Furthermore, there's a growing body of research showing that values-aligned investments can perform as well—if not better than—similar nonaligned options. This is turning out to be true even during the worst economic downturn since the 2008 financial crisis.

The third point about fiduciary responsibility warrants further discussion. Anyone making financial decisions on your behalf should be bound to prioritize your interests. In the US, the Department of Labor (DoL) sets the rules that govern the fiduciary requirements of 401(k) administrators. Due in part to political reasons, the DoL's guidance related to ESG has been inconsistent. It changes somewhat frequently, which has understandably led to confusion among administrators. As of this writing, the rules are under consideration yet again, and it's unknown whether the suggested changes will be implemented.

Advocating for Change Where You Work

The good news is that if you want to work with your employer to build more values-aligned options into your retirement fund, you won't be alone. Others have come before you. There are also resources and values-aligned 401(k) experts who can provide assistance along the way. The ease with which you can create change will depend, in part, on the size of your company. Small firms tend to be more agile and willing to listen to their employees, whereas change tends to happen more slowly in large companies, due to their size and complexity.

Before you start down this path, recognize that reaching your goal will take time—even in a small company. Adding new funds to an existing 401(k) plan is a formal process and can take up to a year to complete, depending on the complexity of the plan. To complicate matters, large companies often have investment committees that meet infrequently. This limits your opportunities to get their attention. In addition, these committees often engage advisory firms to select and manage 401(k) investments, which adds another layer to the decision-making process. However, if you're persistent and bring others along, you might succeed.

These are six well-trodden steps you can follow to bring values-aligned investment options to your employer's 401(k) plan:

1. Figure out where you stand and identify gaps;
2. Build a coalition;
3. Familiarize yourself with key concepts;
4. Be prepared to address potential concerns;
5. Build your case; and
6. Find another administrator.

Step 1: Figure Out Where You Stand and Identify Gaps

Before you begin advocating for change, it's helpful to understand your current situation and to identify the gaps between where you are now and where you want to be. Thus, your first step is identifying the investment options in your company's retirement plan now. A full list of the funds in your 401(k) should be available to you as a plan participant. If you cannot easily find them on your company's portal, talk to the person in your company who oversees your 401(k). The best place to start in a smaller enterprise is with the CEO or CFO, while the human resources department might be more appropriate in a larger corporation.

Once you have the list, look up each fund using the tools described in Chapters 6 and 8. This will tell you how funds in your 401(k) plan align with your values. A great outcome of this exercise is that you're pleasantly surprised and discover there are already values-aligned options available to you that you weren't even aware of. Congratulations! Now you can spread the word.

If your company doesn't offer the options you're seeking, a next step would be to ask the individuals managing the 401(k) if they're considering such a change. You may be surprised to find there are discussions already underway. If that's the case, you could ask if you could support the effort— perhaps through employee education and awareness campaigns.

A Tale of Corporate Advocacy

For over five years, Serena has been interested in climate change because she's concerned about the state of the world that she's leaving to her children. Serena doesn't want them to have to worry about the livability of the planet. So when she realized her employer's 401(k) didn't offer a fossil-free investment option, she decided to do something about it.

Around the time Serena started her advocacy effort, her company's retirement plan shifted to include a socially responsible Vanguard fund. Although this product was better than many in terms of its carbon footprint, it wasn't fossil-free. Serena would like her company to do better. She wants them to offer a completely fossil-free option. Since so many employees enjoy the simplicity of target-date funds, she would also like them to use their corporate power to incentivize Vanguard to develop a fossil-free fund of this type.

Serena is currently working with her benefits department to gather data about the number of employees taking advantage of the socially responsible option offered by her company. She's also educating her colleagues about their opportunity to invest with their values and is identifying collaborators. Serena is finding that women and millennials are most aligned with her objectives and are the most enthusiastic about helping her on this journey. Given that her employer is a large corporation with over 20,000 employees, it's not surprising that effecting change has been a slow process, as Serena readily admits. But like many committed women, she's not giving up.

As Serena learns more about investing through her advocacy, she's also taking those lessons back not only to her children but also to her mom. As a result, she's building financial confidence across generations—a nice side benefit of her efforts.

Step 2: Build a Coalition

Working with your company to bring values alignment into your 401(k) takes time and effort. So it's important to build a coalition around you that can share the work and heighten your influence. Your coalition can include employees from across the company, department heads or other high-ranking staff, and external experts.

The more people you can bring to your cause, the better, as you'll garner more attention from key decision-makers. The information you gather through your research and from initial internal discussions can be helpful tools in your recruitment campaign. If you're comfortable casting a wide net, consider leveraging your company intranet, newsletters, or social media.

Once your group begins to form, work together to articulate your goals and strategy. The more ownership all the participants have in the process, the more power you'll have as a group.

Step 3: Familiarize Yourselves with Key Concepts

As a result of reading this book, you've had a significant education in values-aligned investing. In fact, you probably now know more about this subject than most people. To help the members of your group, you can share some of what you have learned.

The *Responsible Retirement Plan Toolkit* developed by the WBCSD may also be helpful. You can access the toolkit on our companion website. This two-part guide was designed for plan administrators. It addresses common misconceptions related to values-aligned investing and highlights methods that can be used to integrate these options into 401(k)s. It also describes types of retirement plans, explores governance structures, and discusses fiduciary duties.

If you and your team review these materials together, you'll not only deepen your understanding of the issues, you'll also gain perspective on the challenges your employer and plan administrators may face as they consider your request. Try not to underestimate the level of responsibility these individuals feel as guardians of your money. Instead, recognize how hard they probably work to make decisions they believe will benefit you. If you can approach them from the perspective of understanding and openness, your dialogues can be more successful. You might even find they're sympathetic to your cause.

When you feel adequately prepared, schedule an initial meeting with those in your company who are responsible for your 401(k) plan. During the meeting, share your research, express your views, ask questions, and assess their level of receptivity.

Step 4: Be Prepared to Address Potential Concerns

Before meeting with your plan administrators or company executives, be prepared to address issues that might arise. Some of the most common include:

- **Our employees don't really care about this issue**. By pulling together your colleagues and other supporters into a coalition, you've already begun to address this issue. You can also present research that shows participation increases in 401(k)s that offer values-aligned options.
- **Sustainable funds underperform**. This issue has been addressed numerous times in this book. Feel free to pull whatever research and studies you need from the chapters in this book and the content on our companion website to support your claim.
- **There aren't enough viable values-aligned alternatives**. Many administrators will only consider funds that have a three- to five-year track record and at least $150 million of assets under management. Fortunately, there are a number of values-aligned funds that have long competitive records and low fees.
- **There is regulatory uncertainty about our fiduciary responsibility**. Check for links to the current status of this issue at *activateyourmoney.net*.

Step 5: Build Your Case

Are the plan administrators ready to work with you, or do you need to build a case to convince them? Once you know where you stand, you and your team can determine next steps. Your options include:

- Finding responses to the administrator's questions and concerns;
- Emphasizing that your request is about creating options, which means not taking anything away but rather adding choice and letting employees make their own decisions; suggest they add new investments, rather than replace what is already offered;
- Starting small with one US large-cap public equities fund, the type of ESG fund that has the longest track record;
- Demonstrating that other companies of your employer's size have successfully integrated values-aligned options into their 401(k) plans; and
- Contacting values-aligned 401(k) firms to help you build your case. Members of their staff may even be willing to join you at a subsequent meeting as subject matter experts.

Step 6: Find Another Administrator

You might find yourself in a situation where the management team at your company is fully onboard and supportive of your goals, but your plan administrator is not. If this is the case, it may be time to find another administrator.

WHO CAN HELP   In most cases, your company will be working with a retirement plan provider. Some of the biggest are recognized names in the financial industry: Schwab, Fidelity, and Vanguard. Others specialize in working with small and mid-sized companies, and some have a focus on sustainable investing. There are also retirement plan advisors who can help you and your employer create and execute a values-aligned 401(k).

Green Retirement has over 15 years of experience working with companies of all sizes to integrate values-aligned investments into their retirement plans. Timothy Yee, the company's cofounder, strongly advises interested employees to find a companion within their company. If the firm's CEO is committed to this change, as in the case of Stok, a new plan can be in place in less than two months.

Impact Retirement, a relatively new player in the market, has developed a comprehensive values-aligned strategy that can be easily integrated into many employers' existing retirement plans. The company grew out of Mike Grimm's more than 28 years of experience working within the pension and retirement plan industry. He knew that most 401(k)s include the target-risk and target-date funds that employees desire. Since values-aligned alternatives for these types of funds are rarely offered as an employee option, Impact Retirement created a solution that makes it possible to add these choices into existing employer plans with limited effort and relatively low cost.

HIP Investor is another company that works with 401(k) plan sponsors, companies, and employees to help integrate values-aligned options into retirement plans.

These firms are interested in helping you and your employer create change. If you're serious about integrating more values-aligned options into your 401(k), you can find them online and reach out directly for advice and support.

What if You Hit a Brick Wall?

If your employer is not immediately receptive, don't give up. Try to understand their decision-making process, find out who needs to be involved, and ask when it would be convenient for you to raise the issue again. You can also offer to educate employees by sharing the information you've learned so far.

If you make no headway at all, or the idea of trying to shift your company is just too daunting, then you can choose to contribute enough to your 401(k) to get your employer's match and invest the rest in a traditional IRA, Roth IRA, or SDIRA. You could also choose to invest in a Solo 401(k), if you are eligible.

A Range of Options

Whether you're a part-time or full-time worker, self-employed or working for someone else, you have a range of options when it comes to saving money in tax-deferred or tax-free retirement accounts. The path you choose will depend on your particular circumstances. The following points can help guide your choices:

- A key decision will be whether you want to invest through an IRA or Roth IRA model, in other words, using pre- or post-tax dollars. Our companion website provides links to websites that can guide you through this decision point.
- Should you be fortunate enough to have an employer that offers a match through your 401(k), consider taking advantage of it. After all,

this is akin to free money. Don't forget you can invest in an IRA or Roth IRA, even if you have a 401(k). However, once your income reaches certain limits, your contributions to a traditional IRA will not be tax-deferred and contributions to a Roth IRA will be disallowed.

- Since traditional IRAs, SEP IRAs, and Roth IRAs are easier to set up and manage, they're probably better tools if you plan to invest your tax-deferred assets into money market funds, fixed income, and public equities.
- A SEP IRA is an excellent choice if you're self-employed because you can contribute more money through this vehicle than you can with a traditional IRA or Roth IRA.
- A self-directed IRA or Solo 401(k) might be preferable, if you want to invest your retirement funds in nontraditional asset classes such as private investments, real estate, or other alternatives. Also, a Solo 401(k) plan often allows you to contribute more than a SEP IRA when you're self-employed. If you go this route, please seek assistance from qualified professionals and follow the rules.
- We applaud you if you choose to work with your employer to add values-aligned options to their retirement plan. You will be helping yourself and your colleagues. Since you'll be doing this on behalf of many people, your impact will be multiplied because you will ultimately drive greater amounts of money into the things you care about.

Take Action

If you haven't done so already, you might want to evaluate what is currently sitting in your retirement accounts to see if it aligns with your values. Should you discover that it doesn't, then you might want to take steps to move your assets in that direction. Remember, retirement accounts that you control are often the easiest place to start making this transition because you won't face tax consequences as long as your money is not taken out of the account. Imagine how great it will feel to apply the information in this book to those accounts!

Endnotes

1. https://www.businessinsider.com/personal-finance/average-401k-balance.
2. https://www.personalcapital.com/blog/retirement-planning/average-401k-balance-age/?utm_medium=Email&utm_source=ExactTarget&utm_campaign=&utm_content=Day+20+-+Knowledge+is+Power+(From+Advisor)+(QQ3)&c3ch=Email&c3nid=Day+20+-+Knowledge+is+Power+(From+Advisor)+(QQ3).
3. https://udirectira.com/about-us/.
4. https://www.theselc.org/how_to_establish_a_self_directed_ira_and_solo_401k.
5. https://docs.wbcsd.org/2019/06/WBCSD_ARA-toolkit_USA_version.pdf.
6. https://institutional.vanguard.com/VGApp/iip/site/institutional/researchcommentary/article/HowAmericaSaves2019.
7. https://www.im.natixis.com/us/research/defined-contribution-plan-participant-survey-2019.

CHAPTER 14

Gather Your Friends
Get Together for Fun and Profit

Taking control of your money to invest with confidence and in alignment with your values is a lot more fun when you learn alongside other women. Your skills develop faster with less effort, and you are more likely to see success across your entire portfolio. You'll also be part of a time-honored tradition that goes back more than 100 years.

Investment clubs got their start in the early 1900s. Although female-only clubs were part of that early movement, they got their biggest boost in 1991 when the Beardstown Ladies published their bestselling book, *Common-Sense Investment Guide: How We Beat the Stock Market—and How You Can, Too.* Their call to action spawned thousands of female-led investment clubs all over the country. I know because I was in one.

The investment clubs that were formulated along the Beardstown Ladies' model aggregated capital from their members and collectively invested that money into well-researched stocks. The investment strategy worked in its day, but times have changed. The investment approach that was popular then—a focus on individual stocks—is no longer the only, or even the best, approach to constructing an investment portfolio today. There are many more opportunities in the market now, and successful investors need to know more. As women, we also want to ensure our money grows our wealth and aligns with our values—a concept that was in its infancy when the Beardstown Ladies were meeting.

Today's investment clubs can focus on a single asset class like those of yore, but they can also bring a much broader range of subject matter and goals into the mix. They can emphasize knowledge-sharing across all asset classes, offer opportunities for joint angel investing, or serve as accountability forums to actively move members' money into alignment. A new movement is forming, and we invite you to be part of it. The Invest for Better campaign is providing the tools and curriculum for today's women to help them join or activate their own investment clubs.

Invest for Better Circles

Invest for Better is a nonprofit campaign that's on a mission to help women demystify values-aligned investing and mobilize their money for good through women-led investment clubs or circles. Started in 2018 by Ellen Remmer in collaboration with other leaders, Invest for Better Circles bring together novice and experienced investors to increase their knowledge, overcome barriers, and hold each other accountable for taking the actions required to move some—or all—of their money into values-aligned investments. Some of the women involved in this book have partnered with Ellen to bring her vision forward and have even started circles of their own.

Ellen and her colleagues created the initial curriculum for an Invest for Better Circle. We have built upon that material in this chapter to offer additional resources that help you start, manage, and run your own investment club.

Why Women Come Together to Discuss Their Money

You probably already recognize the power we women have when we come together for a common purpose. At the same time, we're all busy, so some of you may be wondering, why would we want to use our precious spare time to join an investment club?

The reason is simple. Investment clubs build your knowledge and confidence, move you into action, and connect you more deeply with a group of likeminded women. If you want to know more about your investments, hope to make better investment decisions, and truly want to activate your money, you will jump at the chance to join one of these clubs.

As Tracy Gray, a leader in the gender lens investment movement, said, "Run, do not walk to get into a network." She believes that organizing or being part of a group of trusted, diverse peers who talk openly about money and commit to making change is the next bold step to our full empowerment as women.

My Investment Club Journey

Over the past 30 years, I have been a member of three investment clubs, each of which was quite different. My first experience was in my early 30s when I wanted to get better at picking individual stocks for my portfolio, which was the way to invest at that time. About a dozen women met monthly at the group leader's home. We talked about our investments over dinner, shared research, and learned together.

The second group I belonged to was co-led and specifically focused on impact investing. The group had already been together for two years when I joined. I participated in person for five years and then became an emeritus member when I moved to a different city. I've come to respect and admire the members of the group for their deep commitment to moving their capital into high-impact investments and helping each other be successful in that endeavor.

As I started writing this book, I launched a women-only, values-aligned investment club. We met over a period of 18 months in the offices of a values-aligned financial advisor who graciously let us use her space after hours. We brought our own food, had guest speakers—many of whom were highlighted in earlier chapters—and talked about our money, our values, and our investments.

I have learned from, enjoyed, and valued all of the investment clubs I have participated in, and I hope this chapter inspires you to join one or to start your own investment club.

They Cherish a Safe Space for Learning

While in her 20s, Angie joined an investment club to increase her overall understanding of investment topics. At the time, she was confused about how to read a brokerage statement and wanted to explore retirement options. For Angie, joining the club was about not feeling alone and not feeling like she should already know a lot about money and investing. Instead, the club was a safe space for her to learn, explore, experiment, and build her investment skills.

This is one of the primary reasons women give for being part of an investment group. It's a safe space for them to learn about financial matters without worrying about looking ignorant. We're less afraid of asking questions when we're in the company of other women. Our deep-held fears around money can emerge among a group of women that we trust. We know these women have our backs, and that can make all the difference!

Being part of a women's investment club is also about breaking down taboos around money. When the club's charter is focused on this issue, the discomfort of stepping forward and discussing all kinds of challenges related to money is much easier. Members are often surprised by the concerns they share in common with other women in the group. This is a relief to many women who've been raised to avoid talking about money even with family members and close friends. Confronting this taboo is like taking a huge breath of fresh air and lifting a heavy weight from your shoulders.

Angie has stayed in her group for almost two decades. Now in her late 40s, with a retirement plan and rental properties to manage, she reminds us that women need support around their money at every stage of their lives. Angie's personal growth through her investment group took her from the basics—learning how to read brokerage statements—into much more sophisticated investment vehicles, such as real estate and other alternative investments. As she grew in confidence, so did the value and diversity of her portfolio.

Like Angie, hopefully you'll be investing your money wisely. If you take the time to make informed decisions, you will be able to watch your money grow while supporting the causes you care about. Although investing is not a sprint, it does get easier and more fun over time as you learn and build your investment muscles. The sooner you dig into understanding how to invest, the sooner you'll be on a path to financial freedom and financial fulfillment.

Knowledge Is Power

Even women who have financial advisors are eager to supplement their knowledge so they can ask the right questions and give their advisors better guidance about their investment objectives. Many women struggle with the traditional male-centric advisory model, which does not value deep listening, values-based goal setting, or a comfortable space for asking questions and learning. This is a particular challenge for women who are committed to moving their money into alignment with their values. In many cases, they're actually dissuaded from these goals by advisors who are uninformed about these investment options or their return potential. Women who know about values-aligned investing can either guide their financial advisors or seek a new advisor that more closely meets their needs.

They Delight in Supporting Each Other

Learning how to invest is easy to put off, especially if you have anxiety around money, finance, or math. Many of us would love a quick fix or a simple investment plan that we could implement and then never have to worry about again. But that's not how money works. Angie didn't resolve all of her financial matters in one year. She worked at it over decades, but now she feels confident in her abilities, secure in her financial situation, and has a close-knit group of friends who continue to support her journey. She's also in a position to mentor other women, which makes her feel great!

We've found that women are consistently delighted to share their expertise and support their peers' learning journeys. One of the great things about an investment club is there's often a wide range of experience and knowledge represented. There's also a spectrum of goals and challenges that members are grappling with. This adds depth to group discussions. Over time, participants gain deeper insight into other members' situations as well as their strengths and weaknesses around money. In turn, they can give each other advice and identify new investing interests based on others' experiences.

Circles Broaden Our Horizons

Irene started hearing about values-aligned investing through a philanthropy group she belonged to and got curious. When a friend invited her to join an investment club, she decided it was the perfect opportunity to get educated. At the time Irene joined, she was interested in private equity—the only asset class she thought could be values-aligned. She became a dedicated member and attended every meeting. What surprised Irene was learning she could invest her values in other asset classes. Before joining the group, she hadn't realized what a difference she could make with the assets she'd invested in fixed income and public equities. It was a real eye-opener for her!

They're Empowered by Group Learning

Women have always been deeply engaged in using their money for good. Traditionally, that involvement came through philanthropy, where we tend to contribute more than men. We're more motivated to give for altruistic reasons, whereas men are more likely to give based on self-interest.[1] New research shows that women are also more likely to use impact investing as an *additional* avenue to achieve their social goals, while men are more likely to *replace* some of their philanthropy with values-aligned investing.[2]

We're starting to recognize the power of not just giving to achieve impact but investing for impact. By investing—whether from a savings account, a public equities account, or a retirement account—in alignment with their values and in pursuit of their social and environmental goals, women's capital comes alive and has purpose. Women are finding they want to learn more about how they can invest their capital to support the revitalization of their communities, to elevate human rights, and to build sustainability into our economic models.

The ability to invest in a way that aligns with their values is waking women up and making the entire investment process more interesting, more engaging, and more relevant to their lives. By working together, we can accelerate a shift of capital from investments that are harming our communities and our world to those that support the things we care about.

A Public Equities Blitz

Alicia Robb is the founder of Next Wave Impact, a movement driving impact, diversity, and inclusion in early-stage investing. Although she's dedicated to putting some of her money to work supporting social businesses with female founders, she realized that other parts of her portfolio were not values aligned. To share the research burden and have fun in the process, Alicia gathered nine friends and colleagues to select environmentally and socially responsible alternatives to their investments in other asset classes.

The group met about nine times over the course of a year. While sharing dinner, the women crystalized their objectives, decided to focus on their public equities, and then got to work. They jointly identified a number of potential investments that included index funds, ETFs, and actively managed investments. The women divided the research among themselves and then came back together to report on their findings.

The group was excited to work together and happy with their outcome. As a result of their joint effort, all the women moved their money from existing investments into more values-aligned options. At the end of their time together, one member told Alicia, "I feel like those were the most memorable social events of my year—having conversations with purpose and substance. Thank you for putting them together!"

They're Moved to Action

Beyond gaining new skills, knowledge, and alignment, participating in a group can move women from anxiety to action. Having a group with specific goals strengthens motivation, offers support, and provides accountability. As one circle member mentioned, "Learning in a group provides the structure to 'get it done.' It helps you to take action when others are taking that step, too." Participating in a circle also gave her a sense of accountability to deal with the financial issues she previously avoided.

Meeting to "Do the Work"

Being a member of an investment group allows women to translate their increased knowledge and comfort with investing into tangible outcomes. Avary Kent is a serial social entrepreneur and the cofounder of Conveners.org, a global nonprofit that brings conveners together to dramatically increase their ability to create positive social and environmental change. So it's no surprise that when Avary decided it was time to move her cash into alignment with her values, she chose to do so in a spirit of collaboration.

Over a three-month period, Avary and a group of her friends met to support each other in the process. During the initial meeting, they discussed what they wanted from their new banks, identified the steps required to make a shift, and developed a set of interview questions for new banking prospects. Once the foundational aspects were established, the group moved into action.

Because everyone in her group led busy lives, Avary structured all three meetings as working sessions where members brought their computers (or joined virtually). After some initial socializing, the participants sat down to work. They developed documents, conducted research, and set up their new bank accounts during the course of the meetings. This approach ensured that participants set aside one or two hours a month to dedicate to changing their banks, and their efforts were encouraged and supported by other members of the group.

By shifting the "doing" portion of the work into the meetings themselves, Avary's group had 100% success. Members of the group moved their cash to financial institutions that made them feel good about themselves and how their money was being used.

Starting an Investment Club

You may be able to find an existing Invest for Better Circle or other women's values-aligned investment club in your community. However, if you don't find one, consider starting your own group. As a leader, you have an opportunity to be thoughtful about who participates, what you want the group to accomplish, and the culture you want to establish.

Our companion site will point you to some resources to help you design, run, and manage an investment club that works for you and your members. In the remainder of this section, we'll lay out some of the fundamentals that you might want to mull over if you're considering start-ing your own investment circle.

Identifying the Leadership

While running an investment club is not overly burdensome, it does take some logistical planning and organization. A key decision will be whether you want to start a group on your own or whether you would prefer to join forces with one or more co-leaders. We've found that having a co-leader can be advantageous, because they share the responsibility and provide thought partnership for key decisions. Bringing the networks of two or more co-leads together also increases the size and variety of the pool of prospective members, which can add diversity to the membership and greater richness to discussions. Many of the Invest for Better Circles were launched by co-leaders with complementary skills and backgrounds. Even though there are advantages to co-leadership, there are plenty of club leaders who opt to go it alone. So do what feels right for you.

Selecting Members

The recruiting process is an important step in creating your circle because the composition of the group will inform the group's goals. So some intentionality is valuable. For example, you should consider whether your group's mission would be better achieved through homogeneity or diversity in terms of age, experience, and level of wealth. You may even want to focus your club on a specific interest or lens, such as gender or climate change. Members of these groups and the curriculum they follow could be quite different than a group focused on a range or a specific set of actions, such as moving cash or public assets, or a group established for general knowledge sharing.

Inevitably, members will have a range of experience and understanding about the investing process. While this can be intimidating for the novice, it generally works out, as women are happy to mentor one another and share their expertise. Some clubs opt to offer special Investing 101 sessions for their novice members while others may choose to focus recruitment on women who already have a base level of knowledge.

Recruitment is typically based on personal networks and referrals. When you reach out to them, you might be surprised at how many of your friends and colleagues are interested in joining a values-aligned investment club. Referral sources can include your accountant, financial advisor, or other women's networks in your community. For best results, be clear about the qualities you are looking for in members, expectations for participation, and your goals for the group. We believe it's important to be clear up front that investment clubs are not places for members to promote their services or products, as this would be counterproductive to creating a safe space for full participation.

We've also found that small groups of 5 to 15 provide the intimacy to build personal relationships yet are large enough to foster good discussions. Continuity is very important to the cohesiveness and value of the group. Therefore, regular attendance should be stressed. Even with that, there will inevitably be scheduling conflicts. We've found that a roster of at least eight means you can be relatively confident that at least five will attend each meeting.

Establishing Goals and Culture

Values-aligned investment circles have three primary goals: to help members build confidence around investing, to actively move money into values-aligned investments, and to provide a community for support and accountability. You may have additional goals, such as focusing investments in your local community, developing a shared pipeline of investments, or even co-investing. We recommend articulating the club's goals in writing up front, regularly reminding participants thereafter, and adjusting your goals as circumstances warrant.

In addition to establishing group goals, encourage each member to define and share her personal goals for participation. Knowing each other's priorities helps achieve accountability, so it can even be a good idea to come back to them periodically. Revisiting personal goals is also helpful because you might find they change as participants' knowledge and confidence grow. In our experience, women who started out with the intention to learn shift to actively moving their assets after just 6 to 12 months in a group.

Starting out with a set timeline or number of meetings you ask members to commit to is also a good idea. This provides additional structure and puts an end date on their commitments. If you find the group has really coalesced and wants to continue past the original deadline, that is fine. You can always adjust that. However, the recruitment process is less demanding from the prospective members' point of view if they know they're only committing for a specified number of months. We find that many members want actually to continue as the end of the commitment period approaches.

One woman enjoyed her club so much that she, and five other members, decided not only to continue for another year after they completed their first six-month commitment but also to expand the circle—which had been quite small to start—and bring in more women.

Other Considerations

You'll also need to decide on some practical matters, such as where and when to meet, how frequently you want to meet, how long the meetings should be, and whether you should charge a fee.

Some groups meet at members' offices during lunch or right after work, while others choose to have their meetings in members' homes or in a secluded room in a local restaurant. If food is included, meal duties can rotate, members can all pitch in to order takeout, or participants can bring their own food.

We recommend you hold meetings monthly or bi-monthly. In our experience, meetings typically last from 1.5 to 2.5 hours, depending on the amount of social time you build in.

Some groups bring in experts—either in person or via Zoom—for part of the meetings to talk about specific asset classes or investment approaches. You and your group members may already have greater access to high-quality speakers than you realize. Individuals employed by values-aligned financial advisory companies are often eager to share their expertise. Invest for Better also offers a Speakers Bureau of experts who can participate. Visit their website for more information.

While many club leaders are volunteers and participation is free, some circles are managed by a paid facilitator or coordinator. In our experience, members pay anywhere from $500 to $5,000 to join. Several fee-based circle leaders contend that participants are more committed to the experience if they have agreed to pay a fee. Fees can also be charged to cover food, instructors, or any administrative costs.

Women with Capital: A Curated Investment Group

Barbara Pierce is an active investor and philanthropist who is passionate about amplifying the power of women's personal and financial capital through investing with intention. She started Women with Capital because she knew women with investable capital are also dedicated philanthropists. These women had not explored other ways they could use their assets to make a difference through values-aligned investing, and neither had their advisors. Yet, the women were hungry to know more. Barbara realized if she could help higher-net-worth women understand the potential of aligning their money with their values, she could help move millions—or even billions—of dollars in support of a better world.

Women with Capital is a curated investment club, based on a membership model with an educational series at its core. It is complemented by speaker luncheons throughout the year to build knowledge and foster a community of women with similar interests, concerns, and dedication to making a difference. One member said, "I especially liked being surrounded by so many women who are all interested in, and capable of, making investment choices that can nourish and support our communities and world, rather than just looking at the financial bottom line."

Members are carefully vetted to ensure a safe space to delve into subjects that are often considered off-limits. One member summed it up: "This community helped me become financially savvy not only because of the amazing instructors but also from having discussions about money that you can't have with your friends and family."

Virtual Options

Coming together in person on a regular basis is a powerful way to build a trusted community. It's conducive to personal connection and sharing, and bonds are built through repeated interactions. But that isn't always practical. Moreover, clubs that meet regularly in person may want to hold occasional virtual sessions due to weather or schedule changes, to listen to a prerecorded expert, or to discuss a specialized topic that doesn't interest all members.

During the coronavirus pandemic, some new groups launched dedicated virtual experiences, allowing the leaders to bring participants together across geographies. And many existing circles shifted to an online format. Virtual groups offer the benefits of access to a broader audience, the ability to host speakers who live anywhere in the world, and ease of logistics for leaders and participants. Eliminating the travel time sometimes means participants are happy to meet more frequently. With the technical tools we now have available, both in-person and virtual gatherings are possible.

Club leaders haven't had great success with meetings where some members are online and others are in the same room. Not only do the online members feel left out of a lot of the conversation, offering the option also becomes an invitation for attrition in attendance.

Using a Curriculum

We recommend that any women's values-aligned investing group conform to a structured curriculum with clear goals and a thoughtful approach to achieving those outcomes through meetings and homework. Without this, the circle runs the risk of failing to achieve everyone's personal goals. As a result, interest will inevitably wane. You can come together with other women to tackle one objective, much like Avary and Alicia did with cash and public equities. Or you can start a club that plans to stay together for a more general purpose over a longer period, like Angie and Irene's groups.

On our companion website, you'll find resources to help you create a structured approach to your meetings. You'll also find guidance on how you can use the content in this book as the basis for some of your meetings. Sessions can be organized around: (1) assignments from the book or expert presentations, (2) group discussions or activities, and (3) updates about members' investments, activities, and needs. Our materials are intended to ensure the leader(s) do not have to be experts themselves. Rather, they can be learners and activators along with the other circle members.

We suggest leaving time at the end of each meeting for members to share something they want to offer. This could be anything from an interesting investment they're looking at to an area of need, such as help engaging in financial dialogues with partners or other family members.

Take Action

When women band together, they can make real change happen. Women draw courage, conviction, and personal satisfaction from gathering together to support each other in their own personal journeys. We encourage you to join an existing Invest for Better Circle, or to create your own, using the suggestions outlined in this chapter and the resources at *activateyourmoney* *.net*. Let's create an unstoppable movement and a better world together!

Endnotes

1. https://philanthropy.iupui.edu/institutes/womens-philanthropy-institute/research/index.html.
2. Women's Philanthropy Institute. "How Women and Men Approach Impact Investing." May 2018.

Stepping into Your Financial Future

Although you've reached the last pages of this book, I hope you see this as a beginning rather than an end. We've traversed a lot of material together. You were invited to think about how your beliefs about money may be undermining your financial freedom. We delved into all the asset classes, looking at what they are, how they work, and where you can find investments that align with your values. We also talked about how you can shift your relationship with money so it is no longer a taboo topic but rather a subject that you can feel comfortable discussing with a trusted group of family or friends. Most importantly, we asked you to consider the possibility of investing in an entirely new way.

If you've reached this point in the book, I hope you've been moved and encouraged in some way. Perhaps you were inspired by the stories you read of the pioneering women who helped launch values-aligned investing or the stories of the women leading the charge today. Maybe you feel more confident in your knowledge of investment terminology, your investment options, and ways you can educate yourself going forward. You might have already downloaded some of the tools and started taking action with some of your assets. I hope all of these things are true—and more!

There are a few core concepts that are important to take with you.

YOUR MONEY MATTERS. My first hope is that you've come to understand that your money matters—probably more than you realized. Where we invest has an impact on the world—for better or for ill. As women, we have the opportunity to use our money to create the kind of world we want to see for ourselves and future generations. The potential is already there. We just need to step into it!

YOU CAN BE A SUCCESSFUL INVESTOR. Second, I hope you feel more knowledgeable, confident, and empowered around your money than you did on page one. I hope you have come to believe that investing doesn't have to be an onerous task, something we need to pass on to the men in our lives, or avoid. It can be interesting, even fascinating. And it is something that we as women can absolutely do—and do well!

While it's true that successful investing takes some work and attention, that doesn't mean the process can't be fun. And that's especially true if you choose to learn, or invest with, other women. Investing is definitely something that you can take on and succeed with. As Oprah Winfrey famously said, "The big secret in life is that there is no big secret. Whatever your goal, you can get there if you're willing to work."

YOUR CAN HAVE IT BOTH WAYS.   Third, I hope that you now know that you can invest with your values without giving up financial return. It's not an either-or situation. You can truly have both. Adding your values to your investments is an integral part of the overall investment process. Not only do you not give up financial return, you also gain peace of mind, a sense of inner integrity, and a new level of fulfillment around your money. You can know your money is growing, be proud of what you invest in, and be endlessly delighted by the positive impact you can have.

Join Us

After reading this book, I hope you got some ideas about investment types and categories that you never thought about before. Maybe you're ready to check out `MightDeposits.org` to move your cash to a financial institution that supports the environment, women, education, or opportunities in your own city. Maybe, like me, you never knew you could invest directly in municipal bonds to improve the lives of women and girls. Maybe you'd like to put some of your assets into a mutual fund or ETF that invests in companies that are creating solutions in renewable energy, clean water, or affordable housing. Maybe you find the idea of joining with other women to make angel investments in female-led start-ups exciting. Or perhaps you are interested in knowing more about investing in your local community. Whichever part of the book intrigued you, inspired you, or made you wonder, we encourage you to use our companion website, *activateyourmoney.net*, to dig deeper.

I sincerely hope you will join me, the 150 women (and a few men) who collaborated on this book, and the thousands of other women across this country who are moving their money into alignment with their values.

Whether you choose to take just one step and move one investment or asset class into values alignment, go for 100% alignment like I am doing, or something in between, the women behind this book applaud you. We are here to help you activate your money, grow your wealth, and build a better world. As women, we have shown, in so many ways, that we really can do it all. Our relationship with our money does not have to be any different! We invite you to step with us into a new future.

Glossary

accredited investor: Anyone whose earned income exceeded $200,000 (or $300,000 with a spouse) in each of the prior two years and who reasonably expects the same for the current year. Or someone who has a net worth over $1 million, either alone or with a spouse, not counting the value of the person's primary residence.

actively managed: Financial products, usually funds, in which investment decisions are made by portfolio managers and designed to outperform an index.

angel investing: Practice of making investments in early-stage and start-up businesses.

annual percentage yield (APY): Total amount of interest you earn on an investment, usually a bank deposit, assuming the funds remain in the account a full year.

annualized return: Return that is realized on a per annum basis, assuming compounding of returns during the period.

asset allocation: Strategy for portfolio management that splits assets among broad categories of investments, such as cash, fixed income, public equities, and alternatives.

asset class: Group of investments that have similar attributes and behave in a like manner in the market. The most common asset classes are cash, fixed income, and public equities.

assets under management (AUM): Total market value of all the financial assets that a financial institution manages on behalf of its customers and for itself.

B-Corporation: Businesses that receive certification confirming they adhere to high standards of social and environmental performance, transparency, and legal accountability. B-Corp certification is not a legal classification.

balloon payment: A large, one-time payment, often of the principal amount invested, at the end of a loan period.

basis point (bp):   Term used to describe percentages for amounts that are less than 1%. Each basis point is equal to one one-hundredth of 1%, or in other words, 100 basis points is equal to 1%. For example, 50 basis points is the same thing as half a percent, or 0.50%.

benefit corporation: Type of for-profit corporate entity that includes positive impacts as part of its legally defined goals. Classification is recognized by more than 35 states.

benchmark: Standard designed to reflect a specific segment of the market and against which an investment can be measured. The best-known standard is the S&P 500.

bond: Loan from an investor to a government, federal agency, corporation, or other entity that is repaid with interest over a fixed period.

broker/brokerage firm: Regulated individual or company that buys or sells financial products on behalf of investors. They act as the intermediary between the buyer and seller.

call: Right of a bond issuer to purchase back any outstanding bonds before their maturity date. The issuer can exercise this right by "calling" the loan and paying it off in full.

call premium: Amount over face value that is paid to the bondholder if the bond is called.

capital gains: Profit realized when you sell an asset, such as a stock fund or a piece of property, whose value has increased over the holding period.

cash: Funds that are immediately available, such as savings and checking accounts.

cash alternatives: Relatively low-risk investments that provide liquidity within 30 days to one year. Examples include CDs, notes, and some specialized products.

certificates of deposit (CD):   Time-bound cash deposits that pay a set interest rate and are invested in for a fixed term.

charity: Tends to be a more emotional, immediate response to an urgent situation or personal request.

collateral: Something that will be relinquished in the event of non-payment of a loan—often a tangible asset, such as machinery or property.

Community Development Financial Institution (CDFI):   Financial institutions that are 100% dedicated to providing affordable lending to disadvantaged individuals and communities.

community investments: Investments, often through lending or real estate development, targeted to local communities.

compound interest: Interest paid on the interest. When interest is reinvested, then subsequent interest is paid on both the original principal and the interest. As a result, the total balance grows at an increasing rate over time.

concentration risk: Risk of placing too high a percentage of assets in the same or similar investments.

concessionary return: A below-market-rate return. An investor may consciously decide to forgo some financial return to achieve a greater social return.

conscious investing: Investing in such a way investors are aware of, and consciously choose, the impact their money is having on the environment and society.

correlated: In investing, refers to assets that behave alike under similar market conditions.

coupon: Term used to denote the interest rate set for a bond on issuance. The coupon does not change over time.

credit union: Non-profit financial institution that is member-owned and exists to serve those members.

custodian: Specialized financial institution that holds investors' assets for safekeeping. Vanguard, Schwab, Fidelity, and many other firms provide this service.

cyclical sector: Group of companies in the stock market that provide products and services that consumers spend more on during periods of economic prosperity.

deal: An investment opportunity, including the potential financial structure. Often used when discussing private investments or angel investing.

defensive sector: Group of companies in the stock market that deliver goods and services that are important during economic upturns and downturns.

deflation: Decrease in the price of goods and services that occurs when the inflation rate falls lower than 0%.

delinquency rate: Percentage of borrowers who default on their loans.

directed: Investment made to achieve a specific outcome or set of objectives. Synonymous with targeted impact.

diversification: The process of allocating capital or adding uncorrelated assets to a portfolio to increase resilience during market downturns.

dividends: Distribution of profits by publicly held companies to their shareholders. Can be used as a synonym of interest in fixed income.

environmental, social, and governance (ESG) criteria: Metrics used to evaluate an investment's sustainability, social impact, and adherence to ESG objectives.

ESG investing: Act of investing in companies, funds, or other financial products with high ESG scores. Although some consider ESG investing as an approach across all asset classes, it primarily refers to investments in public equities, i.e., the stock market.

exchange-traded fund (ETF): Financial product that holds a collection of securities. ETFs have become so popular, you can now find them in virtually every asset class.

expense ratio: Annual fee that investors pay for a financial product, such as a stock or bond fund.

exposure: Amount of money invested in a particular financial product, asset class, or other investment.

face value: Amount that will be paid for a bond to a bondholder at the maturity date, assuming the investment does not go into default. Face value is established at issuance. "Par" is often a synonym.

Federal Reserve System: The central bank of the United States. Also referred to as the Federal Reserve or more simply as the Fed.

Federal Deposit Insurance Corporation (FDIC):   US federal agency established in 1933 to maintain stability and public confidence in the nation's financial system. Among other things, the FDIC supervises the country's financial institutions and insures deposits.

financial freedom: Having enough money to afford the lifestyle you want even into your retirement.

financial fulfillment: Satisfaction that arises from being in full integrity with your money as well as the deep contentment that comes from knowing your money is working for you and the world.

financial independence: Having knowledge about your money, being involved in the financial decisions related to your money, and not being financially dependent on others.

Financially Independent, Retire Early (FIRE):   Movement to aggressively save and invest to retire early, potentially as early as your 30s or 40s.

fixed income: Loans with a term of at least one year that are usually repaid over a set time at a fixed rate. Examples include CDs, Treasury notes, and bonds. These types of investments tend to be safer than other non-cash asset classes.

fund: Collection of individual investments that are collectively held by numerous investors. Mutual funds, ETFs, private debt, and private equity funds are all examples.

general partners (GPs):   Individuals or firms responsible for managing a private investment fund.

Green Bond Principles (GBP):   Set of voluntary guidelines that can be applied during the issuance of green bonds and are intended to promote integrity and transparency in the market.

greenwashing: Making an unsubstantiated or misleading claim about the environmental benefits of a financial product. This practice makes an investment appear more ESG compliant than it is.

growth stock: High-quality, successful company expected to grow above the average rate and outperform the market.

hedge: Investment made to offset potential losses, or gains, from other investments.

high-yield bonds: Non-investment-grade bonds that have ratings of BB+ or less. Speculative grade and junk bonds are often synonyms.

illiquid: Investments that cannot be easily converted into cash without substantial loss.

impact investing: While some use this term to refer to social investing across all asset classes, it often only applies to private investments in companies with a business model or mission directly tied to an intentional positive impact.

index: Often used interchangeably with the word *benchmark*, but they are actually two different things. An index tracks a specific market or segment while a benchmark can be composed of one or more indexes.

index fund: A type of mutual fund built to match or track a particular market index, such as the S&P 500 or the Russell 3000. Index funds tend to provide broad market exposure, low fees, and limited portfolio turnover.

Individual Retirement Account (IRA): A tax-advantaged individual investment vehicle. There are several types of IRAs, including traditional IRA, Roth IRA, and SEP IRA.

inflation: An increase in the price of goods and services over time.

institutional investors: Entities with large asset bases that invest on behalf of other people. Examples include banks, endowments, pension funds, and investment advisors.

internal rate of return (IRR): Metric that describes the expected annual return on an investment. It is used to compare the potential profitability of different investments.

investment-grade bonds: Bonds that have ratings of BBB– or better.

investment lens: *See* lens.

investment policy statement (IPA): Document that captures investment goals, objectives, and strategies.

issuer: Borrower of bond debt.

large cap: A publicly traded company with a market capitalization, or value, between $10 billion and $200 billion.

lens: Investment perspective that elevates one objective or value over others. For example, in gender lens investing the investor prioritizes gender equity above other factors. Virtually anything could be a lens. "Theme" is often used as a synonym.

limited partners (LPs): Investors in a company or private fund whose liability can't exceed their invested amount.

liquid: Investments that can be easily converted into cash with little to no loss in value.

liquidity event: Point at which an illiquid investment converts to cash. In private equity, this is often the time when an investment is sold or goes public.

load: Fee that an investor pays to purchase (or exit) a mutual fund or other investment. Can be paid at the time of purchase (front-load) or at the time of sale (back-load).

locavesting: Act of investing in one's local economy.

maturity: Day when a bond term ends and the initial investment, or principal, is due to be paid back to investors.

maximum drawdown: An investment's potential downside, or worst-case scenario, based on historical data.

mega cap: A publicly traded company with a market capitalization, or value, of more than $200 billion.

micro cap: A publicly traded company with a market capitalization, or value, of between $50 million and $500 million.

mid cap: A publicly traded company with a market capitalization, or value, of between $2 billion and $10 billion.

mutual fund: An open-ended financial product that pools the assets of many people into a single financial instrument. Fund managers invest that money in cash, bonds, stocks, and other securities on behalf of the investors.

nano cap: A publicly traded company with a market capitalization, or value, of less than $50 million.

National Credit Union Association (NCUA): US federal agency established in 1970 to provide credit union oversight, insure deposits, and protect members. NCUA insurance is offered through the National Credit Union Share Insurance Fund.

negative screening: Investment approach that excludes "bad actor" companies and industries from an investment fund or strategy.

non-accredited investor: Anyone who does not meet the criteria established for an accredited investor.

non-concessionary: Investment made with an expectation of achieving or exceeding market rate returns.

par: Term related to bonds that tends to be synonymous with face value.

passively managed: Investments, usually funds, designed to mimic a specific index and use technology to make investment decisions.

philanthropy: More strategic, deliberate approach to grant making that is built on a desire for longer-term outcomes.

portfolio: Collection of all the assets owned by an individual or entity across all asset classes.

positive tilt: Investment approach that considers high ESG scores as a requirement to include a company in a fund or strategy.

prevailing interest rate: The average current interest rate in the economy—also known as the current market rate—set by the Fed.

principal: The original amount of money invested in a financial product.

private debt: Loans made to nonpublic companies.

private equity: When written in lowercase (private equity), refers to an asset class in which an investor purchases shares of a non-public company. When written in uppercase (Private Equity), refers to the act of buying fully operating companies and restructuring them.

prospectus: A document that provides detailed information about a financial product or investment opportunity.

proxy vote: Right as a shareholder in a publicly traded company to vote on shareholder resolutions.

qualified purchaser: Individual or legal entity with at least $5 million in investments.

real estate: Property that includes land and the buildings on it as well as any natural resources, such as minerals, water, or crops, found there.

Real Estate Investment Trust (REIT): Company that finances, owns, and operates income-generating real estate or natural resources. REITs collect rent or generate income from the properties they hold and pass those profits to investors through regular dividends.

registered investment advisor (RIA): Individual or firm that provides advice and manages investment portfolios on behalf of clients.

retail investor: Nonprofessional individual investor.

return: The profit or loss made from an investment.

return on investment (ROI): Simple measure of an investment's return relative to its cost. Often represented as a multiple of the original investment made, such as 2× or 10×.

risk: Potential for financial loss on an investment.

risk-return trade-off: Balance between the level of risk associated with an investment and the potential return of that investment.

risk tolerance: Level of an investor's capacity or willingness to accept risk on an investment.

robo-advisors: Digital platforms that provide online investment selection and portfolio management. Usually offer little or no human advice or support.

Roth IRA: Type of individual retirement account that accepts post-tax contributions. Neither principal nor gains are taxed on withdrawal, assuming rules are followed.

secured debt: Loan backed by an asset, such as property or machinery.

securities: Generic term used to describe financial products, such as stocks, bonds, and funds.

Securities and Exchange Commission (SEC): US federal agency established in 1934 to protect investors, maintain fair and efficient markets, and enforce securities law.

self-directed IRA (SDIRA): Type of individual retirement account that can include a range of alternative investments prohibited in other types of IRAs.

sensitive sector: Group of companies in the stock market that fall somewhere between the cyclical and defensive sectors and include industries such as communications, technology, and heavy equipment.

shareholder advocacy: Process in which stock owners engage directly with corporate executives to drive positive change.

shareholder resolution: Proposal submitted to shareholders for their votes during a company's annual meeting. Often related to business practices, policy, or operations.

slow food: Global grassroots movement focused on preventing the disappearance of local foods, traditional cooking, and related customs.

small cap: A publicly traded company with a market capitalization, or value, between $500 million and $2 billion.

social investing: Any investment strategy that seeks financial return as well as social and environmental good. Sustainable and ethical investing are synonyms.

socially responsible investing (SRI): First widely adopted term, SRI is often associated with divestment or negative screening and is becoming a bit passé.

solo 401(k): Type of retirement account that was designed for business owners with no employees as a "one-participant" 401(k).

special-purpose vehicle (SPV): A legal entity established to fulfill a narrow, specific purpose. In angel investing, they are used to pool investors' money to buy equity in a private company.

speculation: Willingness to accept a high level of risk in the hope of a substantial upside, even though there is limited data to support that outcome.

sustainable investing: Investments that operate in a manner that is sustainable for people and the planet. Green investing is often a synonym.

Sustainable Development Goals (SDGs): Framework that includes 17 goals to achieve peace and prosperity for all people and the planet. The SDGs were ratified by the United Nations in 2015.

syndicate: Self-organizing group of individuals or entities that come together for a shared transaction or to pursue a shared interest. In angel investing, syndicates form to establish SPVs and co-invest in one or more private equity deals.

target-date funds: Investment product, usually a mutual fund or ETF, that holds a diverse mix of cash, bonds, stock, and other investments—all in one fund. The asset allocations automatically readjust as the investor ages.

target-risk funds: Investment product, usually a mutual fund or ETF, that holds a diverse mix of cash, bonds, stock, and other investments—all in one fund. Investors can choose between conservative, moderate, or higher risk investment options.

tax-deferred: Taxes due on interest, dividends, or capital gains are postponed until sometime in the future, often when funds are removed from a tax-deferred account, such as a traditional IRA.

tax-free: Interest, dividends, and capital gains are not subjected to taxes. This is the case if they grow in a tax-free account, such as a Roth IRA or a Roth 401(k).

term: Period of time.

thematic: Investment approach that seeks impact in a specific area or theme, such as climate or gender equity. "Investment lens" is a synonym.

time horizon: Length of time money can remain invested and grow without being tapped for funds.

tracking error: Divergence between the return of an investment, such as an index fund, and its associated benchmark.

turnover: Percent of total holdings in an investment fund that is sold, or turned over, on an annual basis.

two-pocket thinking: Belief that the only way to expend money is to invest it to maximize financial return or to give it away through philanthropy. Doesn't recognize opportunities that are emerging at the intersection of traditional investing and philanthropy.

uncorrelated: In investing, refers to assets that do not behave alike under similar market conditions. Instead, they behave differently.

underwrite: Accept liability and guarantee payment.

unsecured debt: Loan that is not backed by any assets. The only obligation for repayment is the borrower's promise.

values-aligned investing: Total portfolio investment strategy tailored to the values held by the investor.

value stock: Typically, more stable, more mature companies that have lower volatility and often pay investors a dividend.

venture capital: Form of private equity financing that provides capital to start-up businesses and other early-stage ventures believed to have high growth potential.

volatility: Range of price changes an investment experiences over time.

yield: Income earned from an investment, such as interest from a bond or a dividend from stock, and usually expressed as an annual percentage rate.

wealth preservation: Strategy to ensure your money grows over time and is available for family members into the future.

Acknowledgments

A*ctivate Your Money* has been a labor of love for more than two years. I have only been the ringleader and could not have completed this project without the amazing collection of women (and men) who stepped up to contribute their time, talent, and resources as writers, reviewers, thought partners, and more. They shared their insights, wrote material, reviewed chapters, and provided inspiration. Through their support and incredible commitment, they encouraged and buoyed me along the way.

I so appreciate the women who wrote entire chapters and those who reviewed several sections of the book. To my utter amazement, the writers and reviewers willingly read first drafts, then a second, and sometimes part of a third! They never complained. They just showed up, over and over again. I also value the reviewers who gave me critical feedback. This last group pushed me hard, forcing me to go back, tear a chapter apart, and write it again. Though it was painful at the time, I believe that process resulted in a better book.

There is literally no way I can express how deeply indebted I am to all the people who stood beside me on this journey. I am grateful to the women who were friends before this effort started and to those who have become friends along the way. I have been awed by their determination, contributions, and commitment to make the world a better place than they found it. I feel fortunate, indeed, to be in their company.

There are a few people who deserve a special callout. First, I want to thank my husband, Michael Taylor, for his unflagging patience with me as I worked long hours and over weekends to meet my self-imposed deadlines. He made sure I ate and showed his support for me and this project in innumerable ways. Second, I would like to thank Nancy Fish, who was one of the earliest fans of this book. As soon as we sat down at Book Passages to explore the crazy idea I was considering, she encouraged me. She read drafts of my first chapter, provided input to my book proposal, and introduced me to Michele Crim, who became my wonderful literary agent.

Regina Connell, the Joss Collective CEO, put together a club for writers early in my process. Although neither of us realized it at the time, that group was instrumental in helping me get, and stay on, the right path. I also want to thank Rebecca Williams for her work helping me create a vision and brand, Archie Alibasa for building the companion Activate Your Money website, Jill Bamburg for creating the amazing curriculum that works with this book, and, of course the women who helped me with all the editing—Margot Silk Forrest with earlier versions and Diana Ceres, who was enormously helpful later in the process.

The Writers

These women and men, experts in their field, wrote portions of, or entire, chapters. Together, they provided the scaffolding on which I was able to build the final content you see in this book today. Editing someone else's brilliance is so much easier than starting from scratch. I am humbled by their willingness to give so freely of their time and knowledge and apologize to those whose work may no longer be recognizable or was not included in the final draft.

The primary writers are Kate Barron-Alicante (Chapter 2); Lisa Leff Cooper (Chapter 3); Akasha Absher (Chapter 6); Lauren Sercu, (Chapters 7 and 8); Lisa Frusztajer, (Chapter 9); Beth Stelluto Dunaier (Chapter 11); Lisa Renstrom, Megan Morrice, and Kate Simpson (Chapter 12); and Ellen Remmer (Chapter 14).

Other content contributors included: Alicia Robb, Amie Patel, Andrew Behar, Andrew Jones, Astrid Scholz, Barbara Pierce, Caterina Rinde, Catherine Pyke, Clara Brenner, Eileen Freiburger, Jenny Kassan, Johanna Posada, Julie Lein, Laura Oldanie, Luni Libes, Mara Zepeda, Rebecca Young, Sara Lomelin Velten, Steve Murphy, Suzanne Andrews, and Victoria Fram.

The Reviewers and Thought Partners

Content reviewers were critical in helping me identify oversights, fix flaws, and provide greater clarity. Some reviewers were content experts in their own right, while others were potential readers of the book. I deeply appreciate their honest, critical feedback, as it kept me on track. Others provided insight and guidance along the way.

They are as follows: Abigail Ingalls, Alisa Gravitz, Alison Smith, Amir Chandra, Amy Beck, Amy Gudgeon, Anese Cavanaugh, Angela Marciano, Aniyia Williams, Ann Miles, Anna Mabrey, Anne Sapp, Annie McShiras, Arielle Ford, Arno Hesse, Avary Kent, Babbie Jacobs, Barbara Waugh, Beth Bafford, Caroline Yarborough, Carson Faris, Cat Berman, Cheryl Contee,

Dan Murphy, Dana Smith, Daniel Wu, Danielle Eigner, David Stein, Deana Zabaldo, Divya Gandhi, Drew Tulchin, Elana Yohan Rosen, Elizabeth Castro Abrams, Emily Green, Erika Karp, Eve Picker, Felicia Herman, George Calys, Hali Lee, Homero Radway, Isis Krause, Ivka Kalus, Jane Bulnes-Fowles, Jenna Nicholas, Jennifer Leonard, Jennifer Sonderby, Jennifer Tonda Rohlfes, Jenny Wapner, Jessica Chao, Judy Bernstein, Karen Michels, Karin Bauer, Karl Uhlig, Katie Bamberger, Kathy Sonderby, Kimberly Griego-Kim, Kristin Hull, Kristina Montague, Laura Waters, Lauren Dube, Lauren Evans, Lee Clay, Lisa Margulis, Lisa Molinaro, Lisa St. Claire, Liz Fisher, Lynn Marie Auzenne, Marcia Dawood, Mark Herrera, Marilyn Waite, Marsha Morgan, Matt Hoffman, Megan Hryndza, Melanie Firpo, Michael Grimm, Michael Shuman, Michael Taylor, Naila Sharifova, Nancy Fish, Natalie Holm, Nicole Brown, Patricia Farrar-Rivas, Paul Ang, Paul Herman, Paula Liang, Phuong Luong, Rachel Robasciotti, Randi Benton, Rebecca Williams, Regina Connell, Renata Gomez, Sally Outlaw, Sandy Emerson, Sara Gelfand, Sara Olsen, Serena Zhao, Sonia Kowal, Sonya Dreizler, Stacie Rasmussen, Stefania Di Bartolomeo, Stephanie Meade, Steve Zuckerman, Sue Baggott, Suneeta Krish, Susan Bruce, Susan Fairchild, Susan Mayginnes, Sven Gatchev, Sylvia Kwan, Tamara Larsen, Tasha Seitz, Teresa Wells, Tim Yee, Toni Robino, Tory Laughlin-Taylor, Val Red-Horse Mohl, Valeriya Epshteyn, and Vic Griffith.

And, finally, I would like to thank Kevin Harreld, the senior acquisitions editor at John Wiley & Sons, who saw the potential in this book and agreed to publish it.

Now that *Activate Your Money* is completed, it is my turn to support you, the reader, on your investment journey. I also look forward to supporting the amazing work that many of the contributors are undertaking to help women feel more confident with money or by creating investment opportunities that let us shine as women. They allow all of us to fully express who we are and what we value through the choices we make with our money.

About the Author

Janine Firpo is a values-aligned investor, angel investor, and social innovator. For almost 10 years, she has been on a personal mission to invest all of her assets so they align with her values. In 2017 she left a successful 35-year career in technology and international development to focus on how women can create a more just and equitable society through their financial investments.

During her prior career, Janine was often on the crest of what have become massive waves of progress. In 1981 she became a computer programmer in what was a male-dominated, early-stage industry. Then in 1995, she started using technology as a tool for poverty reduction, becoming one of the first practitioners exploring how to do well financially while also doing good socially. And in 2008, she became one of the first mobile money experts in a fledgling enterprise that grew from a handful of implementations to an industry with 900 million customers across more than 90 countries. Now Janine is at the crest of a new wave, as she joins with a group of visionary female leaders who are forging a movement that supports women, their money, and their values.

Janine has held executive positions in corporations, government agencies, start-up enterprises, and foundations. She spun a non-profit out of Hewlett-Packard in 2005, serving as its president for more than 10 years. She also worked for Apple Computer, the World Bank, the US government, and other international agencies. While working for the Bill & Melinda Gates Foundation, Janine and her team designed philanthropic and impact investments to bring poor people out of poverty. She has traveled to almost 80 countries and worked extensively in Sub-Saharan Africa and Southeast Asia.

Today, Janine is one of the lead investors in the Next Wave Impact Fund, an impact fund designed to help more women become angel investors. She also chairs the board of Zebras Unite, an organization that is developing the capital structures, community, and culture that non-unicorn start-up businesses need to thrive.

In partnership with over 40 financial experts and a larger team of reviewers, Janine has written *Activate Your Money* to help others transform their relationship with money and break the taboos related to women and financial empowerment. Today, Janine is taking action to move her money into investments she feels good about and is watching it grow with market-rate returns. She lives in California with her husband, Mike. This is her first book.

Index